EXPERIMENTAL ECONOMICS: FINANCIAL MARKETS, AUCTIONS, AND DECISION MAKING

EXPERIMENTAL ECONOMICS: FINANCIAL MARKETS, AUCTIONS, AND DECISION MAKING

Interviews and Contributions from the 20th Arne Ryde Symposium

Edited by

FREDRIK ANDERSSON
Lund University, Sweden

and

HÅKAN HOLM
Lund University, Sweden

Springer Science+Business Media, LLC

ISBN 978-1-4613-5303-4 ISBN 978-1-4615-0917-2 (eBook)
DOI 10.1007/978-1-4615-0917-2

Library of Congress Cataloging-in-Publication Data

A C.I.P. Catalogue record for this book is available from the Library of Congress.

Printed on acid-free paper.

About the Arne Ryde Foundation

Arne Ryde was an exceptionally promising student in the Ph.D. program at the Department of Economics at Lund University. He was tragically killed in a car accident in 1968. The Arne Ryde foundation was established by his parents, pharmacist Arne Ryde and his wife Valborg in commemoration of Arne Ryde. According to the deed of the foundation from 1971 the aim of the foundation is: to foster and promote advanced economic research in cooperation with the Department of Economics at Lund University. The foundation acts by lending support to conferences, symposia, lecture series and publications which are initiated by faculty members of the department.

Anders Borglin
Chairman

Contents

Part I Interviews with Invited Speakers

1
Peter Bohm 3

2
Catherine C. Eckel 9

3
Werner Güth 19

4
John Hey 29

5
Daniel Kahneman 41

6
Alvin Roth 49

7
Vernon Smith 67

8
Martin Weber 75

Part II Contributions

9
Attitudes towards Risk and Inequality 85
Yoram Amiel, Frank Cowell, with the assistance of Kaspar Richter
1 Introduction 85
2 Theoretical Background 86
2.1 Inequality and Risk 86
2.2 The Meaning of Inequality and of Risk 88
2.3 An Axiomatic Approach 89
3 The Experiment 91
3.1 Issues 91
3.2 Implementation 92

4 Data 93
5 Numerical responses and the Principle of Transfers 94
5.1 Descriptive results 94
5.2 Regression Analysis 96
6 Numerical Responses: variation by Type of Income Transfer 97
6.1 Descriptive Analysis 97
6.2 Regression Analysis 98
6.3 A provisional evaluation 99
7 The Verbal Question 102
7.1 The structure of the question 102
7.2 Verbal question: descriptive results 102
7.3 Regression analysis 104
8 Conclusions 105
Appendix 107
1 Variable definitions 107
2 The Questionnaires 107

10
Pitfalls in Experimental Economics 117
Peter Bohm
1 Introduction 117
2 Monetary Incentive Levels 118
3 Subjects 119
4 Testing Theory in Context or Non-Context Environments 121
5 Stationary Repetitions 124
6 Concluding Remarks 125

11
The Effect of Trading Period Duration 127
Darren Duxbury
1 Introduction 127
2 Relevant Literature and Research Hypotheses 128
3 Experimental Design 131
3.1 Overview of Experimental Procedures and Design 131
3.2 Experimental Markets 132
3.3 Participants and Motivation 132
3.4 Specific Market Designs 135
4 Analysis and Results 136
4.1 Data Considerations 136
4.2 Experimental Markets Group One (PN Markets) 137
Volume of Trade 144
Informational Efficiency 144
Allocational Efficiency 145
4.3 Experimental Markets Group Two (IN Markets) 145
Volume of Trade 148
Informational Efficiency 152
Allocational Efficiency 153
4.4 Experimental Markets Groups Three and Four 153
5 Discussion and Conclusions 153

12
Robust Learning Experiments 159
Werner Güth
1 Introduction 159
2 Auctions and Fair Division Games 161
3 Reputation formation 166
4 Endogenous timing in bilateral negotiations 171
5 Alternating offer bargaining 174
6 Discussion 179

13
The Impact of Fairness on Decision Making 185
Heike Hennig-Schmidt
1 Introduction 185
2 Relevant Literature 187
3 Method 189
4 Experimental design 191
4.1 The Ultimatum Game 191
4.2 The Tripled Take Game 191
4.3 An Alternating Offer Bargaining Game 192
4.4 Procedure 192
5 Results 193
5.1 Fairness is synonymous to equity 196
5.2 The influence of fairness on decision making 202
6 Conclusion 204

14
The Sequential Prisoners' Dilemma 211
Carles Solà
1 Introduction 211
2 Previous Experiments 212
3 Models and Predictions 214
3.1 Inequality Aversion 215
3.2 Altruism 217
4 Experimental Design 218
5 Results 219
6 Conclusions 221
Appendix 222

15
Collusion in Auctions 227
Jana Vyrastekova and *Maria Montero*
1 Introduction 227
2 The Game 230
2.1 Nash Equilibria of the Stage Game 231
2.2 Collusion in the Repeated Game 231
Simple collusion 232
Efficient collusion 232
3 The Experimental Design 232

3.1 Hypotheses 233
4 Results 234
4.1 Average Earnings 234
4.2 Bidding Behavior 236
4.3 Bidding Proposals 237
Round 1 data 237
Overall data 238
4.4 Value Messages 241
4.5 Sidepayments 242
5 Conclusion 243
Appendix: Collusion in Equilibrium 244
Incentives to tell the truth 244
Incentives to bid low 244
Incentives to give sidepayments 245

Foreword

In the spring of 1998 the editors of this volume realized that although a few Swedish researchers had conducted experiments and presented their results in journals and on international conferences, Sweden had not hosted any major conference with focus on Experimental Economics. Furthermore, knowledge of the recent interesting developments in this area were not widespread among economists in general. Inspired by this we decided to plan an Arne Ryde symposium on Experimental Economics with the purpose to further the knowledge of experimental methods and results to the larger scientific community of economists in Scandinavia and to provide an additional opportunity for researchers in the field to meet and exchange ideas. The chairman of the Arne Ryde foundation at the time, Professor Björn Thalberg, was enthusiastic, and promised financial support. In the same summer invitations were sent out.

The 20th Arne Ryde Symposium on Experimental Economics was held November 9-11, 2000 at the School of Economics and Management at Lund University. Invited lectures were given by Peter Bohm, Catherine Eckel, Werner Güth, John Hey, Daniel Kahneman, Alvin Roth, Vernon Smith, and Martin Weber. To document the symposium each invited lecturer was interviewed. Part I of this volume – Chapters 1 through 8 – consists of these interviews. Most of the questions posed to the interviewees are similar and concern issues that we hope to be of interest to researchers of the field but also to a general audience of economists. Although, it might be interesting to compare answers of different prominent researchers we have decided, for the sake of completeness and authenticity, to present interviews author by author and not question by question. This also makes it easier for the reader to follow the interviewees' thoughts through the interview.

Part II of this volume consists of papers of that were presented at the symposium. The papers by Peter Bohm and Werner Güth are related to their invited lectures. Participants that were accepted as paper presenters at the symposium were invited to submit their papers for publication in this volume; following submission there was a peer review process. A subset of the presenters submitted their papers and a subset of these were finally accepted.

An undertaking like the 20th Arne Ryde Symposium cannot take place without support and help from numerous persons. In many cases this help goes far beyond what normally can be expected. We are very grateful to the Arne Foundation for the financial support. In particular we would like to thank Björn Thalberg and his successor as chairman for the foundation, Anders Borglin, for their general support and their understanding that not all expenses can be foreseen. In the planning and completion of the symposium the help from Ann-Charlotte Sahlin and Mona Hansson was invaluable. We have also received substantial help in finishing this volume. The task of making transcriptions of the taped interviews (in Part I) was solved with accuracy and sensitivity by Anna Holmqvist. We are also grateful to a number of anonymous referees that made a substantial effort in evaluating the contributions in Part II.

Lund, January 21, 2002

Fredrik Andersson and Håkan Holm

I

INTERVIEWS WITH INVITED SPEAKERS

Chapter 1

PETER BOHM*

Stockholm University

Q: *It is not uncommon that researchers in the experimental field have backgrounds that are somewhat surprising. Furthermore, far from all have pursued a consistent career in the field. Why did you start with experimental research?*

P.B.: In 1969, I was doing research on public-good decision making and wanted to investigate the extent of misrepresentation of non-hypothetical WTP among potential consumers of a real-world public good. For that purpose, I designed an experiment which turned out to produce pretty surprising results (published in the European Economic Review, 1972) and this got me hooked on doing experiments, primarily field(-like) experiments with real-world subjects and significant incentive payments.

Q: *Today quite a few economic graduate students start directly with experimental research. What are your thoughts about this development?*

P.B.: Directly? If they have taken a year of graduate courses in theory, econometrics and a basic course in experimental economics, I think it is quite OK if they start their thesis work with experimental topics.

Q: *Behaviorally and experimentally oriented economics has often imported methods and knowledge from psychology. However, few economists would argue that experimental economics is a sub-discipline of psychology. To what extent is there a marked division line between experimental economics and experimental psychology?*

P.B.: I assume you mean: concerning economic issues and experimental *methods*. To the extent I have checked what experimental psychologists have been doing I think there is a marked division line in methodology between the two sub-disciplines. What has been particularly problematic in what I have seen is, first, the psychologists' dominant use of hypothetical questions – or insignificant incentives – and, second, their acceptance

*P.B.: Peter Bohm; Q: question. Peter Bohm answered the questions in writing soon after the conference.

of lying to subjects in ways that will eventually become evident to the subjects and, hence, is likely to have detrimental long-term effects on what the experimental approach can achieve.

Q: *To the extent that you think that there exists experimental research in the intersection belonging to both subjects. What would this intersection contain?*

P.B.: I think the potential intersection is considerable concerning both methods and topics – with respect to the latter, relating in particular to consumer behavior and bargaining.

Q: *There have been instances recently of theory being developed from experiments. This seems to be a new phenomenon in the sense that previous theoretical breakthroughs have been initiated by other sources. What is your opinion about the virtue of this development, and do you think it will change the economics discipline fundamentally?*

P.B.: As long as the new theory is based on relevant and robust experimental results, this development is most welcome, of course. But I think that there have been instances where new theory has been developed before there were enough relevant and robust results for doing so. One example: a series of – what I consider to be – pretty biased tests of preference reversal were met by attempts to develop new theories which did not rely on, e.g., the independence axiom. Higher incentive levels and more-than-two-outcome options did not seem to produce anywhere near the initial frequencies of PR (see further below). – With respect to the second question, I think it is hard to believe that experiments any time soon will fundamentally change the economics discipline.

Q: *Can you give some examples where experimental results have preceded and stimulated the emergence of new theories.*

P.B.: There are a number of good examples arising from the experimental findings that "(market) institutions matter," e.g., regarding the properties of double auction markets.

Q: *Some theories have at times found themselves in an "embarrassment of riches" by, in some sense, delivering too much (this is sometimes said about the IO literature of the 1980's). Do you have any concerns that this is a problem in experimental economics? (For concreteness: one may provocatively say that a good graduate student is likely to be able to produce any anomaly he likes by cleverly designing an experiment.)*

P.B.: First, with insufficient incentive levels, a wide range of anomalous experimental results can be established, I'm sure. Second, variations of experimental markets with relatively few agents of various sizes (one large, two small, and three very small, etc, etc) can probably provide the 'embarras de richesse' that was said about the IO literature in the 80's, if a lot of energy and experimental money was spent – or misspent? – on identifying robustness of such results. Part of such problems may be avoided through the establishment of 'methodological rules' such as – as I favor – not publishing experimental results attained from studies using 'trivially low' incentive levels.

Q: *Even small differences in experimental design tend to produce differences in results and it is not uncommon that experimentalists use drastic phrases like "the devil is in the details": With this in mind to what extent and in what way do you think it is possible to make generalizations based on experimental results?*

P.B.: Difficult question and difficult to give a generally valid response. But, again, spending money on expensive experiments with clearly sufficient incentive payments to subjects would help to make generalizations of important aspects of behavior possible.

Q: *When lacking a theory it is not uncommon that empirically oriented economists instead try to generate stylized facts. Do you think there is a difference between generating stylized facts within the lab and generating facts from more traditional statistical sources?*

P.B.: Yes, there may well be such a difference, but in what direction is hard to say. But if attention is paid to the parallelism precept so that the stylized facts generated by results in the lab are tested in the field chances are that the experimental approach comes out on top.

Q: *What do you consider to be the most convincingly demonstrated regularities of behavior in public-goods experiments, and what do you consider to be the key open questions?*

P.B.: If the public-good experiments you refer to are primarily experiments with the voluntary exchange mechanism (VEM), the most convincingly meaningful regularity in my view is the existence of weak free-rider behavior. But the key open question is what happens in real-world applications of feasible demand revealing mechanisms and I am not convinced that experiments with the VEM, and especially the VEM results after a number of stationary repetitions, provide much insight in that respect.

Q: *You have done work on preference reversals indicating that some of the experimental results are artifacts of the experimental settings. In light of this, what is your opinion about the rationality assumptions in economics in light of this? More specifically: what is your views on rationality in its literal sense, and what is your view on "as-if rationality"?*

P.B.: I refer here to my first response to the question on generalizations above. On the basis of my own experimental work, given that the results therein can be replicated, I conclude that the role of preference reversals as a violation of the rationality assumptions in economics has been greatly overstated.

High rates of PR have been found, in particular, (1) for lotteries, two of which subjects are asked to choose between, where one lottery has a high probability of winning a small amount and the other a small probability of winning a large amount and where, for both lotteries the remaining outcome is zero or a small gain/loss, pretty much the same for the two lotteries; and (2) for claims, two of which subjects are asked to choose between, where one claim concerns a small amount at an early redemption date and the other a larger amount at a later redemption date, at other dates no payments are offered.

The evidence of preference reversal in decision making is weak in cases

- where incentives are significant – the important case for which theory has been developed, or
- where each option ('lotteries' or claims with different redemption dates) involves more than two outcomes (i.e., several 'lottery prizes' with different probabilities or claims with a stream of payments at several dates instead of only one payment at one date for each claim), and
- especially for the combination of these two cases, which is the dominant application of the received theory.

For cases with only two outcomes (specified above), similar expected (present) values and modest incentives, significant rates of violations of the rationality assumptions have been observed. To what extent these violations are much more than 'ordinary' non-systematic mistakes (which, of course, is another type of rationality violations) can be questioned.

Q: *There seems to some disagreement regarding the extent to which institutional aspects of specific applications should be "taken into the laboratory." What are your thoughts on this?*

P.B.: I interpret the question as concerning the choice between 'context-meager' (context-free is illusory) and 'context-rich' experimental environments. The former are unfamiliar to subjects, normally without a motive and hence likely to confuse the subjects and likely to yield unrepresentative results, I believe. The latter type of environment is easier to comprehend and it is typically also easier to understand the motive for the experiment. However, as a standard argument suggests, the latter may well allow that decisions are affected by uncontrollable subject attitudes to the particular context and may thus measure something that is irrelevant for the purpose of the experiment. Still, if the objective of experimental research is to identify *robust* findings, it may well be that a large number of different context-rich tests is overall a better basis for real-world relevant results than running identical tests with an outlandish context. The use of the voluntary exchange mechanism is a possible example of the latter type of tests.

Q: *According to certain psychological studies certain contexts to which the individual is familiar will help him to deal with logical problems. This may suggest that while subjects behave in a strange or irrational fashion in labs they may very well act differently in a more realistic situation. Can you think of any situation when it is motivated to use a strongly context dependent description of the experimental situation?*

P.B.: Yes, and I refer to my preceding response. If the purpose of studying the feasibility of consumer demand revelation for public goods, I think potential mechanisms should be tested in series of field or field-like contexts, where participants would understand the purpose of the tests, not in long series of applications of the voluntary exchange mechanisms which in several important respects are dissimilar to the bulk of real-world public goods.

Q: *It has been held that most research in medicine teaches us a lot about white mice; similarly, skeptical economists sometimes hold that experimental research teaches us a lot about undergraduate students. To what extent do you think that this criticism is fair?*

P.B.: Partly only. The problem is that subjects who are 'real-world' relevant for the issue at hand are so seldom used at some stage of a series of experiments, when (particular) student groups may not be obviously real-world relevant and especially when they are definitely not representative of real decision makers.

Q: *Is there any topic in experimental economics (decision-making) that you consider to be relatively exhausted and for which the marginal benefit of additional studies is small.*

P.B.: What I have said above suggests certain topics that I personally would not spend time on dealing with. But things may look differently tomorrow when possibly a new angle has popped up. Furthermore, the only principle for research that I can think of is to let people do what they want to do, but also to let qualified journal editors publish what they want. A problem may be that there are editors around who may not be qualified enough to select qualified and open-minded referees who don't hesitate to use anonymity for their own purposes. Unfortunately, the field of experimental economics does not seem to provide an exception to this rule.

Q: *Do you see any particular pitfalls for EE now or in the future?*

P.B.: The often too low incentive payments, creating in some cases exciting results that set off long series of, in the aggregate, costly experiments that would not have surfaced if large pay-off dominant incentives had been used at the outset; the neglect of the need for parallelism and the rare use of non-student subjects and context-rich field(-like) experiments; the tendency for experimental themes or topics of uncertain or unlikely relevance for real-world applications to set off a cavalcade of experiments with minute variations of the theme; the over-use of smart 'context-exotic' experimental environments (ultimatum games seems to me to be another such example); the lack of convincing reasons for some of the cases where stationary repetitions are used. On this, see Bohm, "Pitfalls in Experimental Economics," this volume.

Q: *What do you think will happen with the market share of experimental research in the future economics discipline?*

P.B.: If the quality of experiments is kept on a high level with substantial incentive payments, more experiments using real-world contexts and increasing the use of real-world non-student subjects, the cost of the average experiment is likely to be high. But with a high quality, the demand for this kind of research is likely to continue to grow and so, I think, will its market share, in spite of high experimental costs.

Chapter 2

CATHERINE C. ECKEL*

Virginia Tech

H.H.: *It is not uncommon that researchers in the experimental field have backgrounds that are somewhat surprising. Furthermore, far from all have pursued a consistent career in the field. Why did you start with experimental research?*

C.E.: In graduate school I was exposed to the early experimental research of Roger Sherman who was one of my professors at the University of Virginia. Later on Charlie Holt visited Virginia for a semester while I was there, and he was also just beginning to dabble in experimental research. This was in the late 70's. Later on, Charlie and I did a paper together, where we were testing a simple agenda-manipulation idea. Soon after that I became really interested in the differences in career paths of women and men. In particular, I noticed that women published less than men in every field, and that they were less likely to get tenure in every academic field. I thought that this was pretty interesting and it occurred to me that the experiment lab might be some place where I could try to learn something about differences in the way people behave and treat each other.

H.H.: *Today quite a few economic graduate students start directly with experimental research. What are your thoughts about this development?*

C.E.: In the US market at least, I think it's better for students to show a portfolio of skills on the job market. Those students who can show skill at theory, at data analysis and at experimental design do the best, with experiments being a component of the portfolio but not the whole thing. In the US at least, there are very few departments that have positions for experimental economists. Most departments are organized along traditional field lines and it's hard for them to fit an experimentalist into their line-up of faculty, so it's best if someone can have expertise in the field, but have experiments as one of their tools, one of the methodologies that they can

*C.E.: Catherine Eckel; F.A.: Fredrik Andersson; H.H.: Håkan Holm.

bring to bear on the questions they're interested in. Eventually I think, most departments will have an experimentalist, like they have econometricians now – the experimentalist will be someone whose expertise is in experimental design and analysis – but we're a long way from there.

F.A.: *Behaviorally and experimentally oriented economics have often imported methods and knowledge from psychology. However, few economists would argue that experimental economics is a sub-discipline of psychology. To what extent is there a marked division line between experimental economics and psychology?*

C.E.: Well, psychologists and economists ask different questions, and the methodologies that they use follow from the questions that they ask, and so naturally there are differences in most of what each field does. But there is an area of overlap, and the overlap is mostly in decision making. Behavioral economists are interested in experiments about the psychology of behavior in economic situations, and so naturally there is overlap. You find psychologists doing economics there, like Colin Camerer, and economists doing psychology, like George Loewenstein.

F.A.: *To the extent that you think that there exists experimental research in the intersection belonging to both subjects, what should this intersection contain?*

C.E.: Well, I have no clear idea what it should contain, but I have a pretty clear idea what it does contain. It seems to me that there are two branches of research where economics and psychology are overlapping, and they are the two that I mentioned earlier today in my talk. One is this that economists are challenged by the richness of behavior in experimental games; that challenge has resulted in their bringing psychological elements into richer theoretical models of preferences. So the preference-based area is one instance of overlap between economics and psychology. The other is in the area of learning. There is so much work on learning now, and it is clear that psychology has a lot to tell us about that, especially the cognitive end of learning – how subjects process information. In other areas, there is work in economics now that is informed by theories from evolutionary psychology – like the work that Vernon Smith was talking about today, for instance, or Tooby and Cosmides and their ideas about cheater detection. And there are two additional areas, not where psychology overlaps economics, but where economics is beginning to talk to other fields: There is a lot of work now in anthropology where anthropologists are using experiments to measure aspects of culture, and in sociology there is a very close relationship between work in the group processes area of sociology and people who are doing experiments in group decision making as well.

H.H.: *There have been instances recently of theory being developed from experiments. This seems to be a new phenomenon in the sense that previous theoretical break-throughs have been initiated by other sources. What is your opinion about the virtue of this development and do you think it will change economics fundamentally.*

C.E.: Well, it's really interesting what is happening with experiments and theory. Theorists are listening to the results of experimental games, and there seems to be a partnership, or a growing partnership, between people developing behavioral theory and people who are doing experiments. I think that it is absolutely critical that this partnership continue. Experiments need to be grounded in theory, and it is very important that theorists pay attention to the kinds of patterns that we observe coming out of the lab.

H.H.: *Can you give some more concrete examples where experimental research has preceded and stimulated the emergence of new theories?*

C.E.: Well, yes. I suppose the most prominent area is the area of richer preferences. There are a number of competing theories now that bring some element of fairness into the modeling of behavior. The work by Fehr and Schmidt, Bolton and Ockenfels, Rabin and Charness, those are all examples of theoretical developments that are the result of progress in experimental games. But there's another area too, and that's in the area of market and nonmarket institutions. Experiments have led to some surprising results – for example that some auction institutions that are equivalent theoretically turn out to not be equivalent in the lab – and that has spurred additional development on institutions and how institutions process information.

F.A.: *Some theories have at times found themselves in what might be called an embarrassment of riches, by in some sense delivering too much. An example might be the IO literature in the 80's. Do you have any concerns that this is a problem in experimental economics?*

C.E.: I remember IO in the 80's being referred to as theory by example, and sometimes we see something in experiments that looks like that. But it seems to me that we just need to be careful about what questions we're asking, and what details of the experimental environment are important for answering the question that we're interested in answering. It's not really so interesting that we can push the results in one way or another. What's interesting is the regularities that you find and their relationship to the questions that you're asking. So the important thing is to pick the right details and design the experiment in a way that is appropriate to the question.

F.A.: *Well, there is this problem with the devil being in the details. With this in mind, to what extent and in what way do you think it is possible to make generalizations based on experimental results?*

C.E.: One point that is important to make is that there are some areas where there are general regularities; you can't make the oral double auction fail for example. It always works. Three buyers, three sellers, it always works. So one of the things that we've learned in experiments is the importance of institutions, and that there are some institutions that are very robust to everything. The details really don't matter. You can run them with 5th graders for candy, you can run them with CEOs of corporations, you can run them with students, it doesn't make any difference how you set the environment. It doesn't matter whether it's hypothetical or there are really big incentives or anything like that. And then there are other environments that are really, really sensitive, and those are other types of institutions that Vernon Smith refers to as "non-disciplining institutions," like the ultimatum and dictator games. And these institutions are interesting because of their sensitivity. That means that they can be used, not to test theory – I think we've finished testing theory with the ultimatum game – but they can be used for things like measuring aspects of culture, so you can measure the degree of cooperation among a particular type of people, or risk attitudes among different types of people. Institutions that are sensitive can be used as measuring tools and there is some movement in that direction. Another point to make is that many times the details will affect the base line of an experiment but not the comparative statics. If you're interested in the difference between treatments, then your base line really doesn't matter so much, and to the extent that the details only affect the base line, they're really not so much of a problem

H.H.: *When lacking a theory it is not uncommon that empirically oriented economists try to generate stylized facts. Do you think there is a difference between generating stylized facts within the lab and generating them by more traditional statistical methods?*

C.E.: Not fundamentally. Fundamentally you are looking for regularities of behavior, and you can find them in all kinds of places. On the other hand, the lab does give you more control over the environment so that you can determine to a greater extent what factors about the environment are producing the regularities in behavior for the stylized facts.

H.H.: *Given the artificiality of some experimental situations, does this raise any particular concerns?*

C.E.: Well, I don't think that it's really a problem. As I said earlier, I think the important thing is to suit the situation to the question, to suit the elements of the context that you want to manipulate to the question you want to answer; as long as we're all careful about doing that, I think we're fine. In some instances it's appropriate to have context-free artificial situations, because that's the way the theory is written. In other situations when you want to ask a more specific contextual question, then you need the appropriate context.

F.A.: *If you were to mention three robust, non-trivial findings in experimental research, what findings would you suggest, and would you suggest the same to Joe on the street as to an economist?*

C.E.: I could point to two categories of contributions that I think are important. One is more important to economists, and that would be findings about what I would call the fundamentals of behavior. What we have discovered pretty robustly is that people share. There is altruism – or there is behavior that appears to be altruistic – in these experiments, and it's robust; the subjects really mean to do it, and it doesn't go away. So that's one thing that we really know now. Of course, the average person on the street wouldn't be surprised by that, they know that already, it is only economists who are surprised. Another result is that people are willing to punish behavior that they think of as unfair. So behavior that violates social norms gets punished in the lab. That is also something that would only be surprising to economists. I would add a third result, which is sort of general to the other two: when there are gains to cooperation, subjects are pretty good at exploiting those gains. They find a way to cooperate when it is in their interest to cooperate, and it is hard to call that irrational; it seems to make sense that the subjects should want to get as much money for less as they can. So this is sort of like a gains version of the Coase theorem. If there are gains to be had, then subjects will find a way to exploit them.

Now, the other category of results is more what I would explain to Joe on the street, and that has to do with applications and institutions. For example, enormous progress has been made in designing auction institutions for special purposes, and that research is completely dependent on experimental results. Another example would be an understanding of bubbles and crashes in the stock market. Here we have an element of psychology, but I think that the experiments have led us to a better understanding of when and where we might expect to see bubbles and crashes in the stock market. And a third example would be the Environmental Protection Agency's auction of tradable emissions permits. This is a market that didn't exist before, and experimentalists have had a lot to say about how to design and implement these markets.

H.H.: *According to some of your recent research, status has economic implications in economic bargaining, with high status sellers obtaining higher prices than low status sellers. Status has been recognized for quite some time in sociology. It is clear that in your paper the status effects are embedded in an economics context, with monetary pay-off etc, that is likely to be different to the context designed by sociologists. Where do you think, in this case, that economics ends and sociology starts?*

C.E.: Well, I think that my work is firmly between the two fields; it has elements of both. So in a way, research is merging from both directions there as it is in psychology; sociologists are doing more work about economics and economists are doing more work that has sociological components. And the area of sociology that's relevant here is the group processes area. I use status characteristics theory and expectations states theory in my own work. And I have talked and interacted with a lot of sociologists who are beginning to do things like incentivise their environments, and pay their subjects for what they do, to sharpen up their own results or to broaden the relevance of their results into more economic settings. So I think that both sides are recognizing that many economic exchanges are social decisions, and there is a social element to that interaction that's important to look at.

H.H.: *You and Phil Grossman have done a number of contributions in experimental testing for gender differences. Do you think that this research has become sufficiently mature to motivate scientific recognition of any well established gender differences in experimental behavior?*

C.E.: I believe that the points I made in my talk today are valid. One is that in many environments women exhibit more altruistic behavior than men do, and in many environments women appear more risk averse than men do. I actually think that the second one is more important for real economic considerations, like the negotiation of wages and investment portfolios and even things like medical treatments which I also mentioned today. To the extent that women have different risk attitudes, they end up with different outcomes that might not look so good to us. If women's greater risk aversion means that they earn lower wages, then that is an area where there might be a call for policy intervention. I'm not sure that we need to be positive that these things are true in order to go forward with policies that might help balance things a little better. We just need to think that there is enough evidence that women's greater risk aversion might be getting in the way of their economic success to think that a policy intervention might be worth while.

F.A.: *I'll go on with some broader questions about experiments. There seems to be some disagreement regarding the extent to which institutional aspects of specific applications should be taken into the laboratory. What are your thoughts on this?*

C.E.: I think I already answered this question. I think that you ought to suit the environment to the question and the theory, so for some things you want an abstract environment and for others you want a context rich environment. I don't think that there's any hard and fast rule on that, as long as we're careful about suiting the environment to the question that we ask.

F.A.: *According to certain psychological studies, certain contexts to which the individual is familiar will help him to deal with the logical problems. This may suggest that while subjects behave strangely or irrationally in the lab, they may very well act differently in a more realistic situation. If any, can you think of any situation when it is motivated to use a strongly context dependant description of an experimental situation?*

C.E.: I think this is a really interesting question, but it is one that I don't know much about. I don't know of any experiments that show that subjects behave irrationally here and then you give them a little hint and then they suddenly behave rationally. First of all, let me say that it's really not irrational. A lot of what we call non-rational or irrational behavior in the lab, really isn't. So if you take the public goods game for example. It's hardly irrational for subjects to cooperate when they get a lot more money out of the experimenter by doing so. And even in something like the ultimatum game, it's not irrational for subjects to make more generous offers if they're anticipating the pattern of rejections, and that appears to be what they're doing. I just think it's an interesting research area and one that I hope that some people pursue.

H.H.: *This is a little bit of a provocative question. It has been held that most research in medicine teaches us a lot about white mice; similarly, skeptical economists sometimes hold that experimental research teaches us a lot about undergraduate students. To what extent do you think that this criticism is fair?*

C.E.: Again we have this difference across institutions. For some institutions it really doesn't matter who's playing the games. For example, I've run public goods games with fifth-graders, and they get it. They can generalize it to things like libraries and parks, and they really understand the concepts involved. So in many cases I don't think the subject pool matters at all; in others it does. In areas where it does matter who the subject pool is, we can find out interesting things about differences between people; there have for example been some experiments on children that measure children's cooperativeness and altruism and risk attitudes and time preference. There are some new experiments underway where researchers are using things like ultimatum and dictator games to measure aspects of culture for primitive cultures, things like the Machiguenga Indians in Peru and others. There's some work that we're starting that will take a set of games designed to measure cooperation, altruism, trust, reciprocity, time preference and risk attitudes. We're going to be running these experiments on children in the high schools in Chicago, and we're also going to be doing the same experiments in a series of senior centers, centers where the elderly meet. I've recently completed a study with a team of researchers in Canada measuring preferences of poor people. This study is designed to inform policy making. There's a survey by Sheryl Ball and Paul Czech that looks at differences across subject pools and surveys all of the papers that have looked at subject pool characteristics. In my own research I'm interested in the characteristics of the subject pool and how that is correlated with behavior and the allocation of resources. These sensitive environments give us tools to use to look at systematic differences in attitudes and behavior.

F.A.: *Is there any topic in experimental economics or decision making that you consider to be relatively exhausted and for which the marginal benefit of additional studies is small?*

C.E.: You know, I used to think that the ultimatum game was finished, but I'm not so sure any more. And for a while there I thought that we were finished with mixed strategies, but it looks like people are coming up with new ways to look at mixed strategies now. I'm not willing to say that any area is really tapped out. I don't suppose that we need to run any more oral double auctions.

F.A.: *It's a small area but still very specific. Are there still any large territories unexplored, on the other hand?*

C.E.: Yes. I think that the largest unexplored area has to do with using experiments to measure other things. So, I mentioned the work that we're doing with children and elderly. I've also been involved with a group that has trained a bunch of anthropologists to go out onto the field and run ultimatum and dictator games with these indigenous populations who have various degrees of market contact, and there are some really fascinating results coming out of the work of these anthropologists. So, they're finding for example that there's a relationship between the degree of marketisation and the extent to which people split things equally in the ultimatum game. And it might not go the way you think – the more the market contact, the more equally they split it, and without market contact they tend to split it unequally and they never reject offers. So there's really a fascinating growth area of research there, I think, and I've seen proposals to use these experimental games to measure culture within organizations, as a way of measuring corporate culture and the effects of corporate culture. It's still an open question whether these games are going to be useful for doing that, but it's quite an interesting area.

H.H.: *Do you see any particular pitfalls for experimental economics now or in the future?*

C.E.: I think that we need to avoid reinventing the wheel, and this is important as we move toward research in other fields. As we move toward psychology and toward sociology it's really important to do our homework and to know what other people have found out. So it seems to me that the only real pitfall in experimental economics is not having enough respect for the research in other fields that we can bring to bear on the questions that we want to ask.

H.H.: *What do you think will happen to the market share of experimental economics in the future?*

C.E.: It seems that experimental economics is growing, there's quite a lot of interest in it, and I expect that the market share will go up. But I think that it will take some time for experimental economics to be sort of a normal component of graduate student training. I think that it will come to that, that students will take an experimental class and that that will be part of what they do. I can imagine a time when all departments will have an experimentalist. That's certainly not true now so that means that the market share has to go up. Certainly it has grown enormously over the past ten years.

Chapter 3

WERNER GÜTH*

Max Planck Institut, Jena

F.A.: *It's not uncommon that researchers in experimental economics have backgrounds in other fields – obviously you have a background in game theory – and moreover far from all have pursued a consistent career in the field. Why did you start in experimental research?*

W.G.: The decisive reason was that I wanted to learn game theory. I was interested in experimental economics, but I thought "maybe, this is nothing for me." Later, the same thing happened with evolution. Then we had a series of local conferences where game theorists and social psychologists met. So, there was a long tradition of experimental research going back to the late 50's. When I came back from one of those conferences in 1977 I had 1000 marks in my bag for running experiments. Actually, in the winter semester of 1977-78, which was my first semester as a professor in Cologne, we ran ultimatum experiments, and also Vickrey-auction-type experiments; it took us four years to publish the results, but ever since I have been involved in experiments. I don't have a life-long plan of running so and so many experiments, of doing so much theory, and so on. When I was invited to this conference two years ago I knew I had to offer something, and this demand effect is pretty much how it works.

F.A.: *Today quite a few economic graduate students start directly with experimental economics. What are your thoughts about this development?*

W.G.: A good background in theory is not bad, of course. It goes both ways, actually. Many experiments are theoretically inspired, and vice versa. In order to do experiments they must know statistics, and they must be trained to solve software problems; they really need to be quite sophisticated. In fact, one thing which is nice is that experiments can be taught differently. I teach experimental economics completely differently compared to other things, I teach it in an "apprentice" fashion. I

*W.G.: Werner Güth; F.A.: Fredrik Andersson; H.H.: Håkan Holm.

use learning-by-doing in small groups from the start. This is a very nice aspect of experimental economics, actually.

H.H.: *Experimentally oriented economists have often imported methods and knowledge from psychology. However, few economists would argue that experimental economics is a sub-discipline of psychology. To what extent is there a marked division line between experimental economics and psychology?*

W.G.: The disciplines become increasingly close. To some extent, they are preoccupied with the same problems. Also, many of the paradigms in psychology are of a game theoretic structure. Sometimes we have a lot to learn. For instance, recently I ran experiments in Bielefeld dealing with the game theoretic concept of mixed strategies. A psychologist (Yaakov Kareev) pointed out that it is not easy for people to randomize. In fact people tend to "over-randomize" – change too often. When people try to randomize there are too few long sequences, like head-head-head; his idea is that we have a short-term memory of about seven draws and people try to balance heads and tails within such short subsequences. In fact, I don't see the dividing line; I was once the president of an economic psychology association. More generally, I think game theory is social science; what we call experimental economics, could as well be called experimental social science. I consider myself a social scientist.

H.H.: *You indicate that there is a substantial intersection between experimental economics and psychology, but is there something that the intersection does not contain?*

W.G.: For instance, I personally would not like to engage in a questionnaire study. If I collect data, I will always provide monetary incentives; I am satisfied with my evidence only if there are significant monetary incentives backing them. Another major difference is that we have slightly other ethics, for instance there is a great reluctance to be untruthful to subjects in experimental economics, whereas in psychology they would simply say "you have to debrief them," that means you have to tell them afterwards. But there are many psychologists who follow the same practice as I do. I don't see a clear dividing line. I am more for crossing dividing lines than drawing them.

F.A.: *There have been instances recently of theory being developed from experiments. This seems to be a new phenomenon in the sense that previous theoretical breakthroughs have been initiated by other sources. What is your opinion about the virtue of this development and do you think it will change the economics discipline fundamentally?*

W.G.: You have to be very clear on what kind of new theories have been developed. There are so-called new equilibrium ideas. I refer to this as a neoclassical repair shop. The starting point is that orthodox theory – meaning that you apply the common laws of rationality to material incentives and derive a solution – is strongly rejected in many instances, for instance in case of the ultimatum game. And then, what those people will do is to somewhat repair the game-theoretic presentation; they have richer utility functions, but they would never question rationality. The same can be said about psychological game theory: there is no questioning of rationality, what people do is that they somewhat change the game-theoretic presentation so that the game-theoretically rational behavior moves somewhat closer to the observed behavior. And that I call neoclassical repairs. Something can be learnt from this. What can be learnt is that maybe one natural type of argument like for instance inequality aversion, can account for many experimental effects. That you can learn from it, but it's never the true explanation. A completely different story would be something where you'd say: "OK, in light of the experimental data, I now really try to develop a theory about how people come up with their decisions." Let me give you one example: I was always very much inspired by the study of Roth and Malouf. They had two people sharing a unit pie – but the pie was probability. Either one or the other wins a monetary prize, and what the two can bargain about is with what probability each wins. And what was varied in the experiment was how much the parties knew about the monetary prize which they could win. Once nothing was commonly known, each knew their own monetary prize, but not that of the opponent, and vice versa. The usual tendency was to split the probability equally, so each won the prize with probability one half. When those monetary prizes became common knowledge and were different, however, they tended to choose probabilities giving the same monetary expectation to each. So what I read from this, and what I see now everywhere, is that we have a hierarchy of equity standards; in the case at hand monetary expectation would rank higher than winning probability. There is hope for developing a more sophisticated type of equity theory here.

H.H.: *Some theories have at certain times found themselves in some kind of embarrassment of riches by in some sense delivering too much. This is said about the IO literature of the 80's. Do you have any concerns that this is a problem in experimental economics?*

W.G.: Yes, I guess we might get the same. In American courts, they consult experts to provide evidence. And for some time they used experimental evidence. For instance, in these new frequency auctions, they also used experimental evidence sometimes to argue that this institutional rule is better than the other one. I guess we know how to frame an experiment to get the right data. Maybe somebody wants a certain type of results, and pays me generously for this, and maybe I would know some ways to make it more likely to get this type of result, in a clean type of experiment. I just want to say this because what I think is that we will get evidence for all kinds of effects. There is a risk that the same thing will happen as in IO, that a second type of folk theorem applies; you could say "OK, give me any type of behavior, I can define a game predicting this behavior and even run an experiment that just explains this kind of absurdity." There may be something like this.

H.H.: *Even small differences in experimental design tend to produce differences in results and it is not uncommon that experimentalists use drastic phrases like "the devil is in the details": With this in mind to what extent and in what way do you think it is possible to make generalizations based on experimental results?*

W.G.: Let me give one idea: Nobody would translate the reactivity numbers you observe in an experiment into real life. But qualitatively you can infer, because people are not brainwashed when they participate in experiments. When participants go into the lab, and they stay there for two or three hours, they can leave it with fifty to one hundred marks. And if you go to shop in a supermarket this is similarly relevant. One artificiality is of course that certain experiments cannot really be used for normal people because they have a quite demanding analytic structure. They could be, for instance, of the game-theory type or something like this. Think about a second, third or fourth-price auction for example, which are very difficult to explain to people; they might understand the English auction, but sealed bids might be very difficult for them. And so sometimes you need students to understand the rules. We sometimes have gone to high schools for participants. Psychologists quite often go to consumers or households. They sometimes go to households and ask questions over three months. But in general, no one is so naive to translate the reactivity numbers, the parameters that you observe directly, but qualitatively you learn a lot.

H.H.: *If you were to mention three robust non-trivial findings in experimental research, what findings would you suggest? Would your suggestions be the same to "Joe on the street" as to economists?*

W.G.: That's really difficult. I see a lot of fairness and equity aspects in certain types of situations, but there are other places where you don't observe fairness, in market places for instance. I think you have to defend theories by restricting their area of application. Equity theory is something about say, joint ventures, and there it's rather robust. But as I said, fairness is not the only motivation we have. It has to fight with competing motivations, and in some situations it's a dominating force and in others it may be dominated by other motivations. That would be one thing. The other thing is that decisions and evaluations have to be derived. They are not readily available. Even some psychological theories, like prospect theory, do not answer how I have to make a decision. But if it's really a difficult decision – like "should I marry girl A or girl B?" – what's really important? What should matter? In economic theory decision making doesn't make any sense, it's just exercise. So that leads to the need to develop the concept of bounded rationality. What else? Of course one important finding is that losses matter more than gains. Going down is something what we don't like very much. We are able to do it, but it is painful. These are three. Also "Joe on the street" is an economist, all people are.

F.A.: *From time to time it's argued that certain theories contain vague concepts that are very tricky to control in empirical tests. Sometimes such concepts are less respectfully denoted as theories garbage cans, since by referring to them as anomalies they can be made consistent with theory. According to your views, are there any garbage cans in economic theory?*

W.G.: There is something like risk attitude for instance. But in economic theory it's just the shape of the utility curve for money, and this is not rich enough to express the concerns which make us sometimes shy away from risk and sometimes search for risk. In actual life people sometimes buy insurance for very stupid minor damages, and on the other hand, people spend a lot on gambling and so on. So, I don't know. Sometimes you learn – I wouldn't call it garbage cans. I also would never refer to anomalies; what the notion of an anomaly says is that we have the norm of rational behavior and you somewhat deviate from this norm. But actual behavior is not just one step away from this kind of norm – it's a universe away. But, of course, we often learn something. Consider the endowment effect; there could be a more basic thing behind it. Maybe the endowment effect is somewhat related to the idea that losses matter more. I wouldn't claim that those effects are simple anomalies but I learn a lot from the observation, and by framing them as anomalies they are easily understood; it serves a pedagogical purpose. Thaler, for instance, became quite popular because of his series of anomalies, but in general I think I really want to explain things rather than referring to them as anomalies.

H.H.: *I think many economists and game theorists associate your name with ultimatum games and you have done quite a few ultimatum game experiments since the beginning of the 80's. In 1995 you reflected on this in an article in JEBO. Now, five years later, what main conclusions can you draw from this research?*

W.G.: Yes, it was the first experiment I ran and there was a time when I was afraid that people would say "he always runs this," but I have started doing it very actively again. And one reason for doing it is that I know much data around this paradigm with certain institutional details varying – for instance, we have considered selling the degree of veto power. So, I'm sometimes interested in other aspects, for instance in why people veto. And I do it quite often by doing something close to the ultimatum game because I have data to compare it with. So partly this is just a working-horse which lends itself to studying new types of questions. My motivation for the basic ultimatum game was that I wanted to study the simplest bargaining situation; actually I wanted to develop a kind of bargaining theory. That was my first idea when I got these 1000 marks. You have to see that just like in game theory, experimental economics also started with characteristic-function type of work. There were many characteristic-function type experiments, and I was a bit scared by these because you just have the characteristic function. Then you have to make sure how this is really run as an experiment since for a cooperative game, it is not clear how they are going to really do it. You need instructions telling them how to announce a coalition and how to announce the payoff distribution, and so on. So you have all the procedure details and this became quite complex since subjects confronted each other face to face with possibilities of free communication. I was a bit scared by those things. So that resulted in studying the simplest kind of situation, and to have a more strategic kind of situation with very exact rules. And I hoped that first you do this and then you slowly proceed with more complicated games; actually, there is a more complicated game in that 1982 paper but nobody reads the second part. And as you see, you got stuck with the original situation because it's game theoretically simple, but apparently it's psychologically very rich. That we have to learn. Other people learn other things from it, they would say for instance, "OK, it was a standard example to show that game theory doesn't predict well." But that was not my main intention, because that would have been beating a dead horse. I knew that game theory is not good in explaining behavior. So that was not the main motivation. But, of course, that may have been the primary reason for why it became so famous. I heard that Robert Aumann often talked about this kind of game, so others also propagated the idea. It came to me as a surprise, but people just caught on and talked about these results, sometimes asking "are those students in Cologne stupid?"

H.H.: *You mention (in the paper you will present at this symposium) that one reaction to experimental results that seems hard to explain by the rational choice approach is that experimental hypotheses about subjects' preferences do not truly reflect the real ones. In your paper you suggest another explanation; by substituting forward looking by backward looking or adaptive behavior. Could you develop your thoughts on this theme.*

W.G.: The main motivation for this kind of robust learning experiments is that I was sometimes attacked in the past, especially because of my work on ultimatum games, along the lines: "OK, he rejects rationality, but does he really offer something else? No it's too difficult." I try to, but the answers are incomplete. Somewhat surprisingly, those people who attacked me because I questioned rationality, now completely deny any kind of rationality. Because in evolution you don't have any cognitive requirements. Some learning theories also have very low cognitive requirements. Sometimes – for instance in stimulus-response learning – you simply would say: "OK, what was good in the past has some reason to be good in the future." That's the only cognitive demand which you have there. So, I said that the truth must be in the middle. We learn from the past, but it's not that we don't deliberate future consequences. First of all I want to show this, and secondly I want to collect stylized facts to get some guidance how I can separate and combine learning from past experience and forward-looking deliberation. And it's a very modest aim: let's get some stylized facts before we rush to develop theories. One thing is, of course, that it depends very much on the type of situation – when social norms are very strong, there's very little learning because people know what to do. If, however, the situation is complex then there is need of adaptation. But there is always, nearly always, consistent evidence of forward-looking deliberation, and we tried to capture this by: "OK, it's a learning experiment where you do not always play the same game." It is the same decision format, but the rules change. And then, if you tell them "now you play another game," then you always see jumps in the decision behavior. We see that as evidence for forward-looking deliberation. The truth is in the middle: behavioral adaptation is neither non-cognitive learning, nor is it complete rationality – i.e. rational anticipation of rule changes – it's in between. And again it's very difficult to organize those things.

F.A.: *There seems to be some disagreement regarding the extent to which institutional aspects of specific applications should be taken into the laboratory. What are your thoughts on that?*

W.G.: Why shouldn't we allow everybody to do it according to his taste? People are interested in different things. I'm not interested so much in economic policy, but if somebody is interested in economic policy he might, for instance, take a macro model and build something on top of it which he carries into the lab, this is now possible. You could have a large econometric model and define a game on top of it – for instance labor negotiations. Some aspects are of course difficult to take into the lab. Once we did a marriage-formation experiment. Of course, we clearly say that we don't capture the romantic aspect. Actually, we refer to it as a joint venture, so certain things are clearly more difficult to get into the lab. And we have an overlapping-generations type of experiment with multiple families, so that you can study whether tax systems and social security systems crowd out solidarity within the family or not. Again, these are not real families. But maybe the economic models about those things also don't have the romantic aspects. You just look at the structural aspects, how they feed into behavior. Certain institutions are clearly difficult to put into an experiment. But if one is ingenious enough, maybe one has new ideas how to do it.

H.H.: *It has been held that most research in medicine teaches us a lot about white mice; similarly, skeptical economists sometimes hold that experimental research teaches us a lot about undergraduate students. To what extent do you think that this criticism is fair?*

W.G.: As I said, you need some training to understand the kind of models we are interested in, and for those things an undergraduate student is quite good. I would love to have more students of mathematics, for instance. They usually capture the situation quite easily because they have an analytic talent. That restricts us somewhat. If the situation is complicated, it might take a long time for normal people to capture the situation. There have been these high-stakes experiments where people would travel to a poor country with a 40 dollar pie. Many results from studies of undergraduate students are rather robust. Especially the ultimatum results are rather robust; other things could be culturally or country dependent. But you have to ask yourselves why should the cognitive and emotional system of undergraduate students be so different?

F.A.: *Is there any topic in experimental economics or decision making that you consider to be relatively exhausted and for which the marginal benefit of additional studies is small?*

W.G.: People might say, for instance, that there are enough ultimatum bargaining experiments – just to attack myself, because I don't want to attack others. And there is of course an almost infinite sequence of prisoners' dilemma type of experiments. But again, people might vary the scenario and I do so. Sometimes these are just paradigms which you use to ask something else. There are always additional questions related to this.

F.A.: *Presumably, you will have a more positive answer on the next question, which is if you think that there are still any large territories unexplored in the experimental field.*

W.G.: I would like to know those territories, I would enter them as a pioneer. Maybe there are large territories, but if it would look promising, I would immediately jump to that. I guess we are all trying to enter the hall of fame.

H.H.: *Do you see any particular pitfalls in experimental economics in the future.*

W.G.: I wonder where all these brilliant young colleagues will find a job. There is so much going on because so many people run experiments. It's a big field now, but there will be some frustration. So I sometimes encourage my younger colleagues to have some additional special field, say law and economics, or import experimental economics to business administration. Experimental economics could have a better future in business administration. They have much more funds, and sometimes they also know much more details. Maybe we could import our ideas in the medical sciences. For instance, I have seen work on an algorithm for the allocation of kidney transplants.

H.H.: *Then I have the last question here and that is what you think will happen with the market share of experimental research in the future in the economics discipline.*

W.G.: I don't know, but in the near future it will be stable, maybe even growing, simply because we attract very brilliant young scholars. But otherwise I don't make any predictions. It's also not necessary. People develop the way they develop.

Chapter 4

JOHN HEY*

University of York and University of Bari

F.A.: *It's not uncommon that researchers in the experimental field have backgrounds that are somewhat surprising, and far from all have pursued a consistent career in the field. Why did you start with experimental research?*

J.H.: For probably the first half of my career I did mainly theory, a bit of empirical work but mainly theory, and mainly applications of expected-utility theory. And I used to do a lot of search theory, this shows how old I am. During the 70's and 80's, search theory was extremely popular. I was working on a theory of search with learning about the distribution, so as the individual was searching over the prices and wages, they were learning also about the distribution. And mathematically it was extremely elegant, it was very satisfying, and I thought it would be interesting just to try and work it out, to get some numbers. So I then tried to solve for particular numbers, in a particular search problem, and I could not do it, my computer was not powerful enough. And at this point I thought, well if my computer is not powerful enough, how on earth is it meant to explain behavior? So I started out doing experiments. I actually gave the search problem to subjects in a very simplified laboratory setting and watched what they did. And it was interesting. They were using very nice simple heuristics. The trouble with that was I could not work out the optimal strategy because it was too complicated for me to solve, so I could not compare it with the actual strategy. That was the way I started. And in those days people were extremely hostile to experimental methods.

F.A.: *Today, quite a few economics grad students start directly with experimental research. What are your thoughts about this development?*

J.H.: I feel very strongly that it is a method, it is not a subject. So if somebody comes to me and says I want to do experimental economics, I say: "Go

*J.H.: John Hey; F.A.: Fredrik Andersson; H.H.: Håkan Holm.

away." I want you to investigate some interesting problem in economics; if experimental methods are appropriate you should use them. So I am really quite discouraging to people who like it as a method without an idea of what they want to apply it to. I think it's quite nice that lots of graduate students enjoy it, but it is a method.

H.H.: *Behaviorally and experimentally oriented economics has often imported methods and knowledge from psychology. However few economists would argue that experimental economics is a sub-discipline of psychology. To what extent is there a marked division line between experimental economics and experimental psychology?*

J.H.: Certainly in methodology I think there is a big difference. The one thing I remember from the conference where I first met Daniel Kahneman is having this argument about incentives, about whether you should pay people. I think many psychologists say it does not matter particularly, and they cite evidence where they have done an experiment without incentives and the same experiment with, and the results are similar. But these of course have been experiments with very small incentives, and I do not think that is a very fair test of whether serious incentives matter. Another methodological difference is deception, which I think psychologists use a lot and perhaps find useful as a tool. I think that is extremely bad. Once your subjects think you might be deceiving them, you change the whole structure of the experiment, and it is very important they believe what you tell them. So I think we differ in methodology in key respects. I think we should also – although we do not necessarily do – differ in our research focus. I think we are beginning to forget that economists are interested in different things than psychologists. In a sense I think psychologists are interested in behavior in the small, while economists should be interested in more aggregate behavior. I do not think my role is to predict your consumer behavior, it is to predict the behavior of a group of people. So I think that we should be focussing on more general issues, and they should be focussing on more particular. I am not particularly interested in the effect of mood on behavior. That seems to be a psychological question – unless somehow you can affect a whole country with a particular mood, make the whole country depressed or something. So I think we have different research focus, which many people I think forget about.

H.H.: *To the extent that you think that there exists experimental research in the intersection belonging to both subjects. What would this intersection contain?*

J.H.: I think the thing we economists ought to look at – and which psychologists could help us with – is the whole process of decision making. Economics really is a black box. You give the subject a problem, and you look at the solution. I would like to see how they tackle it; what the process of solving it looks like. And I think psychologists are much better at that than we are. So we could use their methods much more to see how people solve complicated problems in particular – how they begin to understand the problem, how they break it down, how they sort of analyze the bits of it and then how they put it all back together again. Economists typically do not worry about these issues. The decision process is a big black box, so I think that is a very important area.

F.A.: *There have been instances recently of theory being developed from experiments. This seems to be a new phenomenon in the sense that previous theoretical breakthroughs have been initiated by other sources. What is your opinion of the virtues of this development, and do you think it will change the economics discipline?*

J.H.: I think Alvin Roth made a very important point in his talk at the conference. We should not get obsessed with anomalies which only exist in rather special cases. I think we are getting obsessed with that. So if these theoretical developments are motivated by generalities, I think that is a good thing. But if we are going to develop lots of specific theories for special cases, I think we're losing sight of what economists are meant to be doing. We are not interested in particular psychopaths' behavior, we're interested in a whole economy. We should look at perhaps representative behavior, and too often we do not – we pick a group of subjects, students, totally unrepresentative and look to see how they behave on rather peculiar problems that we have designed because we find them interesting. I think that is very bad in the sense that it could lead to lots of special new theories for particular cases, and that is not what economics is about. If you look at psychology it's tremendously fragmented. They have different theories for lots of different cases. The great thing about economics is that we have one big approach and that is really the strength in it and I think we should not forget that.

F.A.: *Are there any particular examples where experimental results have stimulated and preceded the emergence of new theories that you would like to point out?*

J.H.: Well, obviously in decision making under risk it is obvious that we had expected utility which you can almost say came from the St Petersburg paradox which is a sort of thought experiment. But more recently all these developments, like prospect theory, all these new theories – rank-dependence and regret theory. It is quite interesting that the experimental results have determined the way these theories have been constructed, and that is extremely important. Going on to dynamic decision making, I think that has worked through there too – looking at the process by which people analyze dynamic decision problems, that has been informed by experimental results.

H.H.: *You have already touched the next two questions earlier but I ask them anyway. Some theories have a times found themselves in an embarrassment of riches, by in some sense delivering too much. This is something for instance said about the IO literature in the 80's. Do you have any concerns that this is a problem in experimental economics?*

J.H.: The IO literature is very interesting. The old IO literature was heavily empirical, and then came this game theoretical approach which gave lots and lots of insights. But since then there have just been lots of variations on this theme, and it is rather upsetting that a slight change of the assumptions leads to markedly different conclusions. I think – this goes back to my earlier points – that we should look back a bit, we should not look close, we should not look at the behavior of a particular ant as it scurries around, we should look at the colony of ants as it moves. So I agree that we should stand back and look at more general results, not focus on specific anomalies. This seems to be the thing that drives a lot of the research: let's find an interesting anomaly, like Monty's three door problem, which is a very interesting anomaly, and explore that. But how general are these things, how important are they in day-to-day behavior? Is that what's explaining bubbles and crashes in the stock market? I doubt it.

H.H.: *Even small differences in experimental design tend to produce differences in results and it is not uncommon that experimentalists use drastic phrases like "the devil is in the details": With this in mind to what extent and in what way do you think it is possible to make generalizations based on experimental results?*

J.H.: This business about the devil being in the details is very important because it seems that framing effects are crucial. That is extremely worrying for economists. If we are going to admit that the way we present a problem influences what people do, that destroys a lot of economics, it destroys our whole methodology. I am not sure if it's true or not. If you give a one-off decision problem to inexperienced subjects in a laboratory, framed in different ways, they could well react differently. If you repeat this and they understand it is the same problem, I suspect these framing effects will disappear, and it is extremely worrying if they are there because it means that behavior is unpredictable. It just depends upon the way we frame the problem. But I do not think that's true. I think we should not forget that economics can predict economic behavior better than anybody else can. If you were to predict the behavior of the Swedish economy over the next five years, you would look at a macroeconometric model, built on macroeconomic theory, built on micro theory, and come up with predictions that are a lot better than a sociologist or a psychologist could come up with. So I think we should not forget that conventional economics does produce good results, while happily ignoring framing effects. So looking at these seems to be a psychological problem, not an economics problem. I think economists are forgetting that they are economists. They try to become amateur psychologists.

F.A.: *When lacking a theory it is not uncommon that empirically oriented economists instead try to generate stylized facts. Do you think there is a difference between generating stylized facts within the lab and generating facts from more traditional statistical sources?*

J.H.: I think I now understand this question, I did not before. It depends on what they are used for. For some people it seems to be a very popular trend to take a stylized fact, then build a nice little theoretical model to explain that stylized fact, and that is the end of it. What do you learn from this exercise? You learn that the person is a good theorist. That's all you learn, that the person is clever. But do you learn anything about economic behavior? No. So it depends on how they're used. If these stylized facts are used to produce a theory which is then tested using other facts, then I think it is useful. I do not think it matters particularly where these stylized facts come from. It's just something to build a theory to predict behavior somewhere else. But if the stylized fact is an end in itself, then I do not know, perhaps there is a difference. Perhaps they're more soundly based, experimental stylized facts. We cannot be sure if we don't use representative samples. I find it very difficult to answer that question.

H.H.: *If you were to mention three robust non-trivial findings in experimental research, what findings would you suggest, and would your suggestions be the same to Joe on the street as to an economist?*

J.H.: I started answering this question on the basis of the first sentence, and then I looked at the second sentence and thought, well, what I've written down, Joe on the street would not understand. So I came up with a new list, which I think, perhaps is not a list. I do not know what you have had from other people. The three I have got is: that people make mistakes;

people simplify problems; but people try to optimize. I suspect you got different kinds of propositions, but clearly from all these experiments, from everything we have done, it is obvious that people make mistakes. And in a sense it is rational to make mistakes. It is not sensible to do everything perfectly. So I think that is an important non-trivial finding, that, of course, is not in conventional theory. Then people simplify problems and particularly complicated problems. On the first time they look at it: a) they cannot optimize, it is too difficult; b) it is probably not worth their while to optimize, it is not worth the effort. So they simplify problems, try and make it into a problem they can tackle. But having said that, they try to optimize; if you repeat this problem over and over again, people tend to improve. And I think these three robust non-trivial findings are extremely important.

F.A.: *Then we go on to questions relating to your more specific work. Your work has dealt with people's capacity to learn to act rationally in complicated environments. What is your opinion about the rationality assumptions in economics in light of this? More specifically: what is your views on rationality in its literal sense, and what is your view on "as-if rationality"?*

J.H.: I think as-if rationality is quite powerful. We get lots of theories which actually work quite well based on this, but in its literal sense it is obviously not true. I think there is one dimension that economics completely ignores, and that is the complexity of problems. It is not in our theories, we do not worry about it; we do not say "this is an easy problem, this is a complex problem," and we do not come up with different solutions depending upon the complexity. So this is one dimension that is usually ignored. Having said that, people often take extremely simple problems into the laboratory. They then test rationality and often conclude that people are not rational, even in the simple settings. I think this is a very quick, perhaps trivial, conclusion, because if you repeat these simple problems and people are given a chance to learn about them, they improve. I am talking more about individual decision making rather than games. You have to be a bit careful, because in games, you have to worry not only about your own rationality but about the rationality of somebody else. I think it is much easier for an individual to learn about his own decision problem and improve on that; it is a bit more difficult with two people who are interacting who cannot communicate, so these comments are confined to individual decision making. I think if you give people simple problems initially they do not behave particularly well, but through time they get better. And then the interesting question is what happens if you increase the complexity of the problem. And I think that as you increase the complexity of the problem, people depart further and further from rationality until they are more and more experienced – if it is a complex problem they need more experience to approach rationality. But people are looking for it, people are striving for it, they learn that they could have done better, and they try to modify their behavior. We have done lots of experiments on how people improve and perhaps the one further dimension we ignore is the ability of people to tackle difficult decision problems. You see people who are clever and whose decision making really does get very close to the optimal and you see people who just cannot work it out, and therefore their decision making ability improves but it is leveled off below the optimum. And these people who are not so clever develop simple heuristics which work but are not the best. I do not know why we are ashamed to admit that there are better decision makers and worse decision makers. We are happy to admit that there are better tennis players and worse tennis players, why can we not do the same in economics? So if we include complexity of decision problems and the ability of people to solve them, we can begin to answer this question. With complex problems, good decision makers who have lots of experience of rationality may be good, but with not so good decision makers in very complex situations that they have only seen once, they can be a long way from it.

F.A.: *Then a very broad question. Do you believe that there is a reasonably general theory of behavior under risk and uncertainty within reach?*

J.H.: Well, my feeling is: expected utility plus error, that is it. It is nice and simple, it explains a high proportion of data; it begins to explain things like preference reversals and so on although it does not explain it all. Robin Cubitt has done work on preference reversal that he presented at the conference. If you just take expected utility, add in some story about how people make mistakes – if you give them a preference question, there is a chance that they get their wrong preferences; if you give them a valuation question, they will not give the precise valuation, they will make a mistake. And if you assume these mistakes are biased, and that the variance may depend on the context, you can begin to explain a lot of these anomalies. This is a much nicer story, it's much simpler, than developing all these complicated theories which are manifestly not true. People make mistakes. So I think that is a nice story. And actually, putting errors into lots of theories improves their explanatory power.

F.A.: *The title of your talk is "Investigating Dynamic Economic Behavior in the Laboratory." This indicates that you are going to follow up on earlier work on dynamic behavior. Would you like to elaborate a bit on what you talked about?*

J.H.: There were four main themes, two on dynamic decision behavior under certainty and two on dynamic behavior under risk. The two things under certainty I talked about are, first, observing discounting – trying to observe at what rate people discount the future, and hence to see if they have inconsistent discounting; the other one, which I think perhaps is more interesting, is trying to look to see how a decision maker, who is dynamically inconsistent in the sense of having different discount rates for different periods, resolves this internal inconsistency. So those are the two main areas under certainty. The two under uncertainty are, first, simply observing how people tackle their dynamic decision problems, whether you can do that; the second one is asking if you can infer from their behavior what they are planning to do. I think that trying to work out what people are planning to do and whether they implement these plans is a very important question, because if they're dynamically inconsistent they would not implement their plans. They would plan to do some thing but continuingly change their mind. Now, observing a plan is an extremely interesting problem, because if you say to somebody "OK, Håkan, what are you planning to do tomorrow" and he tells me, it is totally costless, whatever he tells me. There is no way I can ask that question in a way that forces him to reveal his true intentions, because if I do not let him change his mind, then I have forced him to pre-commit, and if I do not force him to pre-commit, he could tell me anything. The fact that he does something different tomorrow does not tell me anything about whether he has changed his plans or simply lied to me. So it is an extremely interesting problem. These are four key areas that I think are wide open, there's very few people working in these fields.

H.H.: *There seems to be disagreement regarding the extent to which institutional aspects of specific applications should be taken into the laboratory. What are your thoughts on this?*

J.H.: I am a bit confused at the moment actually, particularly after this symposium. Morten Soberg gave a talk on permit trading for emissions. This is a very popular area because many countries are introducing marketable permits for pollution, for emissions. Firms are restricted to pollute the atmosphere according to how many permits they have, and they can buy and sell permits and there are different kinds of markets in different countries. So experimentalists are doing work on this, but Soberg's talk was very interesting because he never mentioned the word pollution or emissions or anything like this to the subjects, so in a sense it was just like any old market. And all he was doing was looking at the effect of a particular market structure on the outcome of the market, which has been done for thousands of years – I mean the chapter in the Handbook about that is enormous. And I am not quite sure whether that is valid, whether there is something different about this kind of market. Perhaps on the one hand it is not any different: you ask a firm, they have to buy and sell these permits, it is just like any other factor. But somehow you feel there's something missing, that it is important to talk about pollution. If it is pollution then, and if it is important, you have got this uncontrolled element, you do not know how your subjects value pollution. They may be all environmentalists. So I honestly don't know. It seems that in certain contexts you do need the particular context, but then you get this uncontrolled element about what subjects are getting out of it. So I am extremely confused about that.

H.H.: *According to certain psychological studies certain contexts to which the individual is familiar will help him to deal with logical problems. This may suggest that while subjects behave strange or irrational in labs they may very well act differently in a more realistic situation. If any, can you think of any situation when it is motivated to use a strongly context dependent description of the experimental situation.*

J.H.: You are trying to induce a particular situation on the subjects in the laboratory, which you are deliberately trying to control, and therefore in a sense it is necessarily different from the outside, because they have their own preferences out there. So perhaps we're spending too much time inducing preferences and then observing behavior, rather than doing both. Perhaps we should observe preferences and observe behavior, and not worry too much about controlling those preferences, in which case we could take the laboratory more out into the real world. We could actually observe, somehow, their preferences about pollution, about the ozone layer, and then give them some experiment on that. So perhaps that is the key to it: rather than inducing preferences, try and observe preferences. But that is extremely difficult. We have tried to do that in certain experiments, where we were not sure of the risk attitude of our subjects. We have actually done separate experiments: first observe their risk attitude, and then use that observation to try and explain their behavior in a difficult problem. For my only paper in Econometrica, we ran four experiments, two just detecting their risk preferences and two then exploring how they solve the dynamic decision problem. It is very funny actually, the stuff on risk preferences was published in Econometrica, the other material never got anywhere, we could not understand the data.

F.A.: *Then to a somewhat more provocative question I guess. It has been held that most research in medicine teaches us a lot about white mice; similarly, skeptical economists sometimes hold that experimental research teaches us a lot about undergraduate students. To what extent do you think that this criticism is fair?*

J.H.: Well you can either say "yes, it's fair, face it" or you could compare experiments where they have used students and other people. But more generally, I do not see any reason why we should not use more representative samples. I speak from some experience because we've just done an experiment using the panel at the University of Tilburg. They have an ongoing family expenditure survey at the University of Tilburg, with something like 5 000 Dutch households, and they know the representativeness of these 5 000 households. And we have used a sample from these. They are on the end of a telephone line and they all have a computer at the end of the telephone line, so we downloaded our experiments onto their computers and then they did the experiment. So we know how they behave in a particular experiment. We also know their characteristics and their characteristics relative to the Dutch population. I think this is what we should be doing more of. Either doing experiments on representative samples, or at least understanding how representative our samples are in order to make some generalizations. I mean, the trouble is that undergraduate students are not sufficiently heterogeneous to make general inferences. I think this leads me to the conclusion that this criticism is indeed fair – we are focussing on one particular group of subjects with one particular kind of experiment. Well, I think it is possible to use more representative samples, and at least know how representative our samples are. Collect more demographic data and adjust our results.

H.H.: *Is there any topic within experimental research that you consider to be relatively exhausted and for which the marginal benefit of additional studies is small?*

J.H.: Yes, lots. Public goods, public goods, if I see another public goods experiment. I mean there is so many, so many variations on a theme. And games, far too many games, far too many simple games. I think there should be more applications. So I think on public goods the marginal return must be negative now, and games, I mean it's got too much detail. I think if you do what Alvin Roth says, and take a random set of games, so we can study behavior in a class of games, that might be more interesting, but getting more and more specific results and more and more specific problems, I think that is a waste of time.

H.H.: *Are there still any large territories unexplored in the experimental field?*

J.H.: Yes, there are areas where there's lots of work to do. I think dynamic behavior is wide open. Virtually nothing has been done in that, partly because of the difficulties.

H.H.: *Do you see any particular pitfalls for experimental economics now or in the future?*

J.H.: Obsession with details. I mean obsession with details is quite clearly a serious problem. I am also a bit worried about whether we're going to go the way of some other sciences, that because of the way we publish bad results will be suppressed, either by the authors themselves or by the journals. "Bad results" may be uninteresting results, results that are deemed to be uninteresting by somebody, or results that are not really what the experimenter expected. There are rumors that certain experimentalists will train their subjects until the subjects start doing what they want. Obviously a certain amount of training is necessary, but data, which might be interesting data, is being thrown away; also, this training may be extremely bad because it could be biased training. So lots of results are being generated which are being suppressed and I think that's extremely dangerous. I think journals have a big hand in that. They don't like results which don't tell you anything. So if somebody has tested a hypothesis and the results are inconclusive, journals do not want to know. I think that is a bit dangerous. This is serious; unless the problem is with the experiment, this is actual behavior so it should be published, but it is often suppressed. And then I suppose worried people manipulate their results. There is not enough sort of verification of results. It is so easy, I mean that's happened in the sciences, people have manipulated their results to get published. I think that could happen here.

F.A.: *What do you think will happen with the market share of experimental research in the future economics discipline?*

J.H.: The market share will rise, that's it.

F.A.: *What do you think in terms of faculty and departments?*

J.H.: Well, it is strange because of in the way experimental economics operates. I think you can either get a critical mass in a particular place or nobody. It is very difficult to do experiments by yourself. So you see that there are centers in Europe that are growing quite fast and that are big centers now, where experimental economics is very strong. Elsewhere probably not so strong. It's difficult to do experiments by yourself. In terms of the sort of specific appointments in this field, that is an interesting question because experimental economics is a method, but an experimental economist, he would say "well econometrics is a method too" and people are employed as econometricians, but usually they are teaching the method rather than actually applying the method, while an experimental economist would also be applying the method.

Chapter 5

DANIEL KAHNEMAN*

Princeton University

H.H.: *It is not uncommon that researchers in the experimental field have backgrounds that are somewhat surprising. Furthermore, far from all have pursued a consistent career in the field. Why did you start with experimental research?*

D.K.: My interest in psychology began a very long time ago, about 50 years ago almost – and that was a substitute for philosophy actually. I was interested in philosophy and then I decided that I was more interested in the origins of philosophical intuitions than in philosophy, so that's how I became a psychologist. And then within psychology I evolved into a general psychologist. I'm not particularly affiliated with any special branch of psychology at this time, but I started out in vision as a student of perception and that had a big effect on the work I did later.

F.A.: *Your work with Amos Tversky concerning decision making is very well known. Unfortunately Amos Tversky died a couple of years ago, but you have continued to work in the field. If you do not consider it to be indiscreet, we think that many readers would be interested to know why you decided to work together and how you worked together.*

D.K.: Well, our collaboration started almost accidentally, when I invited Amos to give a talk in a seminar I was teaching. He gave a talk on what was then the prevailing psychological theory of subjective probability. From my perspective as a student of perception, the theory that he described didn't make any sense. We decided to have lunch, and over that lunch, we came up with a lot of the ideas that eventually became our work on the judgmental heuristics of representativeness of availability. And it developed from there. We became very close friends, and worked by spending almost all our time together. For many years we wrote every word together, by discussing sentences one at a time. We also designed experiments in the same way. There was some specialization, but really

*D.K.: Daniel Kahneman; F.A.: Fredrik Andersson; H.H.: Håkan Holm.

not much. We spent so much time together that we could complete each other's thoughts and we could complete each others jokes as well. Then we separated. We worked together from 1969 to 1978, when he went to Stanford and my wife and I went to Canada. For another couple of years we went on meeting almost every weekend or every second weekend but this gradually tapered off. Our active collaboration mostly ended in the early 80's. Since then we stayed in touch and we spoke a lot. A book that he and I decided to edit when we learned that he was dying just came out, four years after he died.

H.H.: *Behaviorally and experimentally oriented economics has often imported methods and knowledge from psychology. However, few economists would argue that experimental economics is a sub-discipline of psychology. To what extent is there a marked division line between experimental economics and experimental psychology?*

D.K.: Oh, that division is really quite sharp. Most experimental economists describe themselves as students of institutions and of markets, whereas psychologists study individual decision makers. Now there are some economists, some experimental economists, who do work that is very directly relevant to psychology. For example, Ernst Fehr's work on reciprocity is very psychological in terms of its implications. But this was not true of classical experimental economics, as in the early work of Vernon Smith and Charles Plott. So the disciplines are really entirely distinct. We mainly study individuals although some psychologists study markets. The best example is Robyn Dawes, who is well known for his experimental studies of social dilemmas and of the provision of public goods by groups, but this work is unusual.

H.H.: *You mentioned Ernst Fehr and reciprocity. Do you consider reciprocity as a mechanism as belonging to psychology?*

D.K.: Well, yes. So does Ernst Fehr. Ernst quite correctly sees himself as someone who is changing our view of human nature. And of course he would agree that human nature is what psychology is about. His work is directly relevant to psychology, and I teach it in psychology classes. Although this kind of interaction is relatively rare, there is an increasing amount of it, now that economists are more willing to give up on their very strict assumptions. There is a fair amount that is being done in Europe; Martin Weber is certainly informed by psychology and some of the things that he does would be relevant to a psychological analysis of decision making. But I should elaborate on one thing. Behavioral economics is distinct both from experimental economics and from psychology, but there is a link between psychology and behavioral economics; there is much less interaction between psychology and experimental economics.

F.A.: *So the next question is a question about experimental economics but we still are interested in your thoughts about it. There have been instances recently of economic theory being developed from experiments and this seems to be a new phenomenon in the sense that previous theoretical breakthroughs were initiated by other sources. Do you have an opinion about this development and do you think it will change the economics discipline?*

D.K.: Well, I think it's a wonderful development. A striking difference between textbooks of economics and of psychology is that the textbooks in psychology are full of facts and the textbooks in economics are basically derivations from postulates, with illustrations of the implications of these ideas for phenomena in the real world. One theme in my talk tomorrow is that some of the basic assumptions that we invoke when we use expected utility theory are flatly contradicted by experimental research, which implies that the deductions from these assumptions are also incorrect. The hallmark of theorizing within behavioral economics is that some theory is now driven by experimental facts. Matthew Rabin is a leading figure in this very recent development. His game theoretic treatment of fairness was inspired directly by experimental results. In the same vein, he and I are currently collaborating in trying to understand seemingly inconsistent findings in experimental studies of the endowment effect. Rabin is working to create a model within which the results that we have will make sense. This is a new and very promising development.

F.A.: *I guess you've answered partly but still I'd like to follow up with if you would stress some particular examples, other examples, where experimental results have preceded theories.*

D.K.: Matthew Rabin has a recent paper in Econometrica which I think is extraordinarily important. He shows that, contrary to a basic assumption of expected utility theory, final states of wealth cannot be the carriers of utility. Rabin did not come into this from a vacuum. I believe that the experimental results associated with Prospect theory provided a background, by convincing some people that something was wrong with the standard assumptions. Matthew Rabin became a behavioral economist and did mathematical research in that context, and applied his tools to bolster the conclusion that expected utility theory just cannot be right as standardly applied. So that's an example of theorizing informed by experiments and there are few others, notably the research of David Laibson on macroeconomics which was inspired by psychological results on hyperbolic discounting. My impression is that behavioral economics advances by the development of theories that are informed by results from experimental research in the psychological laboratory, and are used to guide a search for similar phenomena in the market. The pioneer of that approach was Richard Thaler, who was a graduate student when he began to use psychological ideas – especially prospect theory – to explain observations that are anomalies for standard economic theory. He and I worked very closely together and are very good friends. But we are not doing the same thing. He views himself as a general economist – who allows himself to be guided by psychology in searching for anomalies and in explaining them. His theory of the equity premium puzzle, for example, borrows from cumulative prospect theory and extends that theory by adding an assumption of myopia, in order to generate interesting predictions about financial markets. A book that Amos Tversky and I edited (D. Kahneman and A. Tversky (Eds.), "Choices, Values and Frames." Cambridge University Press, 2000) includes perhaps a dozen examples of work at the boundary of the disciplines. Colin Camerer has a chapter in that book, titled "Prospect theory in the wild," which reviews economic phenomena that can be explained by the concepts of prospect theory.

H.H.: *Some theories have at times found themselves in an "embarrassment of riches" by, in some sense, delivering too much. (In economics this is sometimes said about the IO literature of the 1980's). Do you have any concerns that this is a problem in experimental research, that it produces too many results of very specific experimental contexts?*

D.K.: Well, there is a major problem of the generality of findings – any systematic experimental behavioral research has that problem of generality. Some situations are just a lot better than others at producing generalizable results; other situations just don't generalize to anything else. Now, there are important methodological differences in how people view the generality problem. At least in the past, Vernon Smith had an answer that is completely different from mine. He argued that there is no generality problem because what happens in a laboratory market is not a simulation of something else, it is a special case of a market. In contrast, most psychologists are quite happy with the idea of simulating. It's a matter of taste really – whether one creates a situation (like an experimental market) to explore it in detail or whether one is methodologically eclectic in the choice of tools to study phenomena that have been identified in "the real world." I think that this may be a difference between some kinds of experimental economics and experimental psychology. Some of the research in experimental economics is thoroughly standardized so that you can take an experiment from one laboratory to another to be implemented, validated, and so on. And this is both good and not entirely good. Standardization means that the results are very solid, but the standardization also means that you just don't know how robust the results might be to modifications of the paradigm. My impression is that the differences between the methodological approaches have been reduced in recent years.

F.A.: *The following question also is very much a question of economics but again, we're interested in your views. When lacking a theory it's not uncommon that empirically oriented economists instead try to generate stylized facts. Do you think there is a difference between generating stylized facts within the lab and generating facts from more traditional sources.*

D.K.: No, not really. A stylized fact is a hypothesis, and those can be generated from anything. That's really what I meant when I was speaking of methodological eclecticism. If you look for example at David Laibson's research, this is something that he does very deliberately. He starts out with assumptions about discounting and then looks broadly for relevant stylized facts – for example about the use of credit, about savings, retirement and so on. This information is used in support of a coherent model that explains a wide variety of observations. It's a style of research I like.

H.H.: *Given the artificiality of experiments would that produce a problem when generalizing results?*

D.K.: Well, yes and no. Psychologists don't have a laboratory technique, so they typically invent experiments; the social psychologist Lee Ross calls that "bottling phenomena": you start with the observation of a phenomenon in the real world, which you bring into the laboratory, where you make it happen under conditions that permit a detailed investigation. Good psychology involves a constant interplay between observing the real world and running experiments. This is certainly how I try to work; most of my ideas come from the real world, not from the laboratory. I have occasionally observed unexpected new things in the laboratory, but mostly I start from some observation in the real world.

H.H.: *At a conference in experimental economics the keynote speaker, Peter Wakker, said that now the textbooks in economics have to be changed, because when dealing with uncertainty and risk they must present Prospect theory. Do you consider Prospect theory as it stands today to be unified enough to provide a general theory of behavior under risk and uncertainty?*

D.K.: Well, that question will take me into a discussion of what I think the theory is. The term 'Prospect theory' is applied to two very different things. First, it is a formal theory of how people make choices between gambles that have no more than two non-zero outcomes and with specified probabilities. The theory is truly about that behavior – it is supposed to be both true and refutable within this domain. If it refuted the theory must be changed. But the domain of the formal theory is ridiculously narrow. Prospect theory doesn't even provide an account of selling prices for gambles, and it does not does not generalize straightforwardly to situations with more than two non-zero outcomes. But what makes the theory valuable, if anything, is not its ability to explain a very narrow category of risky choices. From another perspective, the theory consists of a few key ideas, and is useful to the extent that these ideas are novel and have heuristic value. The key concepts are framing, reference points and loss aversion. These ideas can be considered and applied separately. The theory as such cannot be applied to real-life domains of any substantive interest, but the separate ideas can be. You must distinguish between what makes a theory viable from what makes it significant and useful. A theory therefore has to pass multiple tests: it should be true empirically and coherent mathematically, but it should also contain ideas that are interesting and broadly applicable. Prospect theory has so far survived both types of test reasonably well.

F.A.: *The title of your talk indicates that you are going to follow up on earlier work on rationality. Would you like to elaborate a little bit on what you will be talking about tomorrow?*

D.K.: Over the last decade or so I've been interested in understanding two facets of the concept of utility: decision utility and experience utility. Experience utility is Bentham's original concept and decision utility is the modern concept. As I was thinking about this talk, I realized that I've been working on this topic for twenty five years. The first fifteen were mostly on what I call decision utility, but in the last decade I have worked mostly on experience utility. I will be talking about the psychology of both kinds of utility.

H.H.: *According to certain psychological studies, certain contexts to which the individual is familiar, tend to help him deal with logical problems as compared to abstract situations. This may suggest that while subjects behave strangely or irrationally in labs, they may very well act differently in a more realistic situation. Can you think of any situations that motivate it to use such context-dependent description to the subjects?*

D.K.: I think, you are referring to research on Wason's four-card problem. This is a puzzle which is very rarely solved correct when formulated in abstract terms. However, some versions of it which are concrete and specific are really quite easy. So that problem is there. I should point out that most of the research that has been done on judgement under uncertainty – certainly the research that I have done – has not been concerned with formal problems. It's been concerned with vivid scenarios that invite and engage intuitive thinking. Our hope, whether we succeed or not, is to capture the kind of intuitive thinking that people actually apply in the real world. Much as Vernon Smith was arguing about experimental economics, in fact, we argue that there is no necessary distinction between intuitive thinking in the laboratory and in the real world. However, there is a difference, in the laboratory, between tasks that involve formal or more concrete representations. The former are sometimes much more difficult, but this is not relevant to the research that we've been doing.

F.A.: *Well, the next question is somewhat provocative I guess. It has been held that most research in medicine teaches us a lot about white mice; similarly, skeptical economists sometimes hold that experimental research teaches us a lot about undergraduate students. To what extent do you think that this criticism is fair?*

D.K.: No. I mean, I think this criticism is based on ignorance. The people who make it have heard an anecdote or two, which are drawn from demonstration experiments. But most of the interesting findings in studies of both judgment and decision making, have been replicated and extended in other populations – including experts. This criticism is just wrong.

H.H.: *Are there still any large territories unexplored in the experimental field?*

D.K.: We don't know much, so there's just an awful lot to do. Looking at economics from the outside, there is a very interesting question that arises about how to enrich the theory while keeping the basic methodology going. And that can be done in so many different directions – and people have just begun doing that – that I think there are unlimited possibilities for applications and extensions. Really just beginning.

F.A.: *Do you see any particular pitfalls for experimental economics now or in the future?*

D.K.: I see more opportunities than pitfalls. I'll give you an example. A lot of the early research was done on money and money tokens. But if it turns out – like we find in studies of the endowment effect – that people react to goods that they tend to use – like a mug – differently from the way that they react to money, then one could imagine doing experimental economics with goods. Now this is beginning. Ernst Fehr, for another example, does experimental economics but his model of utility is richer than the standard one – it included reciprocity as a prominent factor – and this richer model creates many new possibilities to be investigated. The recent work by Smith and McCabe also illustrates dramatic extensions of the classic paradigm of experimental economics. I these developments continue – and I think they will – the interdisciplinary conversation will certainly expand.

F.A.: *OK, I guess the last question is something you've already answered but if you would like, you may elaborate. What do you think will happen with the market share, so to speak, of experimental economics within the economics discipline in the future?*

D.K.: I have no way of answering this question. It is not even clear to me that the existing boundaries between experimental and behavioral economics will continue to exist. Until recently, the two groups have been talking to each other, but have remained quite distinct. But my impression is that the boundaries are crumbling, and also that other economists do not see the two sub-fields as distinct. The joint market share for behavioral and for experimental economics is certainly growing in the top departments in the United States.

Chapter 6

ALVIN ROTH*

Harvard University and Harvard Business School

H.H.: *It is not uncommon that researchers in the experimental field have backgrounds that are somewhat surprising. Furthermore, far from all have pursued a consistent career in the field. Your own research does for instance also contain quite a number of contributions to theory. Why did you start with experimental research?*

A.R.: Well, I prove theorems only very slowly, so I have to know which theorems are interesting and which are not. I did a theoretical dissertation. And when I came to my first job at the University of Illinois, I wondered whether the kinds of things I had studied could predict behavior. One of my new colleagues who also came as a new assistant professor in 1974 was a social psychologist named Keith Murnighan, and he and I started teaching each other how to do experiments about economics, and we did quite a few together. The first ones started by exploring the theoretical ideas in my dissertation. Some of those ideas don't organize behavior very well, and that helped me move on to other things.

H.H.: *Today quite a few economics graduate students start directly with experimental research, what are your thoughts about this development?*

A.R.: I think that the ideal dissertation would be three essays, one would be the theory of some problem, another would be an experiment concerned with the theory, and the third would be field observations also concerned with the theory (not necessarily in that order), so the dissertation would tie together the theory and the experimental observations and the field observations. Now, because you have to develop certain kinds of human capital to do each of those kinds of work, it's hard to get someone ready to do this at the dissertation level. But I see no reason why experiments should be sharply separated from other ways of investigating things in economics.

*A.R.: Alvin Roth; F.A.: Fredrik Andersson; H.H.: Håkan Holm.

F.A.: *Moving on to the relationship between experimental economics and other subjects. Behaviorally and experimentally oriented economics have often imported methods and knowledge from psychology, but few economists would argue that experimental economics is a sub-discipline of psychology. To what extent is there a marked division line between experimental economics and psychology?*

A.R.: I had a view on this subject initially that I think has proved to be quite mistaken. I think that the big differences between experimental economics and psychology or between economics and psychology have to do with the kind of questions we're interested in, and therefore the kinds of experiments that we want to do. But my mistaken idea was that there would be a division of labor and that psychologists would do most of the experiments. And to this end, I published one of my early experimental papers on bargaining, with my student Mike Malouf, in a journal called Psychological Review, which is a little bit like the AER for psychologists. It concerned Nash's solution to the bargaining problem, and this was a subject that had received some attention in the psychology literature also. There were psychologists who studied bargaining, and, mostly, they had written that Nash's solution was an untestable theory because it involved unobservables like utility of the bargainers; my idea at the time was that I would show how you could create an experimental design that properly controlled for the unobservables. This is where the binary-lottery games were introduced. My mistaken idea was that I thought that once I could demonstrate to psychologists that it was possible to experiment with theories like this, they would do the experiments and I would read the results. It turns out that this became in some sense quite a well known article among economists because of the binary-lottery game design, but to publish it in a psychology journal was like dropping it into a hole; psychologists weren't interested in economic theories of bargaining. And, of course, that's not surprising. So as economists, if we want to have experiments done that tell us about the theories we are interested in, then we will have to do the experiments ourselves. I think much more than other kinds of differences between economics and psychology, the big differences between experimental economics and experimental psychology have to do with the fact that the pressing experiments are the ones that help you distinguish between the theories that you find interesting and important, and we are concerned with different things. Psychologists are interested in many things to better understand the human condition, how your mind works; economists are interested in understanding how the world works, how markets work, how people interact. I think that we will have to do our own experiments.

F.A.: *To the extent that you think that there exists experimental research in the intersection belonging to both subjects, what would this intersection contain?*

A.R.: Well, there have certainly been some areas where psychologists and economists have, at least for a time, talked to each other quite productively; consider for example individual choice behavior, bargaining and small group behavior, and public-goods provision. And when people from both disciplines are interested in the same questions they can talk very fruitfully, but there have also been times when it appears that they are interested in the same questions but are interested in very different things. For instance in the 1970's when I began to study bargaining, there were quite a lot of social psychologists who studied bargaining as well and I would go and talk to them and give talks in psychology departments and they were always astonished at what boring experiments I would do. They would say "Look, you put your subjects in a bargaining situation or a market situation, you change some variable, and everyone reacts the same way. You have bidding and everyone bids the same way, doesn't that tell you that you're doing something boring – the introverts and the extroverts, everyone acts the same way?," and I'd say no, no I'm an economist, I study the situation, if you change from one situation to another, how everyone's behavior changes. And at that time, what psychologists would do is that they would do a personality inventory, and find out what kind of person you are and then try to categorize your behavior. But I would look at their experiments and say that of course small things like whether you are shy or not make a big difference, because there are no incentives in their experiments. We would look at each others' experiments ostensibly on the same subject, and be surprised. So there are intersections. Sometimes they are real and not just apparent, but that can change over time too, because whether you are studying the same thing has to do not only with the phenomena you are studying but also with what you hope to learn from the things you are studying.

H.H.: *There have been instances recently of theory being developed from experiments. This seems to be a new phenomenon in the sense that previous theoretical breakthroughs have been initiated by other sources. What is your opinion about the virtue of this development and do you think it will change economics fundamentally?*

A.R.: Yes. I think that experiments are coming of age in economics. When there were very few experiments it wasn't reasonable to spend lots of effort to try to explain the results of experiments because you weren't sure how robust they were. Now that we are seeing lots of experimenters and people from different laboratories, and from different theoretical predispositions starting to see some of the same robust phenomena, it makes sense that we should try to explain. And part of the same trend is also the fact that old theories that don't explain robustly observed phenomena fade away because of experimental results. This is equally important, or perhaps more, because the big thing that experiments do is they increase the speed with which theory can be confronted with appropriate data. I mentioned the paper I published in the Psychological Review earlier. The subject of that paper and the subject of a number of experiments that I did in the seventies and eighties was Nash's model of bargaining. Now if you spoke about bargaining to economists when I was a young economist, you mostly heard about Nash's solution to the bargaining problem. It was the predominant theory of bargaining in the literature at the time. Today, it strikes me, there's an excellent chance that you two don't know what Nash's solution to the bargaining problem is, nor should you necessarily, because, among other things, experiments show that it's not a very good theory. Interestingly, I was one of the principal theorists of Nash's solution. My first book was called "Axiomatic Models of Bargaining" and it was published in 1979, and it was a book developing the theory of these models of bargaining. When we did experiments on them we found that they weren't good models of bargaining and, more or less, the world was convinced. This is what I meant when I said I prove theorems slowly so I need to know what's interesting. You could still prove lots and lots of very elegant theorems about that family of theories of bargaining, but on the other hand they missed what we now think of as some of the most essential phenomena, and so one of the early successes of experiments was that theorists were convinced to look for other models of bargaining.

H.H.: *I have a little follow-up on this. Psychologists often use metaanalytical studies. You discussed that there are quite a number of results now, and this is the case also in social psychology. They use these kinds of statistical methods to study certain mechanisms or effects in similar but not identical experiments. What are your thoughts about these methods?*

A.R.: You know, it's hard to develop formal statistical methods to study very different experiments. I spoke a little bit in my talk yesterday about how Ido Erev and I in our 1998 paper in the AER looked at a bunch of studies by people who had studied matrix games over the years. And part of the problem is you realize that the frequency with which different kinds of games are studied depends partly on the accidents of who did them and when and how many games they studied, so that you don't have a random sample from which you could draw some meaningful statistical conclusions. So when you have a lot of studies and the results are very different, I don't know that there are adequate statistical ways to combine and understand them. But even without random sampling, there are plenty of areas where some robust features leap out at you when you look at them, and then it is reasonable to suspect that those might really be robust features. Think again about bargaining and why we're now seeing theories of learning and theories of fairness and things like that emerging from the experimental literature. Partly it's because you look at bargaining and you see a whole lot more equal splits than anyone had anticipated, and there are lots of ways to approach these, there are focal points, and you guys had a focal point conference a couple of years ago, but now people are exploring other things as well. And partly it's because you saw those kinds of equal splits occurring in lots and lots of environments, so even without a formal metastatistical analysis of very different experiments you start to suspect that you're seeing some robust results. I think that the proper unit in which to learn things from experiments is not the experiment but the series of experiments, to see what's robust. What metastatistical analyses often miss is that different experimenters chose the particular games they studied, and the detailed experimental methods they used, to advance the goals of a particular kind of investigation. Without understanding how these experimental design choices influenced the outcomes, it may be difficult for a metastatistical analysis to produce meaningful results. That's why we feel most confident in experimental results that come from within-experiment comparisons.

H.H.: *Can you give some examples where experimental results have preceded and stimulated the emergence of new theories? You mention in the Handbook of Experimental Economics for instance the deadline effect.*

A.R.: The deadline effect is a good example; people had talked about it in non-experimental data, but experimental data made it very sharp and allowed you to really gather appropriate data, so that certainly was a stimulus to new theory. Theories of learning – which is one direction my work is going now – is an example because we see lots of differences between the first play of a game by inexperienced players, and subsequent play, as they become more experienced. So experiments have really made us look more seriously at models of learning. Another example is the theories of fairness in the manner of Gary Bolton and Axel Ockenfels, or Ernst Fehr and his colleagues. Also think of all the non-expected utility theories, theories of choice that can accommodate the Allais paradox, the Ellsberg paradox or any of these other things. So I think there's been quite a rich set of theories that have grown very directly out of experimental results.

But to name three examples: theories of learning, theories of fairness, and non-expected utility theories.

F.A.: *Some theories have at times found themselves in what might be called an embarrassment of riches, by in some sense delivering too much, and an example might be the IO literature of the eighties. Do you have any concerns that this might be a problem in experimental economics?*

A.R.: I do, and my talk yesterday was addressed to that. I think that there is a chance that if you try to explain every data point you can overfit the data, and that we should be concerned with developing simple theories that have predictive value – theories that allow you to predict novel situations correctly, or better than other theories; that's in a sense the test. But I think prediction, out-of-sample prediction, is the touchstone. And part of the problem when you speak of the IO literature is that you can show that anything can happen – it depends on expectations and beliefs. So, if you tell me what happened I can explain why it happened. That is not an approach that lends itself to prediction very well. And so I think that if we keep our eye on the goal of prediction we will avoid this embarrassment of riches that you speak about.

F.A.: *With the importance of detail in mind, to what extent do you think it is possible to make generalizations based on experimental results?*

A.R.: I think again, that the right unit to be looking at is series of experiments. When John Kagel and I edited the Handbook of Experimental Economics we were pretty clear that what we wanted to focus on was sets of experiments big enough to get some idea of what the robust generalizations where. Incidentally, experimental economics – in this respect, in the ability to look at series of experiments and get robust generalizations – has gotten a lot more fun since there have been more experimenters. There was a time in the 1970's, when experiments were really thin on the ground; different groups of experimenters concentrated on what they were interested in. If you wanted to see another experiment on double auctions you had to wait until Vernon did one, if you wanted to see another bargaining experiment you had to wait until I did one. As a result, if you thought that I was all wrong – if you thought that there was something fundamentally flawed about my experimental design, and that maybe I was seeing all these equal splits because of some stupid thing that I did in the laboratory – then the next experiment that I did wouldn't likely satisfy you because many of the things stay the same from experiment to experiment; you only change the few that you think are interesting. So if you, reading my experiments from across the water, thought: "he's missed the whole point from the beginning, and therefore he gets all these results as an experimental artifact," then you would find all my subsequent experiments uninteresting. On the other hand, as soon as you have lots of people doing experiments, as soon as you have Werner Güth, for example, doing very different bargaining experiments, all of a sudden you say: "look at that, you can get lots of equal splits even when you do the experiment entirely differently." And all of a sudden, which parts are robust and which are not leap out.

H.H.: *When lacking in theory it is not uncommon that empirically oriented economists try to generate stylized facts. Do you think there is a difference between the arise of stylized fact within the lab and generating them by more traditional statistical methods?*

A.R.: Well, in the lab you can try to explore the regularities in a more systematic way than you can in the field because the big thing about the lab is you can control and observe much more than you can in the field. To take an example from my own history, we were looking at bargaining experiments with these binary lotteries, and we were seeing lots of equal splits of probability and also equal splits of expected value; we were seeing bimodal distributions, and we noticed that there was a big difference, unpredicted by the theories at the time, between bargaining in which the players know each others prizes and bargaining in which they don't. So I had an experiment with Keith Murnighan published in Econometrica in which we said: "let's just try to develop some stylized facts." In previous experiments, when we changed the experimental condition from the players not knowing each others' prizes to the players knowing each others' prizes, we were actually making a big set of complicated changes. We were changing the information of the guy with the smaller prize, by letting him know the larger prize; we were changing the information of the guy with the larger prize by letting him know the smaller prize; and, in addition, when we went from this partial to full information we typically made this common knowledge. So in the laboratory we can break all those changes into smaller pieces. Murnighan and I broke up the change from full to partial information in a four-by-two design, so the four-way variable was which player knows what about the other's prize, and the two-way variable was the knowledge structure, common knowledge or not. And all of a sudden, without having a theory to guide us, we could really break up the effect of bargainers' information about each others' prizes into some of its component parts. So we weren't testing a theory, we were developing stylized facts about what was happening. On the other hand, you couldn't possibly hope to develop stylized facts, on those kind of detailed information variables, from any sort of field data. But economists are mostly interested in naturally occurring environments, so stylized facts from field data tell you what's important, and stylized facts from experiments allow you to try to understand how it works.

H.H.: *Given the artificiality of some experimental situations, does this raise any particular concerns?*

A.R.: Not in general. The virtue of experiments is that they are simple and therefore sometimes artificial, that's why we go into the lab; it's not as messy as the world. The most reliable conclusions you can draw in the laboratory have to do with within-experiment comparisons. The laboratory is not a wonderful way to estimate universal constants about the world. If I want to know the average risk aversion of the Swedes when they make their retirement decisions, I probably can't generalize that from the laboratory. On the other hand, if I want to know some comparison: "Will people choose riskier investments in environments of greater uncertainty?," this is something I might be able to look at in the laboratory by making some within-experiment comparison. And the reason that it is within-experiment comparisons that are so important is that when you do an experiment, you make a thousand decisions, and then you vary one of these, that's your experiment. And of course there can be important interactions with the other 999, but unless you are unlucky, the interactions won't reverse the main effect. Of course, it might – and other people may come along and test it, as they should – but when you speak of the artificiality of experiments, what you're really speaking of is those 999 decisions that you make in order to bring it into the laboratory. And, of course, they can have an effect and they certainly have an effect on magnitude, so unlike physics, where there's a feeling that there are universal constants that can be measured in any laboratory, I think that's not primarily what we look to experiments for in economics, but rather for doing comparisons between big treatment variations.

F.A.: *A somewhat different question. If you want to mention three robust non-trivial findings in experimental research, what findings would you suggest and would your suggestions be the same to Joe on the street as to an economist?*

A.R.: Well, first my suggestions would not be the same to an educated layman and to an economist because their interests are very different. I think for an economist I would talk about how experiments have changed our theoretical views. So speaking to an economist I think I might say: What are the three things we've learned? We've learned that learning is very important in strategic environments and that it's adaptive and slow and that learners interact with each other. So, when we look at strategic environments, games and markets, we are likely to be seeing not only learning about the market, but, learning about the other participants. When you have a new market – when, say, eBay opens up, and there's now an auction that everybody can participate in – everyone is inexperienced, and then they learn over time. What they learn, however, depends in part on how everyone behaved when they were inexperienced. And so the fact that everyone learns, but not instantly, has important implications for the dynamics of how market behavior develops. That being the case, the second thing is that initial propensities are important; that is, markets have histories and part of their histories are how people behave in the beginning. Especially in environments that we think of as having multiple equilibria, experiments and theories of learning tell us that we shouldn't expect to be able to deduce from first causes what will happen, it might depend also on history. An almost separate third thing is nevertheless that some games, some environments, some markets, move quickly to equilibrium, and some do not, and so the level of generalization that we expect to get is not going to be that equilibrium always happens or never happens, as a non-experimental style of theorizing might have led us to suppose; what we have to learn is rather which games go quickly to equilibrium and which do not, and what happens and why. Joe on the street would find that pretty unintelligible. When I talk about experiments to non-economist colleagues, I think it's easier to talk about the use of experiments in economic design. The idea that economists are now prepared to test designs for new markets in the laboratory before bringing them out into the field is clearly a useful idea. It's quite expensive to bring out a new market, and you see this now again with Internet companies. If you are planning to open a market, before you let the world in, you might like to see what will happen, and experiments are very good for this. And that is a useful thing because it turns out there are strong parallels between behavior in the laboratory and behavior in the field. So, we start to feel that testing new designs in the laboratory makes lots of sense, and I think that's going to be one of the chief contributions that experiments make to the way economics is used in the world.

H.H.: *You have done quite a number of contributions to the theory of economic design. It seems that one of your favorite topics is two-sided matching problems. In these problems theoretical analysis, traditional field studies, as well as experimental research seem unusually tightly connected. Do you agree on this description and can you elaborate on the role of different approaches to generate knowledge in this case?*

A.R.: I more or less agree with the description. I'm in the process of struggling to write up a paper that comes from a kind of old-man talk that I was invited to give last year called the Fisher-Shultz lecture. The working title of the paper is "The Economist as Engineer" and the subtitle is "game theory, experimental economics and computation as tools for design." Loosely speaking, if you are motivated by problems rather than by methods, then you have to attack them with every means available, especially when the problems you are interested in are too hard to solve conclusively. Design problems are often of this sort, so in matching – where I've gotten a chance to help design a number of markets, the best known of which is the market in which American doctors get their first jobs – you need to know about the history of these markets, you need to do some theory to understand what can be done, and often although there's quite good field data, it's not as good as you would like. I've looked at lots of entry-level professional labor markets for example, but you can't always see in them what you would like to know. So for example, in this area, the best natural experiment that I ever came on, that is, the most closely comparable different markets, had to do with the different regions of the National Health Service in Britain. So I studied a bunch of pretty similar markets, that all failed in a certain way and that were then reorganized in an attempt to fix the market failures by adopting different kinds of labor clearing houses, some of which worked and some of which didn't. I wrote a paper about it and I had a pretty good idea, a good conjecture, of what was going on; my conjecture was that differences between the markets in which a clearinghouse failed and those in which one had succeeded had to do with market design, with the design of the clearinghouse. But there were other differences also between these markets: The successful markets were in Edinburgh and Wales, which are not in England proper, and the failed markets were in Birmingham and Newcastle which are in England proper. I mention that just to suggest that there are other differences between Edinburgh and Newcastle than just the way they organize their markets. When John Kagel and I brought this into the laboratory though, we could take a look at those different markets in an artificial laboratory environment in which we could be sure that there was no difference between them except the market organization; that is, we looked just at the Edinburgh organization and just at the Newcastle organization, using subjects from the same subject pool and using the same supply and demand and all of those things. So if you think of it that way, I've looked at many markets and the markets in the laboratory are some of those markets, and you can learn different things from different markets that you look at. The laboratory markets don't tell you some of the things the field markets do but the field markets don't tell you some of the things that the laboratory markets do, so I think all of these tools are perfectly complementary to each other.

F.A.: *The title of your talk yesterday was "The Predictive Value of Approximations," would you like to elaborate a little on what you talked about?*

A.R.: Well, I'm interested in robust prediction and therefore I'm interested in approximations, so what I talked about yesterday is how to think about whether approximations are useful for prediction even though we can confirm that the approximations themselves are false. So I was suggesting that we shouldn't focus too exclusively on hypothesis testing, to the exclusion of all else in our experimental research, because then we will always find that theories with more parameters fit the data better than theories with fewer parameters. And indeed, even when we look at theories of learning we're starting to see some of this. The danger is that you get involved in overfitting the data, and lose the ability to predict novel situations. And so I was talking about ways to think about how theories can be useful approximations even though they are demonstrably false.

H.H.: *There seems to be disagreement regarding the extent to which institutional aspects of specific applications should be taken into the laboratory. What are your thoughts on that?*

A.R.: I think it depends entirely on what you are trying to accomplish in the experiment. When you are testing market designs you bring in lots of institutional features, because you want to know if a particular auction will work, if a particular labor clearing house will work as an institution. If you think that something about the supply and demand characteristics of the market are important then you bring them into your experiment. On the other hand if you want to test a general proposition like, "people tend to play subgame perfect equilibria," that's a proposition that's meant to be sort of institution-free; it's a theory that could be false, but you don't need to test it in particular context, and in fact if you restrict yourself to very particular contexts you will be subject to the criticism that something about your particular context adds or subtracts from the ability of the particular theory to organize the data. So there are virtues to looking at very abstract environments if you're testing very general theories. Although, if your theory fails in abstract environments, it might nevertheless succeed in environments in which people have enough context to recognize familiar situations. I don't think these are questions of principle, these are strictly questions of experimental design. Experiments are part of conversations, and you have to design experiments that allow you to keep the conversations going in a productive way with a community of scholars. So I think that we should be quite eclectic about what kind of experimental designs we want. Different circumstances will call for different experimental designs.

H.H.: *There is a follow-up. According to certain psychological studies, certain contexts, to which the individual is familiar, will help him to deal with logical problems, as for instance the so called four-card problem. This may suggest that while subjects behave strangely or irrationally in labs they may very well act differently in more realistic situations. Can you think of any situations when it's motivated to use strongly context-dependent descriptions of the experimental situation.*

A.R.: Well you mention the four-card problem, by which I assume you mean the Wason-Laird selection task. That's of course an example of people performing well in some high-context situations, while in abstract situations they often perform badly, failing to detect the contra-positive. And it seems to me that we learn something from both of those experiments. From the fact that people know whom to ask for their ID-card in a bar, you might conclude that everyone understands the implication of the contra-positive. That would be a false conclusion, as the abstract task shows. From the abstract task you might conclude that people are just idiots, and that would also be a false conclusion. So I like both kinds of experiments. And I can think of many experiments where the abstract tasks and the high context task complement each other, for example John Kagel, David Cooper, Wei Lo and Qing Gu, did an experiment in the US and China, where they were looking at the ratchet effect – someone sets a budget for you, a goal, in the first period and they can conclude something about your costs from whether you meet it or not, and that causes them to reset your goal in the second period. What Kagel and company found was that American students and Chinese students and Chinese managers all behave more or less the same in the abstract low-context situation but that the Chinese managers quickly recognize the situation in the high-context situation. That tells you that you want to know both of those things.

F.A.: *Next, a somewhat provocative question perhaps. It has been held that most research in medicine teaches us a lot about white mice; similarly, skeptical economists sometimes hold that experimental research teaches us a lot about undergraduate students. To what extent do you think that this criticism is fair?*

A.R.: First of all it doesn't strike me as a very sharp criticism. White mice tell us a lot about medicine to the extent that white mice can be infected by some of the same bacteria that infect people, for example. You can detect whether antibiotics kill the bacteria without killing the mice. That doesn't prove of course that it will help people without hurting them, or, vice versa; if penicillin kills mice it doesn't mean that penicillin will kill people. But nevertheless, as a screening device, in many ways it is preferable to start with mice rather than people. So I wouldn't at all be sorry if undergraduates told us "no more," than white mice do. I'm not at all sure that that's the case though. Many people were once undergraduates, and there's a much closer connection therefore between adult behavior and undergraduate behavior than between white mice physiology and people physiology. But also these are empirical questions. In other words, we tend to use undergraduate subjects because they are a convenient sample, they are easily available. But when you are studying something that might be subject-pool dependent, then you should look at other subject pools. For example, if I can mention another experiment by John Kagel, he and his colleagues studied the winner's curse. They saw it appear and they saw how it could come to disappear with experience, but one of their questions therefore was "Is this purely an experience effect, how about if we looked at people who make bids for a living?" So they did an experiment with a subject pool of construction industry executives who were involved with bidding on projects as part of their jobs, and in an abstract setting the construction industry executives looked just the same as the undergraduates; they were subject to the winner's curse in the same way. So that raises all sorts of additional hypotheses about why they don't go out of business in the construction industry and suggests that there may be high-context things that allow you to either coordinate as a cartel or to correctly assess the costs in a common-value environment. But that moves you along right there: It's not the case that simply because you're accustomed to making bids that you can generally avoid the winner's curse. That was a very appropriate use of different subject pools. And of course you get different answers sometimes. That's a case where undergraduates looked like expert bidders, but for instance if you want to study how well calibrated people are, how well they understand their confidence intervals, I gather meteorologists are better calibrated than anyone else; meteorologists make probabilistic forecasts every day and then they get feedback: "you said there was an 80% chance of rain and it didn't rain, you know you shouldn't do that more than 20% of the time." So if you wanted to understand how well it's possible to be calibrated, you might not want to study undergraduates. On the other hand, meteorologists would also give you a very different sample of the general population. My loose impression – I don't have lots of data at my fingertips to support this – is that undergraduates are probably not a bad sample of the population for tasks that no one performs as their profession. In other words, when you look at abstract tasks and when you look at unfamiliar tasks, I don't think that there have been a lot of studies that have found important differences between undergraduates and other subject pools. On the other hand, when you are looking at things that someone does as their profession, if your particular concern is with the people who do it, then you shouldn't be surprised to find, for instance, that bond traders are quicker at spotting arbitrage opportunities than undergraduates. Depending on what kinds of conclusions you want to draw, you should be prepared to look at appropriate subject pools.

H.H.: *Then we have some more perhaps speculative questions about future experimental research in economics. Is there any topics in experimental economics that you consider to be relatively exhausted?*

A.R.: Sure. I mentioned before that I think of experiments as being parts of a conversation. So you can think of conversations that lost their interest a while ago. For example, think of the theory and the experiments concerned with equilibrium refinement. Ten years ago you could hardly call yourself a game theorist if you didn't have an equilibrium refinement of your own, and initially you had guys who did experiments that would show that this equilibrium refinement works better than that one. But when we started to understand what was going on – the nice thing about having many experimenters is that these experiments would be followed up by more careful and more general broader experiments – we saw that that was not the right generalization to draw from those observations. So, on the one hand experiments tended to show that we weren't seeing deep refinements in any generality, and at the same time the theory was showing that looking for deeper and deeper refinements was like peeling an onion; it didn't stop, and when you finished there was nothing left. So I think partly, both in the experimental community and in the theoretical community, that's a subject that's sort of exhausted itself; not that there weren't appropriate experiments to do at the time as part of that conversation, but I wouldn't encourage a student to today try to think whether sequential equilibria with or without the intuitive criterion was a better general description.

H.H.: *Do you consider there to be any large territories left unexplored in the experimental field?*

A.R.: Yes, I guess most things are still unexplored. Experimenters are still very thin on the ground. I guess if you asked a European before the voyage of Columbus: "Do you think there are any large territories left unexplored?" They might say no; after all, everywhere you go lots of people live. But of course they'd be entirely mistaken. Most of the unexplored territories in economics are so unexplored that I couldn't begin to name them. It's clear that there are many areas that we have just begun to explore and some of these are the areas where new theories have developed. Think of learning and fairness. Those are things that just came on the radar. They might both be very important or perhaps one of them will supplant the other; or we'll still see new ideas to organize some of the unexpected experimental results that those theories are brought up to explore. The whole issue of market design raises all sorts of questions. Lately it seems like almost every time I look at a market, the tough design problems have to do with complementarities. In labor markets you have married couples, in auctions you have people who need bundles of goods. And we don't have elegant theoretical solutions to these things, but perhaps there are going to be regularities that we can assess as we develop better theory and appropriate experiments. So when you say "are there any large territories unexplored in the experimental field," I tend to think of things that are just unexplored in economics, things that we need to develop both theory and experiments for. So certainly the area of complementarities; it's clear that the practical problems of market design are telling us that we need to understand more about complementarities and how markets work when people need to bundle things. And so I would guess that there will be valuable experiments to do there as well.

F.A.: *Do you see any particular pitfalls for experimental economics now and in the future?*

A.R.: Well, one pitfall of course is that we should avoid developing dogma about what's the right way to do experiments, and thereby rule out interesting ways to go. I think that there have been some attempts in the past to suggest that: "if you don't do experiments my way you are making a mistake, maybe we shouldn't publish your papers." I think that the worst thing that could happen is that you get a bunch of old guys together, like me, and we tell you how to do experiments and then things that seem like they might be appropriate for some investigation that we haven't yet thought about is ruled out because we've laid down rules about how to do experiments. And things like that of course happen. It's not that we haven't developed any dogma. Think about things like conventional levels of significance in statistics. Why is 5% the magic number? Well you need to get things published in journals and at some point they decided that 5% was a good number. That has some costs and some benefits as well. So we have to be a little careful in something new like this, that we don't develop some rules that will exclude valuable experiments, of kinds that we just haven't had occasion to anticipate yet, and prevent them from being done.

F.A.: *Well then, finally, what do you think will happen with the market share of experimental economics in the future?*

A.R.: Well, you know, it's been growing and since I don't like to be a market timer, I don't like to predict a turnaround; it will continue to grow. Think of the market share of experiments in chemistry. It's much bigger than the market share in economics, so there's room to grow. Probably, in economics as a mature science, experiments will not play quite the large role that they do in chemistry, but I anticipate that they will play a much larger role than they do now. For several reasons. One is the apparent scientific benefits of doing experiments, but another, and I think it will be one of the entry ways into more departments, is that experiments are also an extremely powerful teaching tool. So right now, if you think about where experiments have come from just in the course of my career as an experimenter - I mentioned to you that early on I published a number of my papers in psychology journals – well now, every good economics journal publishes experiments; the experimental revolution has been won in the journals. It hasn't yet been won in the departments; I'm not very familiar with the European labor market for economists but in the US there are lots and lots of good departments that don't have an experimenter and don't necessarily feel like they miss one. And although more and more are feeling like they miss one, part of the problem is that experimenters need laboratories. If you think about hiring an experimenter, you go to your dean, and he says: "you know, we love economists but the reason we love them is that they don't need laboratories, they are cheaper than chemists, go find a different economist." And so I think that one of the ways that experimenters will enter the profession is that you say to the dean, "we use the laboratory also for teaching," and he says: "oh, here, let me write you a check." I think that as we learn to use experiments better in teaching, it will be easier to get economics departments to invest in facilities, which incidentally are also getting cheaper. When I started to do experiments, our first computer system was a system developed at the University of Illinois called Plato; it was a network computer system and it was used for language laboratories and things like that, and it was a unique set of hardware. They had plasma screens and a language called Tutor, and whenever we would write a paper we would mention this, we would say that we did this on the Plato system, because it was a big deal. Now of course, you can point your browser at my server and anywhere in the world you can do an experiment that I might have programmed in Java on my desktop at Harvard. So the costs that are needed to organize even computerized laboratories have gone way down. Mostly now, as a practical matter, it's a question of space in universities: who controls the room and when you can schedule an experiment. And these things are just getting cheaper, they'll get easier and as experiments become more important in the intellectual life of the profession, the share of faculty positions for experimenters will go up, so I think it's going to be a good century for experimental economics.

Chapter 7

VERNON SMITH*

University of Arizona

H.H.: *It's not uncommon that researchers in the experimental field have backgrounds that are somewhat surprising. Furthermore, far from all have pursued a consistent career in the field. Although you belong to those that started very early with experimental research, and has continuously kept on with it, can you tell us something about why you started?*

V.S.: I think of two things. One was that I had a curiosity about how things worked, even before I started college. My father was a machinist and tool and die maker, and my undergraduate degree was in electrical engineering. Then I got interested in economics, but that interest in how things worked carried over. Also more specifically in terms of getting into experiments, there were just all kinds of questions that I felt I didn't have any answers to. It wasn't ever clear to me, in the studying of economic theory of markets, how that was related to anything you saw. Then I got started, originally in markets of course, and I was interested in how well they worked and under what conditions they were efficient and competitive. It seemed that all those questions were left unanswered in the economics that I studied circa 1950. Unfortunately, the way economics is taught, most students still do not have answers to these questions. And then, after I got out of graduate school in 1955 and soon thereafter, I got started in experiments.

H.H.: *Today quite a few economic graduate students start directly with experimental research. What are your thoughts on this development?*

V.S.: The graduate students I know in the United States take fairly traditional programs in economic theory, econometrics, game theory, and the like, and then do research in experimental economics. So in the cases that I'm familiar with, if they're going into experimental economics early it's not without going through a lot of the traditional training. Actually I think that some of that could be shortened. I would like to see graduate

*V.S.: Vernon Smith; F.A.: Fredrik Andersson; H.H.: Håkan Holm.

programs have fewer core courses, and more apprenticeship-type courses early on, not only in experimental economics but in empirical economics and in theory. I usually advise graduate students to read narrowly within economics and fairly broadly outside of economics. The reason is that it seems to me that within economics it's the same models applied over and over again to different circumstances. I mean that it's more interesting to read in anthropology, read about primate behavior and evolutionary biology, to look for sources of inspiration that are outside the usual economics literature. So if they read Nature and Science, and other science journals and fewer journals in economics, I think they're more likely to change what they do by more than an epsilon from what other people have done, and maybe find some new directions. Of course a lot of that may be dead ends as with all research, but I think that the potential breakthroughs that are possible make it worth doing.

F.A.: *This touches on the next question which has to do with the relationship between experimental economics and other subjects. Behaviorally and experimentally oriented economics has often imported methods from psychology; however, few experimental economists would argue that experimental economics is a sub-discipline of psychology. To what extent is there a marked division line between experimental economics and experimental psychology?*

V.S.: I think the questions are more likely to be different. Psychologists are more interested in cognitive processes and less in the effect of decision making on market and social and group outcome. But when I started out I was very much influenced by psychologists. I knew Sidney Siegel shortly before he died and I still know Ward Edwards. I see him occasionally; he was in Michigan, and I was at Purdue. Anatol Rappaport was in Michigan. We had a Purdue workshop or seminar series and we'd bring some of these people down. We had other members of the faculty there from Carnegie Mellon and they have always had a pretty non-traditional kind of graduate program with a behavioral orientation. So I really see the fields as having a lot in common even though they tend to go in different directions, with very different methodologies. Psychologists don't use written scripts or pay real money, and are heavily into the use of deception. And Danny and I, Danny Kahnemann, had two or three conversations at this conference about how there seems to be a lot of convergence compared with when we first met, which was probably 15 or 20 years ago. And I think what's causing the convergence is that we're looking at the same data and trying to understand it. That's bound to bring some convergence even if we had different questions. He thought it was because I had changed, but we both have under the influence of learning from experience. If you are not changing you are not learning. I worry about people who still teach what I learned to forget as a graduate student.

F.A.: *Is there anything in particular that you would point out as defining the intersection between the two subjects?*

V.S.: Well, I think both economics and psychology will change what they do and the questions they ask because of the developments in neuroscience. I think behavior is now being looked at much more from a perspective of biology, and evolution. How does the brain work? How does the mind work? I think those questions are inevitably going to change both psychology and economics. I think that 25-30 years from now it will be really quite different, the orientation will be quite different. And neuroscience technology is moving so fast. Imaging machines are changing and becoming more powerful and less cumbersome, cheaper, and easier to use. All of these things are going to impact both the sciences. I think all sciences are influenced far more by the machine builders than either the theorists or experimentalists. Just think of how microbiology, astronomy, geology instrumentation – microscopes, telescopes and technology contained in those – have changed what those sciences can do, can attempt to do. I think computers and the communication revolution and now things like neuroscience scanners create new tools that will change the questions asked and what kinds of answers we're able to give.

H.H.: *Then I have a question about generalization. There have been instances lately of theory being developed from experiments. This seems to be a new phenomenon in the sense that previous theoretical breakthroughs have been initiated by other sources. What is your opinion about the virtue of this development?*

V.S.: I think both theorists and experimentalists should be in the business of modifying theories in the light of evidence. And this can only be done by people who appreciate both experimental and theoretical faces of things. We use the rhetoric of testing theories and we like theories that are predictive and all that sort of thing. But our tests will always find deficiencies in theory, and predictive failures, and so the natural thing to do is to learn enough about why that's happening to be able to reformulate the theory. I think we're very weak in that regard; in economics theory has tended to be driven by its own literature, and driven by techniques and tools and not by data that is sharp enough to give you some idea of which directions the theory should go in. Actually, on this business of modifying theory, in the light of experimental results, I first saw that in Sidney Siegel, the psychologist. He was interested in modifying utility theory, to take into account observations in certain kinds of games that he was doing, and he was modifying it in ways that took into account what he saw as kind of physiological limits to decision making, and this was 1959-1960. I can't claim a tremendous amount of originality in that regard, even though I have taken some of the stuff he was talking about in different directions.

H.H.: *Can you give some examples where experimental results have preceded and stimulated the emergence of new theories?*

V.S.: Well Sid Siegel was interested in varying payoffs and determining how that effected outcomes. An early kind of primitive model that he's used has been generalized, and I worked it out with Jimmy Walker in the first iteration. Then, more recently, Ferenc Szidarovszky, who's an applied mathematician at Arizona, and I worked out a generalization that can handle strategic interaction games. The idea there is really fairly simple, that the reason why rewards matter is that they help you to overcome cognitive decision costs. Think of there being an effort cost to calculating, deciding, implementing decision; monitoring what's going on. If you think of there being an effort cost connected with that and the brain as a scarce resource, those costs have to be weighed against the benefit. I think that kind of model helps you understand why increasing rewards can improve matters, and also why increasing rewards sometimes doesn't improve matters because the productivity of the effort is so low and the task is so complicated; you need help, that's why you hire consultants and experts, you can't do it yourself. So that kind of model tells you that it isn't optimal to be optimal because models of optimality don't take into account these other costs, whereas the individual has to in order to make a decision. So optimization can't really proceed without looking at the kind of cognitive limitations of the individual. Of course, people call that bounded rationality but the term bounded rationality begs the question of in what sense it's bounded. And how do you model it so that you get something explicit other than just a claim that people don't have infinite capacities to process information? You have to get more specific than that in order to come up with anything that enables you to organize data.

F.A.: *Some theories have at times found themselves in what might be called an embarrassment of riches by in some sense delivering too much. An example might be the IO literature of the 80's. Do you have any concerns that this might be a problem in experimental economics?*

V.S.: I don't think it's a problem if we work carefully to replicate the work of others before we start doing treatment variations. And I think there's a very, very bad habit in both economics and psychology of picking up an experimental task that someone else did and doing a treatment variation on it and then claiming that "my treatment is giving different results and accounts for the difference." But you can't say that until you've replicated his experiment with your subjects. And when you replicate someone else's experiment with your subjects and it doesn't work, that leads to questions of whether the whole thing isn't sensitive to procedure and that sort of thing. I think a lot of experiments and experimental areas are sensitive to procedure, and unless we actually explore those, it's very hard to differentiate between the kind of economic treatments that we want to study and aspects of doing experiments where it's difficult to control whatever it is that is creating variability in the data. And I think that this requires a deeper treatment of some subjects and less exploration of constantly new fields. I'm not sure I know the IO literature of the 80's, but I think people take hold of cranks and like to turn them because they produce publishable results. And although that's a danger I think it can be avoided if we ask why it is we're getting different results and whether they're really due to the treatments or to something about the procedures we use.

F.A.: *Would you like to briefly elaborate on the extent to which you believe that it is possible to make generalizations based on experimental results?*

V.S.: I think it's not really feasible to generalize until you know why small differences produce a difference in results. In fact, the differences aren't small if they produce important differences in results, and therefore they need to be understood. I think one result of that would be for researchers to standardize procedures more and to reduce sources of variation.

H.H.: *Do you think there is a difference between generating stylized facts from laboratory experiments compared to more traditional sources?*

V.S.: I really don't think there's that much difference; I think both methods are important and they require a lot of attention to detail. Of course we see more and more work in experimental economics that's very close to field work. The Iowa electronic market is something that grew out of the laboratory with laboratory experimentalists. But almost all the experimentalists I know are interested in the world, they're not just interested in the laboratory, and so they do think a lot about those sorts of things. They came up with this Iowa electronic market and that's kind of a blend of field and laboratory results. In principle generalization is always hazardous in the sense that you cannot say that observation imply theories, only that theories imply observational consequences. Observations can always be rationalized by a host of theories.

H.H.: *If you were to mention three robust non-trivial findings in experimental research, what findings would you suggest?*

V.S.: I can give you those, I've jotted them down here. One is very well known, it is the strong equilibrium convergence properties of markets organized under the rules of double-auction trading and of course that was a surprise. Some economists have told me, well, it just shows that markets work so it's a victory for the theory, but actually, the theory never predicted that it would work so well with such small numbers. The theory argued that people had to be price takers; double auction traders are both price makers and takers at the same time, so that's not a big victory for theory. I think it's mostly an encouragement to redo theory. And then we've studied open book uniform-price call auctions that converge on competitive equilibrium fairly quickly, and what's interesting about it is that the equilibrium involved a lot of tied bids and asks, and a number of tied bids and asks tend to exceed the capacity of any one buyer or seller, and as a result no one can manipulate the market, and that's really interesting. In fact, all we have from theory is theorems that say that any market can be manipulated if the subjects or the participants are sufficiently sophisticated, and here's a case where the subjects work out their own form of an equilibrium; each side, by producing a lot of tied bids and asks protects itself from price gouging on the other side, and it's efficient. They don't even know that's what they're doing, but their instincts are that if you see the price kind of converging here, then you don't need to bid much higher than that or offer for much less to trade. So that in itself creates a strategy-proof equilibrium. And then also we've recently been able to show that in electric power trading, if you introduce demand side bidding (and almost no one does that – I think New Zealand and Australia are about the only systems I know of that have any kind of very extensive provision for demand side bidding), it not only controls market power on the supply side but it cuts off all the price spikes. The tendency in these markets to get big price spikes are cut off by demand side bidding, because people interrupt their demand at certain prices represented by limit bids, and that means of course that they have to have contracts with their customers to allow that interruption. But that technology is here and can be introduced and basically that's cheaper than new generation and new transmission lines and everything that it takes to meet peak demands.

H.H.: *The title of your talk is "Personal Exchange." Would you like to elaborate a bit on what you talked about?*

V.S.: Humans are born social creatures, who learn early to engage extensively in social exchange. We trade favors, information, assistance as well as goods and services among friends and associates. Those who do not fail to develop social relationships. Although this might involve some altruistic elements, it appears to be largely based on reciprocity. If some people fail to reciprocate your favors and assistance, you stop the relationship. This is judged to be why people are too cooperative and too trusting, compared with the predictions of noncooperative theory, in two-person extensive form games between anonymous players. Half the subjects in single plays of such games attempt to cooperate, and often they make more money than those who do not – hardly irrational!

I think this human propensity for reciprocity emerged early in our evolution 1-2 million years ago, allowed gains from exchange, which supported limited form of specialization within the family, extended family and tribes. This was very adaptive and eventually led to trade outside the tribe, and laid the basis for an incredible growth in human wealth and enterprise. Certainly this is consistent with the anthropological record and the early development of long distance trade as described in the important work of Douglass North who has done more than anyone to develop these implications.

Chapter 8

MARTIN WEBER*

University of Mannheim

F.A.: *It is not uncommon that researchers in the experimental field have backgrounds that are somewhat surprising. Furthermore, far from all have pursued a consistent career in the field. Why did you start with experimental economics?*

M.W.: Actually, I started with experimental economics right after my Ph.D. I did my pH in multi-attribute utility theory and I wanted at that time to know whether the methods we developed were really able to predict people's behavior, and that's how I started. Then I went on doing work on risk and then as I went for what in Germany is called habilitation I got a grant to go to the US where I learnt about market experiments.

F.A.: *Today, quite a number of economics grad students all start directly with experimental research. What are your thoughts about this development?*

M.W.: I think that, of course, as we're here, experimental research is important, but I think it is a method, it's one method; there are other things you should do too: you should learn about statistical procedures, theory and so on. It's one method, it's one of the methods you should use and learn in your study.

H.H.: *Behaviorally and experimentally oriented economics has often imported methods and knowledge from psychology. However, few economists would argue that experimental economics is a sub-discipline of psychology. To what extent do you think there is a marked division line between experimental economics and experimental psychology?*

M.W.: First I think it's really in the heads of the people. One important thing is that in economics you have one type of models, and in psychology you have different types of models. Another thing is that you have different questions: In economics as well as in psychology you are interested in descriptive research, but descriptive in psychology means that you want

*M.W.: Martin Weber; F.A.: Fredrik Andersson; H.H.: Håkan Holm.

to describe a process, whereas descriptive in economics mostly means that you want to describe results.

H.H.: *To what extent do you think there is an intersection between both subjects?*

M.W.: There is an intersection but the intersection really depends on how do you define experimental economics. For example, if you think about preference reversal, the research on that was done by psychologists and then it was rediscovered by people in experimental economics. These days people in experimental economics think it is really an economics question, and some of them even don't know that it was actually initiated by psychologists. So, as I said before, it's in the head of the people, and there is an intersection and it's mostly related to choice and decision making.

F.A.: *There have been instances recently of theory being developed from experiments and this seems to be a relatively new phenomenon in the sense that previous theoretical break-throughs have primarily been initiated by other sources. What is your opinion about the virtue of this development and do you think it will change the economics discipline fundamentally?*

M.W.: If I anchor on that word, "fundamentally," I don't think it will change fundamentally. As I said before, I think it's another method. It's a positive method to produce data and it's a positive method to more sharply test theories, and there you come up with new ideas, but it's nothing totally different. Even if it's important, otherwise, hopefully, we wouldn't be here.

F.A.: *Can you give some examples where experimental results have preceded and stimulated the emergence of new theories?*

M.W.: My teaching and research is in behavioral finance, and currently there are theories being developed and coming out in the best journals in that field. These are a new type of market-equilibrium theories and they clearly have been triggered by experimental research. There's a paper by Barberis, Huang and Santos where they take two ideas – prospect theory and gambling on the house money – and cook these things together, and come up with a different asset pricing model. So this is clearly stimulated. And there are other things, like overconfidence, which are clearly stimulated by experimental research.

H.H.: *Some theories have sometimes found themselves in what could be said an embarrassment of riches by in some sense delivering too much. This is sometimes said on the IO literature of the 80's. Do you have any concerns that this is a problem in experimental economics?*

M.W.: Well again, I don't think it's a problem, because I don't see experimental economics as the only thing, the only heaven. It's one tool, it's an additional tool. We should carefully take advantage of it, and that's the reason I don't see this problem.

F.A.: *When lacking in theory it's not uncommon that empirically oriented economists instead try to generate stylized facts. Do you think there is a difference between generating stylized facts within the lab and generating facts from traditional sources?*

M.W.: I don't think there's a big difference. I think the difference is in what type of questions you can answer. Of course, if you do it in the lab you can do more individual decision making, and with traditional statistical sources you might be able to do more on aggregate data. That might be a distinction.

F.A.: *Given the artificiality of some experimental situations, does this raise any particular concerns?*

M.W.: Again, as an experimental economist, I am positive about this. I don't think it raises any particular concerns, but it raises a little bit of concern. I think the context is a key problem. When you have a context, subjects might need more training in that context to cope with the decision situation, but on the other side, if you have a context, there might be a strong demand effect coming into the lab. People who come know something, they know something about the context and they don't really listen to what you are doing in the experiment; they come to the experiment and answer the questions you ask with their own context in mind. Let me give an example, because I think this is a very important question and it was also raised during the conference: There is a study where the authors have trades in a double-auction experiment, and they get real traders – the best thing – but the real traders trade as they do during the day. They don't trade as the experimenters want them to do and they get results which are puzzling. The experimental manipulation does not really get into the head of the people because the context is so rich that they bring their own context into the lab.

H.H.: *If you were to mention three robust non-trivial findings in experimental research, what findings would you suggest and would your suggestions be the same to Joe on the street as to economists?*

M.W.: First, thanks for the possibility to give a statement about life: If it's not important for Joe on the street it shouldn't be important to economists; that's why I'm always using my grandmother as a hypothetical listener when I'm teaching, and that's the reason it's the same. I thought about three different examples. One thing is the double auction, which I think is fascinating – that it converges with just twelve people, even with eight people. It converges to the competitive equilibrium, and you can tell Joe on the street that "you just have a couple of guys together and the results are really efficient." The other thing is the insights you get from game theory – from the sort of guinea-pig game like the ultimatum game – that people are just not as egoistic as game theory predicts; there are other issues like fairness and so on, and this has triggered a whole new literature. And then in individual decision making, as this is more my field, you think about loss aversion as one of the key insights: That people hate losses more than they love gains, and this has triggered all types of research. Those are the three.

F.A.: *Then, more specifically, do you believe that there is a reasonably general theory of behavior under risk and uncertainty within reach?*

M.W.: Clearly no. First, it would get us out of business. The other thing, which was also discussed during the conference, is that I think the traditional theory – expected utility – is not correct. There are systematic deviations which we want to model, but it is clearly not correct in the overall way, so it's not well in reach, no way.

F.A.: *Your talk at the conference, was about ambiguity, would you like to elaborate briefly on what you talked about?*

M.W.: The most modern way of thinking about ambiguity is like it's a state of mind. Your attitude towards ambiguity is a state of mind which you have towards the event that you have to judge. And when you have to judge the event it's important to which extent this event – and the associated outcome – contribute to your decision, and here two things intertwine: it's the probability of the event and how much you believe in some way that this probability is the correct one. And this is what I tried to present in what I call a two-stage approach, that these two things are intertwined and that they depend on the type of event; that's what I think could be the key insight of my talk.

F.A.: *How would you more generally assess the experimental evidence regarding ambiguity aversion?*

M.W.: I don't think one should talk these days about ambiguity aversion. It's an attitude towards ambiguity and it can be ambiguity seeking or aversion; it really depends on your state of mind, how confident you feel in evaluating the event. And this is a fact that is sort of new but found in a lot of decision contexts. You find strong ambiguity aversion if you don't feel comfortable, if you don't know the situation. It's like I said in the talk, when your grandmother tells you to keep your fingers away from that type of events, there may be reasons to exhibit ambiguity aversion. At the other end of the spectrum, you can think of American college students who love basketball – they're even ambiguity seeking, for they are so sure about their probability that they really believe in this probability more than in the chance probability, meaning that they're ambiguity seeking.

F.A.: *It seems from what you said yesterday and what you said now that you consider the competence idea very close and not really competing with ambiguity.*

M.W.: They're different ways. The competence idea is that competence, knowledge or whatever you call it matters, and you can see that you can manipulate this competence very nicely. There's a paper by Fox and Tversky in the QJE where they give people Ellsberg-type of urns and people do not show any ambiguity aversion. It's like you see a naked context free Ellsberg urn and you give the same certain equivalence as with a regular risk urn, but as soon as you shatter the competence in evaluating by showing the people the risk urn in a comparison people say "well I don't know anything about it so" and then it drops down. We did the following in a new study which should be finished once I sit two hours on a plane on the way back: We asked people something about the inflation rate in Holland, and they gave some answers, but then we gave them additional information about how the inflation rate is calculated and what is driving the inflation rate, and then they saw that they really don't know anything about it. So we changed the perceived competence of the situation and then the ambiguity aversion got stronger. And you can do all types of different things, you can evaluate an event in light of someone else who knows more and suddenly you say "oh, I'm sitting here with Fredrik, I know less than he, so I'd better sort of be less, feel less competent and be more ambiguity averse." So it's a driving factor.

F.A.: *Thank you. Well I go on to ask the last question on ambiguity and it is what's your view on the usefulness of ambiguity in applications and if there are any applications of ambiguity that you consider particular successful.*

M.W.: If you look at the research, it's very new so people can think about ambiguity but haven't seen very much. The key thing is, I think, that ambiguity research has to go away from the original Ellsberg-paradox type of thing, so you have to go away from balls and urns and come to real-world events, like I tried to present in the talk. And from that you can understand that people in real-world events behave differently in the presence of ambiguity. One application which suddenly comes to mind is what we call a "home bias" in finance, the observation that people tend to invest more in the stocks in their own country. There's a recent study forthcoming in, I think, the Journal of Finance, where they show that, for Finland, the more you know about the company and the closer the company is, the more you invest in it. There are studies on the "Baby Bells": when they were separated, people invest more in the Bells in their areas of residence. So in all these cases you feel more competent, you feel more positive about, some things. It's all intertwined, and this is a clear application of these ideas.

H.H.: *There seems to be some disagreements regarding the extent to which institutional aspects of specific applications should be taken into the laboratory. What are your thoughts on this?*

M.W.: It really depends on the question. I mean if you do too many institution things in the lab you might overburn the people. We once were in Frankfurt talking to the bosses of the stock exchange about doing something for the Frankfurt stock exchange. I asked them "how do you really determine the price?," I mean, asking "is a double auction OK if we do it?" and then they had this huge chart with markets and market makers and so on. If you bring all these things – which are really the institutional features of the Frankfurt stock exchange – to the lab, forget it. No one, beside the real traders, will be able to do it, so you can as well use the Frankfurt market stock exchange real data. So there, you have to test a clear theory in a context free way. If you bring too much context then that's a problem. It depends on the question but you don't always have to do it.

H.H.: *There are psychological studies, where it seems that a context helps people to act more rationally. For instance, when certain formal logical problems are presented in a context it seems that they are easier for people to grasp.*

M.W.: It's clear that when you set people in an environment and they don't know anything, they look for clues, and if you put them in an environment where the context gives them help concerning which type of clues to use then it's a different thing. But the context I was thinking about when I answered the question before is the context of market institutions in, for example, a finance setting. And there the context normally doesn't help to solve these complex problems.

F.A.: *It has been held that most research in medicine teaches us a lot about white mice; similarly, skeptical economists sometimes hold that experimental research teaches us a lot about undergraduate students. To what extent do you think that this criticism is fair?*

M.W.: I enjoy criticism because you learn something from it. Of course, I don't think it's correct. We did some experiments on ambiguity in markets, where first we had students trade ambiguous assets in experimental markets, and then we had traders of J.P. Morgan coming out from the trading desk, and the results were exactly the same. In this ambiguity study a trader doesn't have any specific knowledge and so on. The same thing can be done with other more psychological things like overconfidence. I have asked children, and they exhibit overconfidence. I then gave a seminar for practitioners, and I asked people about overconfidence – about what the German stock market index was – and those people had overconfidence to an extent you wouldn't believe, they exhibit even more overconfidence.

F.A.: *Your answer indicates that there might be some kind of selection issue. How do you think this issue should be addressed?*

M.W.: You may have to make a value judgement about the type of question you are investigating. Going back to my behavioral finance or finance background, of course, traders are more trained. An even better example could be teaching banking and credit loans: If you have a loan officer, he's in some way used to dealing with certain situations so he brings the expertise in the lab and you like that. So for certain questions I can see that you want to have that loan officer. However, if you have given the loan officer just a simple lottery and say "what is your certainty equivalent?" then you might as well use a student for then the context might even be bad, because the loan officer can come along and say "oh the certainty equivalent of this lottery is too bad, for if I don't do anything like blah blah blah then my boss will kick me and so on." The loan officer would bring in all this context, and you don't want to have it. So it's very important that you know what the context is, and if you need that context then you might also use more experienced people. But I'm really convinced that you cannot have a general answer to that question. So it's a nice discussion – it depends on the question. In order to be scientifically correct, sometimes you have to use the other type of subject to see whether it makes a difference or not.

H.H.: *Is there any topic in experimental economics that you consider to be relatively exhausted and for which the marginal benefit for additional studies is small?*

M.W.: The answer is clearly no, but that has nothing to do with experimental economics, it's just a basic question when you think about research. I liked one thing that Werner Güth was saying in his talk a lot: people have done this research extensively ten years ago and now they forgot about it, they think it's over, so then it's time to rethink it. I think that is very insightful. And that's the reason – who am I to judge if someone comes up with a good idea?

H.H.: *Do you consider there to be large territories still unexplored in the experimental field?*

M.W.: Here the value judgement kicks in of course: it's your own research. I think, and I have at least some arguments, that behavioral finance is important. It gets more important in research and it gets more important in theory. But in behavioral finance there are just a couple of people who have done experiments if you compare to game theory and other theories. It's an area where there's individual decision making in markets, and why not have more experiments in this area? You should do research when you have puzzles in the real world, and there are puzzles in the real world: It's by no means clear why people trade so much, it's by no means clear why people buy all these sort of brochures or all these magazines about investors. There are other things – there are market-price momentum effects and so on, but all these things are not clear. So there's a need to do research to understand these better and experiments, as one tool as I keep emphasizing, might be helpful for that.

F.A.: *Do you see any particular pitfalls in, for experimental economics now or in the future?*

M.W.: As you can see in my message the whole time, I think the main pitfall is when experimental economists stay among each other. And I think in finance what you should do is to convince people like Fama that there are results from experiments which are important for people who are interested in the field. It might be a pitfall if you mingle too much among the same people, and that's the reason why I wouldn't even call experimental economics a field, I would just call it a tool to solve problems.

F.A.: *Speaking of that, I will ask you the last question. What do you think will happen with the market share of experimental research in the future?*

M.W.: It will increase but it won't explode.

II

CONTRIBUTIONS

Chapter 9

ATTITUDES TOWARDS RISK AND INEQUALITY: A QUESTIONNAIRE-EXPERIMENTAL APPROACH*

Yoram Amiel
Ruppin Institute
yoram_a@ruppin.ac.il

Frank Cowell
London School of Economics
f.cowell@lse.ac.uk

with the assistance of Kaspar Richter

1. Introduction

Attitudes to inequality and risk can be interpreted in a number of ways. A standard approach is to think in terms of strength of inequality aversion or risk aversion. There are several studies which examine these questions from the standpoint of economic orthodoxy in these two fields, and some which investigate risk and inequality jointly within the standard theoretical framework for analyzing income distributions.[1] However such an approach presumes acceptance of the basic premises of this framework. In this paper we examine a deeper question that addresses the basis for statements about inequality or risk comparisons without incorporating *a priori* the key assumptions that impose structure on inequality indices, measures of risk or other distributional criteria. Instead of posing the question "what is the degree of inequality (risk) aversion"

*This paper forms part of the research program of the TMR network Living Standards, Inequality and Taxation [Contract No. ERBFMRXCT 980248] of the European Communities whose financial support is gratefully acknowledged. Rajeev Bhattacharya, Liema Davidovitz, Leonardo Gasparini, Wulf Gaertner, John Lane, Mårten Palme, Avraham Polovin, Erik Schokkaert and Tony Venables assisted in running the questionnaire. The paper has benefited from the comments of seminar and conference participants at the LSE, Ruppin Institute, Bar-Ilan University, CERGE, Keele University, the Institute for Fiscal Studies and the Arne Ryde Symposium.

we address the logically prior question "on what basis can one say that one distribution is more unequal (risky) than another?" We further address the question of whether there is a linkage between distributional comparisons in terms of inequality and those in terms of risk. This is accomplished by use of a questionnaire-experimental study that permits one to investigate the way in which individuals' perceptions of income-distribution comparisons conform to, or depart from, the orthodox analytical framework.

Previous studies have analyzed the underlying structure of attitudes towards risk and inequality using separate experiments (Amiel and Cowell 1999a, 1999b; Amiel et al. 2001). However, in this case we are able to examine the structure of both types of comparison simultaneously by means of a device explained in Section 3. We analyze questionnaire responses of over 1100 students from seven countries in a joint inequality-and-risk questionnaire experiment.

The paper is arranged as follows. Section 2 describes the background theory. Sections 3 and 4 describe the experiment and resulting data set. Section 5 looks at all the responses to the numerical questions jointly, and Section 6 studies the variation in responses for specific numerical questions dealing with different types of equalizing income transfers. Section 7 examines the implications of responses to the verbal part of the questionnaire. Section 8 concludes.

2. Theoretical Background

As we outlined in the introduction there are two distinct types of question that are relevant to the present paper, namely: What do we mean by inequality and by risk? How are the two related? Strangely enough it is convenient to discuss the second issue first – it is useful to consider in principle why and how the two fields are connected.

2.1 Inequality and Risk

The literature on the ranking of probability distributions forms one of the most important intellectual sources of the modern inequality literature. As noted in Amiel and Cowell (1999b):

> One of the most important intellectual sources of the modern inequality literature is the literature on ranking probability distributions. Some of the seminal pieces in inequality analysis – Atkinson (1970) foremost among them – started from the insight that the problem of ordering income distributions in terms of inequality is essentially similar to the problem of ordering distributions in other contexts.

Some links between inequality measurement and risk measurement are evident – inequality measures such as the coefficient of variation and the variance of logarithms have obvious counterparts in the analysis of risk, since the standard deviation or variance is conventionally used as the measure of spread, either for "income" or its logarithm; the entropy measures of Theil (1967) have their roots in the economics of information and there is also a case for considering the generalized entropy concepts as a measure of risk. However to focus solely the parallelism of approach between these two aspects of distributional analysis would be to omit three important issues for consideration.

1. The special interest of risk-analysis is not just that one can find useful and suggestive parallels between the analysis of income distribution and the analysis of risk – as one can also with, say, the distribution of firms by size or the geographical dispersion of rainfall Dalton (1920). On *a priori* grounds one can argue that the analysis of probability distributions may be an appropriate basis for the analysis of income distributions. The similarity of structure of the two issues lies at the core of a number of key contributions in the literature on distributional analysis – see Rothschild and Stiglitz (1970, 1971, 1973), Nermuth (1993).

2. Second, in both literatures there is a connection to a concept of utility or welfare. In the inequality literature there is an implied relationship between social welfare (W) and inequality (I)

$$W = \phi(I, \mu) \tag{9.1}$$

where μ is mean income: (9.1) may be used to map an inequality ordering into a welfare ordering. Of course, given (9.1), one should be able to use the inverse relationship

$$I = \phi^{-1}(W, \mu) \tag{9.2}$$

to obtain inequality rankings from welfare rankings, conditional on mean income; one can imagine the inequality concept as being "inherited" from the particular system of values represented by W. The counterpart of (9.1) in the context of ranking probability distributions

$$u = \phi(R, \mu) \tag{9.3}$$

connects utility (individual preference) u to a measure of risk R and expected reward. The representation of investor's utility as a function of variance and the mean,[2] is a well-known example of this. Once again, if one takes the inverse of (9.3) one can see the risk concept as "inherited" from the system of values represented by u.

3. Finally, some researchers take a position based on the work of the philosopher John Harsanyi[3] that, rather than risk orderings being just an appropriate basis for comparison with inequality counterparts (as in point 1 above) they are *the essential* foundation for the axiomatisation of inequality comparisons. In some instances the argument linking the two

would also invoke an explicit welfare-theoretic link as in point 2. The core of the argument is that social values to income distribution can be derived from the values that guide individual choices in the face of uncertainty. Imagine a representative individual behind a veil of ignorance who perceives that there would be the same probability of being endowed with the identity of any one of the persons in the population. Then, asked to rank a collection of income distributions, he/she would rank them according to a set of values u; these values for the representative individual making choices in the face of risk then become the social values W for ranking income distributions. Given this equivalence of W and u under this interpretation of the veil of ignorance, there is an equivalence of the "inherited" concepts I and R.

2.2 The Meaning of Inequality and of Risk

However, both inequality and risk can appear to be elusive concepts. There is a variety of ad hoc inequality indices and risk measures. Standard reference works on risk either offer generalized descriptions such as "risk reflects the variability of future returns from a capital investment" (Pass et al. 1993) or list a variety of interpretations[4] and it is easy to concur with the view that "People disagree more about what risk is than about how large it is."(Fischloff 1985)

Nevertheless in the case of inequality – apart from cases where an arbitrary inequality index is used for the sake of convenience – the majority of the mainstream literature on inequality either adopts a direct axiomatisation of the concept or an indirect axiomatic approach through a social-welfare relationship such as (9.2). The view that emerges is consistent with the standard Lorenz-curve comparisons (see section 2.3 below) and is rich enough to encompass a very large range of inequality measures and other tools. Furthermore, as far as risk is concerned, there is also a consensus approach in the mainstream literature of economics and finance that sets the definition of risk within the analysis of individuals' preferences and choices under uncertainty.

This suggests that for risk we reconsider point 2 of section 2.1 – the risk-counterpart to (9.2). A well-known example of this relationship is the use of mean-variance analysis: this incorporates both a natural measure of risk and a simple preference structure, but of course this relies on the use of a specific, and perhaps questionable, utility function. By contrast comparatively little use is made of the more general counterpart to the Lorenz-curve approach as a means of characterizing risk, although clearly one could "build" a Lorenz curve for risk upon the equivalent of the axioms used in inequality analysis (Cf Laffont 1989, page 27). However, this itself begs two questions

1. Whether the inequality axioms are themselves appropriate.

2. The nature of the relationship ϕ in (9.1) and (9.3).

A conventional microeconomic argument might suggest that these ambiguities could be disposed of by invoking the standard stochastic dominance approach (Hadar and Russell 1969). If one is prepared to apply the criterion of second-order dominance to a set of income distributions one can clearly derive the Lorenz order for any subset in which all the distributions have the same mean. However, stochastic dominance is not principally about the nature of *risk* per se but about the structure of *preferences* under uncertainty.

The argument for the stochastic dominance approach encounters a further difficulty. In the literature on inequality and social welfare it is sometimes argued that the chain of connection from W to I introduces overly strong *a priori* assumptions. A similar claim may be made in the case of the analysis of preferences under uncertainty. There is a good case for arguing that the von-Neumann-Morgenstern formulation of preference structures does not adequately capture people's rankings of uncertain prospects. It should be recognized that, even if peoples' preferences violate the von-Neumann-Morgenstern assumptions, they may yet have a coherent perception of risk.[5] There are several strands to the argument:

- It is not clear that people think in terms of preferences over prospects as the standard theory suggests.
- If people do have well-defined preference orderings over prospects, it is not clear that their attitudes to risk can be well represented by a utility function that conforms to the standard axioms.
- There may be a confusion between "better-than" relationships and pure risk comparisons. However, it should be noted that in the corresponding discussion of inequality this confusion does not usually arise.
- People may or may not be risk-averse in the sense of disliking mean-preserving spreads.

A comprehensive study that successfully disentangled the concept of risk *per se* from the language of preference would clearly be demanding. For this reason we seek an alternative approach.

2.3 An Axiomatic Approach

Instead of invoking an apparatus that involves social welfare or preference under uncertainty we can approach the meaning of inequality and of risk directly using an axiomatic approach. The core axioms that are taken as standard in the literature on these two fields are given in Table 9.1. Alternative commonly used distributional tools can be derived by selecting different combinations of standard axioms from the list: for example, for the regular Lorenz curve one invokes Axioms 1, 2, 3 and 5a.[6]

Table 9.1. Standard axioms in the analysis of income and probability distributions.

	Inequality	Risk
1	*Anonymity*	*Anonymity*
2	*Transfer Principle*	*Mean-preserving spread principle*
3	*Population Principle*	*Normalization*
4	*Group Decomposability*	*Independence Axiom*
5a	*Scale independence*	*Scale independence*
5b	*Translation independence*	*Translation independence*

The interpretation of some of these axioms is straightforward – anonymity implies that individual identities can be permuted without affecting inequality (states-of-the-world can be permuted without affecting risk); the population principle implies that a cloning of the population leaves inequality unaltered; scale-independence and translation-independence are two alternative characterizations of what should happen if all incomes in the distribution are increased simultaneously.[7] The interpretation of group-decomposability (the independence axiom in risk) is less straightforward but implies a type of additive separability on inequality indices and risk measures.[8] The transfer principle Dalton (1920) and its counterpart in risk analysis (concerning mean-preserving spreads) are of special interest because they are central to almost all of the modern literature in the two fields.

Definition 1: ***The transfer principle.*** *Let x_i and x_j be the income of any two persons i and j such that $x_j > x_i$; if ceteris paribus a small amount of income is transferred from i to j inequality must rise.*[9]

For the principle of mean-preserving spreads simply reinterpret x_i and x_j as the payoffs associated with two particular elementary uncertain events with known probabilities in Definition 1.

Clearly the transfer principle is appealing and it is certainly powerful in that it is the basis not only for the Lorenz curve for all stochastic dominance criteria of the second-order and higher.[10] But it may be too powerful, and too easily appealing in that it rules out of consideration the some information about income distributions that are actually used by people in making comparisons involving inequality or risk. For example, if one assumes that there are no "externalities" involved in the distributional comparison (Amiel and Cowell 1998, p. 198). Accordingly it may also be useful to consider a weaker version of same idea that allows for the possibility that more complex criteria could be applied by individuals to inequality or risk comparison. An obvious example would be this criterion.

Definition 2: ***"Lowest-to-Highest"* (*LTH*) *principle*.** *If ceteris paribus a small amount of income is transferred from the person with the lowest income to the person with the highest income inequality must rise.*

Note that both the principle of transfers and the LTH principle are silent on rerankings in the income distribution that do not affect both the donor and recipient. The principles in Definitions 1 and 2 are at the core of the analysis of this paper.

3. The Experiment

In previous contributions we have argued the case for analyzing inequality in a way that leaves open the question of whether the "basic" axioms are to be adopted or not, and that a suitable way of discovering whether the commonly used axiomatic structure is appropriate is to adopt a questionnaire-experimental approach (Amiel and Cowell 1992, 1999b). Clearly the same argument could be applied also to risk analysis – it may be the case that in risk comparisons people do not routinely follow the principle of mean-preserving spreads. Furthermore, given the parallel structure of risk and inequality it is also of interest to see whether the structure of the of individuals' judgements is the same – as one would expect it to be if one accepted some of the arguments outlined in section 2.1. Of course one could likewise perform a parallel study in which social welfare and individual preference under uncertainty were the focus of attention. In each case one is comparing like with like. However it is less clear that, say, a comparative study of inequality and preference under uncertainty would be appropriate. In the present study we concentrate on which distribution is more unequal, on which is regarded as riskier, not on which is thought of as "better."

3.1 Issues

Accordingly the main question to be addressed is as follows: are inequality and risk comparisons viewed in accordance with orthodox economic theory as enshrined in the transfer principle that characterizes distributional dominance relations? If there are deviations from the orthodox approach, what form do they take, and what appear to be the factors that predispose people to take a viewpoint that differs from the conventional economic methodology?

A second question is whether the distributional comparisons are viewed in the same way irrespective of whether the problem is framed in the context of inequality or the equivalent version of risk.

Clearly the first question can be tackled by separate questionnaires in risk and in inequality, but to tackle the second question satisfactorily one really needs a joint experiment.

3.2 Implementation

During 1998/99 a questionnaire experiment was carried out on twelve samples of undergraduate students from seven countries. The majority were economics students of some sort – others came from disciplines such as politics and law. Our target base of respondents was those who were sufficiently numerate to reason from simple examples and who – although they may have had contact with economics – had not been specifically trained in the economics of risk or the economics of inequality and so could not be considered "experts".[11]

The questionnaire was organized as follows. During regular class or lecture time the teacher found a slot to distribute two sets of questionnaires to the students. Each student received just one questionnaire and completed it under the supervision of the class teacher or lecturer in about 10 or 15 minutes.[12]

The reason for there being two sets of questionnaires was that we wished to obtain simultaneously two samples from the same population, one for each of the two issues, inequality and risk. The two documents required for the joint study were deliberately designed to be very similar – so that, at a glance, each respondent's questionnaire would appear to be the same as his neighbor's – see Appendix 10. Respondents were presented with the questionnaire in their own language: the translation was carried out by colleagues expert in the inequality and risk fields and the accuracy of translation was checked by re-translating the text back into English. Examples of the translation can be viewed at http://darp.lse.ac.uk/demo.htm.

Students were simply told that they were to complete a "questionnaire on income distribution", and were not informed that there were actually two separate versions of the questionnaire study. The questionnaires consisted of three parts:

1. First respondents were asked to rank six pairs of income vectors (A and B) in terms of inequality or risk. This was motivated by a brief story about a country called "Alfaland": the five components of each vector represented incomes in the five regions of Alfaland; in each of the six questions each (A,B)-pair of vectors was supposed to represent the outcomes of two policies; in the risk context respondents were invited to suppose that a newcomer to Alfaland would be assigned at random to any one of the five regions, and that risk should be judged from the standpoint of such a newcomer: this story is clearly motivated by the Harsanyi veil-of-ignorance analogy (see page 87). For each question, B was obtained from A by an equalizing income transfer from a rich to a poor region without reversing the ordering of the two regions involved in the transfers. As we have seen, according to the Principle of Transfers, an equalizing income transfer reduces inequality. Therefore, the Principle of Transfers would imply that A is more unequal (riskier) than B in all six numerical

Table 9.2. Students by Country.

	Number			Percentage		
	Total	*Inequality*	*Risk*	*Total*	*Inequality*	*Risk*
Argentina	74	38	36	6	6	6
Australia	124	62	62	11	11	11
Belgium	137	87	50	12	15	9
Germany	264	126	138	23	21	24
Israel	180	93	87	16	16	15
Sweden	63	31	32	5	5	6
UK	311	150	161	27	26	28
All countries	*1153*	*587*	*566*	*100*	*100*	*100*

questions. In all but one of the numerical questions the structure of the income distribution is fairly rich in that no two regions have the same income; Question 5 is obviously different in that the implied transfer in switching from A to B or vice versa inevitably involves the richest and (one of) the poorest (there are four of these).

2. Respondents were then invited to look at the issue of the transfer principle (mean-preserving spreads) in terms of a simple extension of the story about Alfaland; this time an exclusively verbal approach was used for both inequality and risk versions. It was possible for respondents to check more than one answer possible. The details of this part of the questionnaire are discussed further in Section 7 below.

3. Finally respondents were asked for details about themselves, their backgrounds and their attitudes, although the questionnaire was conducted anonymously: the details of these questions are presented in the Appendix.

4. Data

Table 9.2 gives a summary of the number of students by country. The data set comprises students from seven countries (Argentina, Australia, Belgium, Germany, Israel, Sweden, and the UK). A roughly equal number of students responded to the inequality and risk questionnaires (52% versus 48%). Students from Australia responded to both inequality and risk questionnaires. The results presented here include the Australian responses, but excluding them does not affect the main findings.

The students provided information about basic personal characteristics – see the Appendix for the complete list. Key amongst these was the main subject of study since it is known that studying mainstream economics may predispose individuals to respond to questions about inequality or risk in a

Table 9.3. Personal Characteristics of Students.

	Inequality		Risk		P-value*
	Mean	*SD*	*Mean*	*SD*	
Gender	0.63	0.48	0.61	0.49	0.66
Age	22.95	4.44	23.21	4.01	0.32
Employment	0.40	0.49	0.44	0.50	0.24
Political Opinion	4.03	1.05	3.97	1.05	0.39
Income 1990	4.32	1.01	4.25	1.10	0.33
Income 2010	5.04	0.91	4.91	1.00	0.02
Economic Subject (core)	0.29	0.45	0.30	0.46	0.64
Economic Subject (broader)	0.75	0.43	0.72	0.45	0.24

*Equality in means across risk and inequality subgroup.

manner consistent with economic orthodoxy.[13] Also of particular interest *a priori* were individuals' political views (it may be the case that those who are politically concerned about inequality have a more carefully articulated view of the meaning of inequality comparisons) and estimates of their own income background and prospects relative to others (it is known that in some contexts income perceptions affect inequality rankings).[14]

The distribution of characteristics for the inequality and risk subsamples are very similar, as shown in Table 9.3.[15] With the exception of income in 2010, a t-test does not reject the null hypothesis of equal means across inequality and risk samples for all characteristics at standard significance levels. Differences in the responses between risk and inequality are unlikely to be driven by systematic variation in the characteristics of the two subsamples.

Table 9.4 compares the characteristics of male and female subgroups. The t-statistics indicate some differences between the two groups, in particular for the inequality subsample. Male students tend to be older, to have more work experience, to be more conservative in their political opinions, and to have a higher estimated income in 2010. It will be important to control for these covariates when we want to isolate the influence of gender on attitudes towards risk and inequality.

5. Numerical responses and the Principle of Transfers

5.1 Descriptive results

The issues that one can address with part 1 of the questionnaire concern inferences drawn from respondents' choices on each pair of vectors or on the pattern of responses over all six numerical problems: do they view a particular equalizing income transfer as inequality and risk reducing? Are their responses jointly consistent with the Principle of Transfers – see section 3.1? Table 9.5 shows simple summary statistics of the responses.[16] For both inequality and

Table 9.4. Personal Characteristics of Male and Female Students.

	Male		Female		P-value*
	Mean	*SD*	*Mean*	*SD*	
RISK					
Age	23.77	4.52	22.27	2.81	0.00
Employment	0.48	0.50	0.36	0.48	0.00
Political Opinion	4.04	1.06	3.88	1.03	0.08
Income 1990	4.27	1.20	4.23	0.94	0.66
Income Change 2010	0.73	1.42	0.48	1.23	0.00
Economic Subject (c)	0.33	0.47	0.27	0.44	0.10
INEQUALITY					
Age	23.40	4.99	22.14	3.26	0.00
Employment	0.45	0.50	0.32	0.47	0.00
Political Opinion	4.10	1.10	3.90	0.96	0.02
Income 1990	4.39	0.98	4.18	1.05	0.02
Income Change 2010	0.77	1.15	0.60	1.31	0.11
Economic Subject (c)	0.30	0.46	0.28	0.45	0.75

*Equality in means across risk and inequality subgroup.

Table 9.5. Percentage Shares of Answer A – Numerical Questions.

	Inequality	Risk
Equalizing Transfer Reduces Inequality?*		
Total	59	61
Male	61	67
Female	57	53
Consistency with Transfer Principle?**		
Total	17	23
Male	21	31
Female	10	11

*Percentage of answer A.
**Percentage of answer A in all six questions

risk, about 60% of the responses view an equalizing transfer as inequality/risk reducing. However, no more than about one fifth of the students ticked response A for all six questions. The consistency with the Principle of Transfers is higher for risk (23%) than for inequality (17%).

Male and female subjects differ markedly in their responses in both risk and inequality subsamples: women are more likely to answer A if the question is in the inequality context than in the context of risk; men are more likely to answer A if the question is in the context of risk rather than inequality. The differences in responses between the genders are stronger for risk attitudes: male students are 25% more likely to check answer A, and almost three times more consistent with the Principle of Transfers than female students.

5.2 Regression Analysis

The question immediately arises whether gender remains an important determinant of heterodox responses once one controls for other personal characteristics. To address this we use a standard probit regressions of the form

$$\Pr(\text{Response Pattern}) = \Phi(b_1 y_1 + b_2 y_2 + ... + b_n y_n) \tag{9.4}$$

where y_j is a measure of personal or background characteristic j, $(b_1, ..., b_n)$ is a vector of coefficients and Φ is the normal distribution function. Given that there were m separate numerical questions (where $m = 6$ in our case) in which only the answer A is consistent with economic orthodoxy there are two main interpretations of "Response Pattern" in (9.4) that of particular interest to us:

1. m separate responses (each of which could be A or B or $A\&B$). This gives us in principle mN observations.
2. a single response pattern in which only $AA...A$ is consistent with economic orthodoxy. Clearly there are just N observations here

Table 9.6 and Table 9.7 display the results of these two interpretations.[17] Again, we look at both responses across all questions, and consistency with the Principle of Transfers. For the regression in Table 9.6 (interpretation 1 above), the response A was indexed as unity, and as zero otherwise. For Table 9.7 (interpretation 2), the response *A in all six questions together* was indexed as unity, and any other response as zero. The dependent variables are age, political opinion, income rank in 1990, the expected change in the income rank from 1990 to 2010, and dummies for gender (1 for male), previous work history, economic subject and country origin: the Appendix discusses the specification of these variables further.

On either interpretation the story is extremely clear. There are four main features to it:

- First, studying an economic subject is significant in both specifications and is highly significant if one takes each question separately.[18] This is to be expected from previous studies (Amiel and Cowell 1992) and accords, perhaps, with intuition: on the whole, those studying economics are more likely to make distributional comparisons in line with economic orthodoxy.
- Second, gender has a similar impact. Male students view more often an equalizing transfer as inequality-reducing risk-reducing (taking each of the six questions separately) and are more consistent with the Principle of Transfers (all questions together). This is striking because, in the nature of the specification of the model, it is a factor separate from that

Table 9.6. Probit Regression of Response A.

Variable	Inequality		Risk		P-value**
	*Coef**	*P>|z|*	*Coef**	*P>|z|*	
Gender	0.05	0.01	0.13	0.00	0.00
Age	0.00	0.63	0.00	0.50	0.37
Employment	0.02	0.35	0.00	0.94	0.55
Political opinion	0.00	0.52	-0.01	0.29	0.75
Income 1990	0.00	0.75	0.01	0.40	0.72
Income Change 2010	0.01	0.19	0.00	0.85	0.40
Economic Subject	0.10	0.00	0.15	0.00	0.16

Explanatory variables include dummy variables for countries.
Number of observations 6767
*Marginal effects. **Equality of coefficients across subgroups.

Table 9.7. Probit Regression of Consistency with Principle of Transfers.

Variable	Inequality		Risk		P-value**
	*Coef**	*P>|z|*	*Coef**	*P>|z|*	
Gender	0.12	0.01	0.21	0.00	0.16
Age	0.00	0.90	0.00	0.41	0.60
Employment	0.02	0.54	-0.01	0.88	0.58
Political opinion	-0.01	0.45	-0.01	0.33	0.90
Income 1990	0.00	0.88	0.00	0.76	0.74
Income Change 2010	0.02	0.21	-0.01	0.48	0.15
Economic Subject	0.10	0.09	0.14	0.01	0.56

Explanatory variables include dummy variables for countries.
Number of observations 1153
*Marginal effects. **Equality of coefficients across subgroups.

of economic subject. The phenomenon cannot be explained away by the fact that more males choose to pursue economic subjects than females.

- Third, the coefficients on gender and economic subject are larger for risk than inequality.

- Finally, the other personal characteristics are on the whole not significant.[19]

6. Numerical Responses: variation by Type of Income Transfer

6.1 Descriptive Analysis

Up to this point, we have considered all questions jointly, ignoring any variation in responses amongst questions. Table 9.8 shows the percentages of

Table 9.8. Equalizing Income Transfers Reduce Inequality/Risk?*

	Total	Male	Female
INEQUALITY			
Question 1	40	44	34
Question 2	74	74	74
Question 3	61	62	60
Question 4	60	64	56
Question 5	72	70	76
Question 6	48	52	42
RISK			
Question 1	49	55	39
Question 2	68	74	60
Question 3	59	66	52
Question 4	68	74	60
Question 5	67	71	60
Question 6	55	62	46

*Percentage of answer A.

response A for each of the six questions. It compares the responses for inequality and risk for the entire sample and across the male and female subgroups.

There is more variation in the proportions of answer A for inequality than risk but the overall pattern is broadly similar. Students are more likely to view an income transfer as inequality or risk reducing if it involves the richest region (Question 2 and Question 5), in particular if the recipient region is at the lower tail of the income distribution (Question 2). They are less likely to attribute an equalizing impact to a transfer among regions, that are located near the middle of the income distribution and ranked next (Question 1) or in close proximity (Question 6) to each other. However, in the case of risk, the response to question 4 that involves an implied income transfer that is large enough to induce a reranking of individuals is also viewed as risk-reducing.

The responses of female respondents vary more by question than those of male respondents. Apart from Question 5 for inequality, male students are more likely to choose A. Across questions, the differences between male and female proportionate responses are uniformly larger for risk than inequality.

6.2 Regression Analysis

One might wonder whether the clear differences in response patterns across questions carry through to the regression analysis. To address this, table 9.9 shows the result of re-running the probit regression from Table 9.6, adding fixed effects for each question.[20] It is clear that the results from the descriptive analysis are indeed confirmed. All question dummy variables are negative, indicating a lower proportion of A responses relative to Question 2 (where the

Table 9.9. Probit Regression of Response A with Question Dummy Variables.

Variable	**Inequality**		**Risk**	
	Coef	*P>|z|*	*Coef*	*P>|z|*
Gender	0.04	0.03	0.13	0.00
Age	0.00	0.85	0.00	0.36
Employment	0.03	0.10	0.00	0.99
Political opinion	0.00	0.75	0.00	0.93
Income 1990	0.00	0.82	-0.01	0.55
Income Change 2010	0.00	0.78	0.00	0.92
Economic Subject	0.12	0.00	0.15	0.00
Question 1	-0.33	0.00	-0.19	0.00
Question 3	-0.13	0.00	-0.09	0.00
Question 4	-0.14	0.00	0.00	0.93
Question 5	-0.01	0.68	-0.02	0.60
Question 6	-0.27	0.00	-0.13	0.00
Number of observations	3522		3396	

*Explanatory variables include dummy variables for countries.

transfer is from the richest to the poorest region) . In the case of inequality Question 5 (where the transfer involves the richest) has the highest coefficient, while Question 1 and Question 6 (where the transfer is among middle-ranking regions in close proximity) have the lowest coefficients. In the case of risk Question 4 (involving the rerankings) has the highest coefficient.

Table 9.10 estimates probit regressions for each question separately. The results are by now familiar. First, responses for both inequality and risk vary typically only by gender and economic subject, while other personal characteristics remain generally insignificant. Second, the coefficients on gender and economic subject are (with one exception for gender) positive, indicating a higher probability of response A. Third, the coefficients on these two variables tend to be higher for risk than inequality (except for question 6), even though the differences are typically not significant.

6.3 A provisional evaluation

It has been known for some time that support for the Principle of Transfers does not enjoy universal support (Amiel and Cowell 1992). However the results reported here yield a deeper insight in that, first, we allow for a broader interpretation of the transfer principle as well as the conventional version that is attributable to Dalton (1920) and that, second, we look at whether the corresponding issue corresponds with individuals' ranking of distributions in terms of risk. There is clear support for the LTH principle that says "a transfer from the highest income to the lowest must reduce inequality (risk)" but not the transfer principle proper – which says "a transfer from a higher income to a

Table 9.10. Probit Regressions of Response A by Questions.

	Variable	Inequality		Risk		P-value*
		Coef	*P>|z|*	*Coef*	*P>|z|*	
Question 1	**Gender**	0.13	0.01	0.16	0.00	0.68
	Age	-0.01	0.24	-0.00	0.38	0.80
	Employment	0.02	0.65	0.01	0.79	0.89
	Political opinion	-0.01	0.58	0.01	0.53	0.40
	Income 1990	0.01	0.61	-0.01	0.50	0.38
	Income Change 2010	0.02	0.31	0.01	0.62	0.68
	Economic Subject	0.11	0.08	0.15	0.02	0.69
Number of observations 1134						
Question 2	**Gender**	0.00	0.99	0.11	0.01	0.05
	Age	0.00	0.29	-0.00	0.32	0.11
	Employment	-0.03	0.56	-0.04	0.31	0.78
	Political opinion	0.01	0.71	0.00	0.97	0.77
	Income 1990	0.00	0.99	0.03	0.13	0.29
	Income Change 2010	0.01	0.73	-0.00	0.97	0.82
	Economic Subject	0.11	0.04	0.12	0.01	0.84
Number of observations 1126						
Question 3	**Gender**	0.05	0.31	0.13	0.00	0.17
	Age	0.01	0.22	0.00	0.38	0.79
	Employment	-0.02	0.68	-0.01	0.89	0.85
	Political opinion	-0.01	0.55	-0.01	0.64	0.93
	Income 1990	0.00	0.94	-0.01	0.58	0.74
	Income Change 2010	0.01	0.66	-0.02	0.30	0.30
	Economic Subject	0.14	0.02	0.18	0.00	0.63
Number of observations 1130						

[continued...]

*Equality of coefficients across subgroups.

Variable		Inequality *Coef*	*P>|z|*	Risk *Coef*	*P>|z|*	P-value*
[...continued]						
Question 4	**Gender**	0.09	0.04	0.12	0.01	0.55
	Age	-0.00	0.92	0.00	0.99	0.93
	Employment	0.00	1.00	0.02	0.71	0.79
	Political opinion	-0.00	1.00	-0.01	0.67	0.75
	Income 1990	0.00	0.89	-0.01	0.67	0.83
	Income Change 2010	0.02	0.40	0.01	0.70	0.73
	Economic Subject	0.06	0.27	0.18	0.00	0.10
Number of observations 1124						
Question 5	**Gender**	-0.07	0.12	0.09	0.04	0.01
	Age	0.00	0.70	-0.01	0.18	0.43
	Employment	0.07	0.10	0.03	0.53	0.47
	Political opinion	-0.01	0.46	-0.05	0.01	0.17
	Income 1990	0.00	0.92	0.03	0.13	0.32
	Income Change 2010	-0.01	0.47	-0.00	0.85	0.68
	Economic Subject	0.06	0.31	0.14	0.00	0.21
Number of observations 1127.						
Question 6	**Gender**	0.08	0.08	0.15	0.00	0.31
	Age	0.00	0.63	0.00	0.53	0.92
	Employment	0.06	0.19	0.00	0.92	0.39
	Political opinion	-0.00	0.82	0.00	0.85	0.77
	Income 1990	0.01	0.74	0.02	0.44	0.76
	Income Change 2010	0.03	0.19	0.02	0.46	0.65
	Economic Subject	0.14	0.03	0.10	0.10	0.59
Number of observations 1126						

*Equality of coefficients across subgroups.

lower must reduce inequality (risk)" . Although the overall pattern of responses looks fairly similar in the cases of risk and inequality – see for example Table 9.5 and the left-hand column of Table 9.8 – the picture differs markedly when one breaks down the respondents by gender: then it is no longer possible to maintain that the pattern of inequality attitudes is essentially the same as the pattern of risk attitudes either among men or among women.

7. The Verbal Question

As explained in Section 3 the respondents were also asked to fill out a verbal question in part 2 of the questionnaire. The responses to this question can give further insights as to the respondents' conformity, or otherwise, with economic orthodoxy.

7.1 The structure of the question

First a brief description of the question itself:

- The story of Alfaland is extended by asking individuals to consider the effect of transferring income exogenously from a rich region to a poorer region.
- There are five possible responses, including "none of the above". The choice of these responses was guided by the considerations set out in Amiel and Cowell (1992) pp 6,7 and was designed to cover views corresponding to the transfer principle and LTH (Definitions 1 and 2).
- Individuals are allowed to check more than one response.
- Only response "d" is consistent with the orthodox view.

Because the questionnaire is structured so that respondents come to the verbal question and its various explanations *after* completing the numerical questions we gave people the opportunity to indicate whether they would have wanted to change their responses on the numerical problems.

7.2 Verbal question: descriptive results

The fact that respondents were allowed to make multiple selections from question 7 means that we can interpret consistency with economic orthodoxy in either a broad or narrow sense. On the narrow interpretation – whether for inequality or for risk – people should have checked "d" and nothing else. However, it might be reasonable to look at cases where, because of difficulties with understanding the question, or some perceived ambiguity, respondents checked both "d" and one or more other possibilities. These two interpretations correspond, respectively, to the lower and the upper halves of Table 9.11. We

Table 9.11. Percentage of "d" responses on verbal question.

	Inequality	Risk
Equalizing Transfer Reduces Inequality/Risk?*		
Total	28	28
Male	28	31
Female	28	23
Consistency with Transfer Principle?**		
Total	23	24
Male	22	28
Female	24	19

* Percentage of answers that include "d"
**Percentage of answers "d" *only*

can see that, overall less than one quarter of respondents are consistent with economic orthodoxy on the narrow interpretation, and a little less than thirty percent for the broader interpretation; this applies to inequality or risk.

However, it is also evident that gender now plays an intriguing role. Recall that (from Table 9.5) women were more likely to answer A if in the first part of the questionnaire if the context of the problem were inequality rather than risk whereas the reverse was true for men. This pattern is exhibited again in Table 9.11, but more strongly now so that, *on the inequality interpretation*, women's responses are more consistent with economic orthodoxy than those for men. In the case of risk we have a confirmation of the earlier result – men's responses are more in line with orthodoxy than women; but in the case of Table 9.11 the effect is even stronger in that men are now 50 percent more likely to give a "d" response than women. Finally note that the number of respondents in line with economic orthodoxy on both the numerical part and the verbal part is quite small: the proportion of responses with straight A's on questions 1-6 and "d" on question 7 is only 8 percent in the case of inequality and 10 percent for risk.

Given that support for the transfer principle was rather low, it is interesting to look at the responses on other views in the verbal question. The strongest support for each of the five responses offered on question 7 was for "b", the case where transfers from/to the extremes is considered to reduce unambiguously inequality or risk, but other transfers are not necessarily considered. If we focus on this response the results are as in Table 9.12. The significance of this is that support for the LTH principle (covering both responses "b" and "d") is quite high.

Finally note that the proportion of those who indicated that they wanted to change their responses to each of the numerical questions in the light of their answer on the verbal question was only about 1 to 2 percent on each of questions 1-6.

Table 9.12. Percentage of "b" responses on verbal question.

	Inequality	Risk
Percentage of answers that include "b"		
Total	41	37
Male	43	38
Female	38	36
Percentage of answers "b" *only*		
Total	31	28
Male	32	28
Female	30	28

Table 9.13. Probit Regression of Response "d".

Variable	Inequality		Risk		P-value**
	*Coef**	*P>|z|*	*Coef**	*P>|z|*	
Gender	0.00	0.92	0.06	0.15	0.33
Age	0.01	0.12	-0.00	0.26	0.04
Employment	-0.04	0.34	-0.01	0.76	0.64
Political opinion	-0.01	0.66	-0.05	0.00	0.06
Income 1990	0.00	0.83	0.02	0.32	0.57
Income Change 2010	0.01	0.42	0.03	0.06	0.05
Economic Subject	0.01	0.89	0.19	0.00	0.03

Explanatory variables include dummy variables for countries.
Number of observations 1153
*Marginal effects. **Equality of coefficients across subgroups.

7.3 Regression analysis

Let us look once again at the role of personal factors on the response to the verbal question using probit regressions. Table 9.13 deals with responses that are either "d" or "d combined with something else". Table 9.14 deals with the more restrictive interpretation: here we consider responses "d and only d" against alternatives. Economic subject continues to be significant for the risk subsample on either the broad or narrow interpretation. Political opinion is also important, but again, only for risk: the more you are self-reportedly left-wing the greater is your probability of responding in line with economic orthodoxy: as we noted on page 93 this might be understandable in the case of inequality, but it is not clear *a priori* why this should hold in the case of risk. However Gender is only significant at the 10% level for the risk subsample – men are more likely to respond in an orthodox fashion.[21]

Table 9.14. Probit Regression of Consistency with Principle of Transfers.

Variable	Inequality		Risk		P-value**
	*Coef**	*P>|z|*	*Coef**	*P>|z|*	
Gender	-0.02	0.56	0.07	0.09	0.10
Age	0.01	0.01	-0.00	0.38	0.01
Employment	-0.05	0.18	-0.02	0.69	0.49
Political opinion	-0.01	0.73	-0.03	0.03	0.16
Income 1990	0.00	0.94	0.01	0.49	0.57
Income Change 2010	-0.02	0.23	0.04	0.04	0.04
Economic Subject	0.01	0.81	0.18	0.00	0.04

Explanatory variables include dummy variables for countries.
Number of observations 1153
*Marginal effects. **Equality of coefficients across subgroups.

8. Conclusions

Our focus has been on a fundamental question of the way in which people make distributional comparisons in the context of inequality and risk – whether they do so in a manner that is consistent with model that is conventionally constructed in theoretical and applied economics, and whether the same structure of comparisons is used both for inequality and for risk. Focusing on these issues raises the question of what determines attitudes towards risk and inequality: we might reasonably expect personal characteristics, like gender, income, and subject of university degree, to play a role.

The main finding is that – apart from the expected role of economics education – gender matters for attitudes towards risk and inequality, particularly for ranking judgments based on numerical comparisons. Based on the evidence in Sections 5 and 6 female students are less likely than male students to view an income transfer from a rich to a poor person as risk- or inequality-reducing. In particular:

1. The difference in male and female responses is particularly large for risk.

2. According to the descriptive analysis, more male than female students attribute an inequality or risk reducing impact to an equalizing income transfer. The difference is larger for risk than inequality. This pattern applies both for all responses jointly and for each question separately. Male respondents are also more consistent with the Principle of Transfers and, again, the difference is larger for risk than inequality.

3. The regression analysis shows that gender remains important once we control for other personal characteristics. The gender dummy is significant, and larger for risk than for inequality. The same applies for economic subject. These results apply regardless of whether we look at

the responses jointly, separately by question, or with regard to consistency with the Principle of Transfers.

4. Respondents are most likely to view an income transfer that occurs from upper to the lower end of the income distribution as inequality/risk reducing. They are less likely to attribute an equalizing effect when the transfer occurs 'within' the income distribution amongst regions ranked in close proximity to each other. The type of income transfer matters more for inequality than risk, and more for female than male students.

Appendix

1. Variable definitions

Respondents were asked about seven background variables and, in addition, we had information about the particular subsample in which they were included from the location of the experiment. Of the seven two were binary – "Are you male or female?", "Were you employed before University?" – and one was numerical – "What is your age?"; these are all self-explanatory.

Viewpoint questions were based on a seven-point scale as depicted at the end of each questionnaire in Appendix 10.

Individuals wrote their own unguided response to "What is your special subject of study?" unless they were in a class where the subject was homogenous. Given that the study of economics could be argued to play a role in shaping individuals' attitudes in these areas we chose two possible definitions of the concept:

"Core Economics" subject categories:
economics
econometrics
economic history
mathematical economics

"Broader Economics" subject categories:
Core economics plus
Accounting & finance
Business
Management science
MBA

"Non-Economic" subject categories:
Behavioral science;
Engineering;
Government/politics;
Geography;
History;
International relations;
Law;
Philosophy;
Operational research.

2. The Questionnaires

Following are the two questionnaires that were distributed to each of the response groups. As explained in the text the experiment was run so that each respondent had approximately an equal probability of receiving either of the two questionnaires.

INEQUALITY QUESTIONNAIRE

This questionnaire concerns people's attitude to inequality. We would be interested in your view, based on hypothetical situations. Because it is about attitudes there are no "right" answers. Some of the possible answers correspond to assumptions consciously made by economists: but these assumptions may not be good ones. Your responses will help to shed some light on this, and we would like to thank you for your participation. The questionnaire is anonymous.

Alfaland consists of five regions that are identical in every respect other than the incomes of their inhabitants. Everyone within a given region receives the same income, but personal incomes differ from region to region.

Two economic policy proposals A and B are being considered for implementation in Alfaland next year. It is known that - apart from their impact on personal incomes - the two policies would have the same effect on the population. The impact upon the regions' incomes would depend upon the particular state of the Alfaland economy at the time the policy (A or B) is to be introduced.

In each of questions (1) to (6) two alternative lists of incomes A and B (in Alfaland local currency) are given. Each of these pairs represents the outcomes of the A-policy and the B-policy on the five regions in each of six different situations in which Alfaland might find itself next year. In each case please state which policy you consider would result in **higher inequality** in Alfaland by circling A or B. If you consider that the two policies will result in **the same** inequality then circle both A and B.

1)	A = (2, 5, 9, 20, 30)	B = (2, 6, 8, 20, 30)
2)	A = (2, 5, 9, 20, 30)	B = (3, 5, 9, 20, 29)
3)	A = (2, 5, 9, 20, 30)	B = (2, 6, 9, 20, 29)
4)	A = (2, 5, 9, 20, 30)	B = (2, 10, 9, 15, 30)
5)	A = (10, 10, 10, 10, 30)	B = (10, 10, 10, 20, 20)
6)	A = (2, 5, 9, 20, 30)	B = (2, 6, 9, 19, 30)

\...Continued

A4a

In question 7 you are presented with a hypothetical income change and some possible views about the effects on inequality of that change. The views are labelled a),..., e). Please circle the letter alongside the view that corresponds most closely to your own. You can check more than one answer, provided that you consider they do not contradict each other. Feel free to add any comment that explains the reason for your choice.

7) Suppose we transfer income from the inhabitants of a relatively high-income region to those of a relatively low-income region, without changing the income of any other region. The transfer is not so large as to make the "rich" region "poor" and the "poor" region "rich", but it may alter their income rankings relative to the other, unaffected regions.

a) Inequality in Alfaland must fall if the ranking by income of all the regions remains the same. If there is any change in the income ranking of the regions then it is possible that inequality increases or remains the same.

b) If the transfer is from the richest to the poorest region, and after the transfer the richest region remains the richest and the poorest remains the poorest, inequality must fall. In other cases we cannot say a priori how inequality will change.

c) The transfer may change the relative position of other regions. So we cannot say a priori how inequality will change.

d) Inequality in Alfaland must fall, even if there is a change in the income ranking of the regions as a result of this transfer, and even if the transfer is not from the richest region to the poorest.

e) None of the above

In the light of your answer to question 7, would you want to change your answer to question 1-6? If so, please state your new response here.

1) 2) 3)
4) 5) 6)

Finally, we would be grateful for some information about yourself:

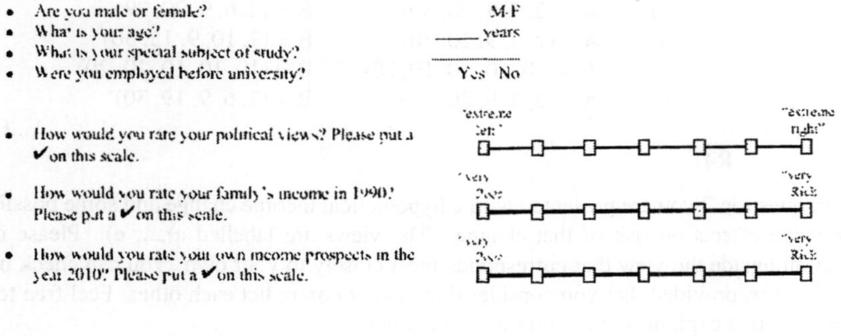
- Are you male or female? M-F
- What is your age? ______ years
- What is your special subject of study? ....
- Were you employed before university? Yes No
- How would you rate your political views? Please put a ✔ on this scale. "extreme left" … "extreme right"
- How would you rate your family's income in 1990? Please put a ✔ on this scale. "very Poor" … "very Rich"
- How would you rate your own income prospects in the year 2010? Please put a ✔ on this scale. "very Poor" … "very Rich"

Figure 9.A.1. Personal information form.

RISK QUESTIONNAIRE

This questionnaire concerns people's attitude to inequality. We would be interested in your view, based on hypothetical situations. Because it is about attitudes there are no "right" answers. Some of the possible answers correspond to assumptions consciously made by economists: but these assumptions may not be good ones. Your responses will help to shed some light on this, and we would like to thank you for your participation. The questionnaire is anonymous..

Alfaland consists of five regions that are identical in every respect other than the incomes of their inhabitants. Everyone within a given region receives the same income, but personal incomes differ from region to region. An immigrant to Alfaland would be assigned at random, with equal probability, to any one of these five regions. Such a person would therefore have a 20\% chance of being on any one of five income levels.

Two economic policy proposals A and B are being considered for implementation in Alfaland next year. It is known that - apart from their impact on personal incomes - the two policies would have the same effect on the population. The impact upon the regions' incomes would depend upon the particular state of the Alfaland economy at the time the policy (A or B) is to be introduced.

In each of questions (1) to (6) two alternative lists of incomes A and B (in Alfaland local currency) are given. Each of these pairs represents the outcomes of the A-policy and the B-policy on the five regions in each of six different situations in which Alfaland might find itself next year. In each case please state which policy you consider would result in **higher risk** for a person immigrating to Alfaland by circling A or B. If you consider that the two policies will result in the **same risk** to a potential immigrant then circle both A and B.

1)	A = (2, 5, 9, 20, 30)	B = (2, 6, 8, 20, 30)
2)	A = (2, 5, 9, 20, 30)	B = (3, 5, 9, 20, 29)
3)	A = (2, 5, 9, 20, 30)	B = (2, 6, 9, 20, 29)
4)	A = (2, 5, 9, 20, 30)	B = (2, 10, 9, 15, 30)
5)	A = (10, 10, 10, 10, 30)	B = (10, 10, 10, 20, 20)
6)	A = (2, 5, 9, 20, 30)	B = (2, 6, 9, 19, 30)

\...Continued

R4

In question 7 you are presented with a hypothetical income change and some possible views about the effects on risk of that change. The views are labelled a),..., e). Please circle the letter alongside the view that corresponds most closely to your own. You can check more than one answer, provided that you consider they do not contradict each other. Feel free to add any comment that explains the reason for your choice.

7) Suppose we transfer income from the inhabitants of a relatively high-income region to those of a relatively low-income region, without changing the income of any other region. The transfer is not so large as to make the "rich" region "poor" and the "poor" region "rich", but it may alter their income rankings relative to the other, unaffected regions.

a) Risk for a potential immigrant to Alfaland must fall if the ranking by income of all the regions remains the same. If there is any change in the income ranking of the regions then it is possible that risk increases or remains the same.

b) If the transfer is from the richest to the poorest region, and after the transfer the richest region remains the richest and the poorest remains the poorest, risk must fall. In other cases we cannot say a priori how risk will change.

c) The transfer may change the relative position of other regions. So we cannot say a priori how risk will change.

d) Risk for a potential immigrant to Alfaland must fall, even if there is a change in the income ranking of the regions as a result of this transfer, and even if the transfer is not from the richest region to the poorest.

e) None of the above

In the light of your answer to question 7, would you want to change your answer to question 1-6? If so, please state your new response here.

1) 2) 3)
4) 5) 6)

Finally, we would be grateful for some information about yourself:

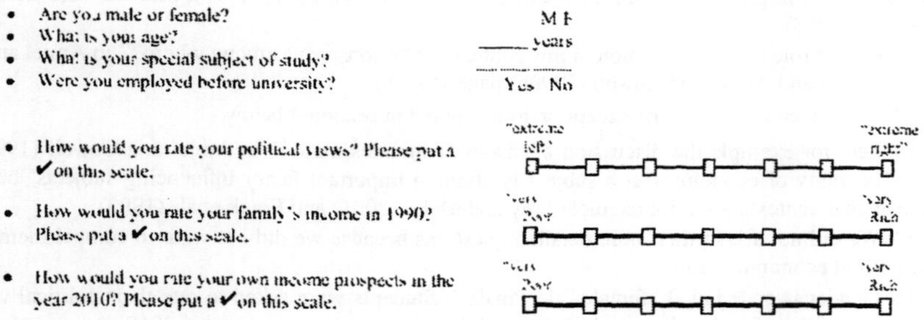

- Are you male or female? M F
- What is your age? ______ years
- What is your special subject of study? ______
- Were you employed before university? Yes No
- How would you rate your political views? Please put a ✔ on this scale. "extreme left" … "extreme right"
- How would you rate your family's income in 1990? Please put a ✔ on this scale. "very Poor" … "very Rich"
- How would you rate your own income prospects in the year 2010? Please put a ✔ on this scale. "very Poor" … "very Rich"

Figure 9.A.2. Personal information form.

Notes

1. On the first see Cowell and Gardiner (2000) or Cowell and Shokkaert (2001) for an overview. On the second see, for example, the experimental approach of Kroll and Davidovitz (1999). See also Barsky et al. (1997) for estimates of risk preferences from survey responses Amiel et al. (1999) for estimates of inequality preferences from an inequality questionnaire responses and Andersson and Lyttkens (1999), Carlsson et al. (2000) for preferences over distribution in non-income contexts.

2. See, for example Hirshleifer (1970), chapter 10.

3. See Harsanyi (1953, 1955) and also Rawls (1971).

4. As an example, take the list of ten different definitions of risk in Yates (1992) page 1. Cf the nine different concepts of inequality listed in Rein and Miller (1974).

5. Cf the discussion by Laffont (1989) of alternative axiomatisations of preferences.

6. Some of the more recondite points in the two subject areas can also be related: for example the issue of violations of the independence axiom in the analysis of risk – manifested in the phenomenon of "regrets" in choice under uncertainty – and the issue of externalities in the assessment of income distributions.

7. See Amiel et al. (2001) for a detailed examination of the experimental evidence on support for either of these axioms and for alternative approaches to the impact of across-the-board income increases on inequality and on risk.

8. The principle is widely discussed in both contexts: see e.g. Pollak (1973), Shorrocks (1988).

9. The usual convention is to define the Principle of Transfers in the other direction – a richer-to-poorer-transfer transfer inequality – but the definition here makes it easier to maintain the comparison with the analysis of risk.

10. On distributional rankings and second and higher-order concepts of dominance see for example Atkinson and Bourguignon (1982), Fishburn and Willig (1984), Kolm (1969), Marshall and Olkin (1979), Shorrocks (1983).

11. On the role of expert opinion in this context see "a consensus among whom?" in Amiel and Cowell (1992) page 4 and Amiel and Cowell (1999b) page 19.

12. In practice there was one exception to this noted in section 4 below.

13. See, for example the discussion of "Does economics matter" in Amiel and Cowell (1999b) page 123. The study of economics as a subject is often an important factor influencing subjects' behavior in experimental contexts – see for example Frey and Meier (2001) and Frank et al. (1993).

14. We did not ask further more detailed questions because we did not want to compel them to reveal their current economic status,

15. Gender is coded as 0: female," 1: "male." Students were asked to rate their political view, their assessment of their family's income in 1990, and their own income prospects in 2010 on a scale from one to seven. For political view "1" means "extreme left" and "7" means "extreme right"; for income "1" is "very poor" and "7" is "very rich." Employment refers to any work history before university. Income Change 2010 – defined as the difference between Income 2010 and Income 1990 – is used rather than Income 2010 in the regressions in order to avoid problems of multicollinearity. Economic subject comprises economics, econometrics, economic history, mathematical economics, and development economics. The main results of the paper remain unaffected if we use a wider definition, including in addition MBAs and the subjects accounting and finance, management science, and business studies.

16. Throughout the analysis we lump the responses "A and B have same level of inequality/risk" and "B has higher inequality/risk than A" into one category. Distinguishing between these responses does not affect the qualitative results of the analysis. Percentages are of the total (not of just those who responded). There was a small number of missing answers on the numerical questions (from 19 to 27) – and 84 missing on the verbal question.

17. The "marginal effect" in these tables and elsewhere is interpreted as follows. Let P denote the relevant probability on the left-hand side of (9.4). Then, given the probit model, it is clear that for the ith explanatory variable, the marginal impact of an increase in y_i on the probability is proportional to the coefficient b_i thus:

$$\frac{dP}{dy_i} = b_i\, \varphi \left(\sum_j b_j y_j \right)$$

where $\varphi(\cdot)$ is the normal density function.

18. It is significant at the 10% level in Table 9.7. This result is robust under changes in the definition of "economic subject" - see the Appendix.

19. The country dummies for Germany and Sweden were positive and significant if the questions were taken separately; but no country dummy is significant for the case where all questions are taken jointly.

20. Question 2 was the omitted category. Again the country dummies for Germany and Sweden were positive and significant in the case of inequality and risk. Argentina was also significant in the case of risk.

21. The country dummy for Israel is significant in Table 9.14 but otherwise no country dummy is significant at the 5% level in either table for either inequality or risk.

References

Amiel, Y. and F. A. Cowell (1992). "Measurement of income inequality: Experimental test by questionnaire," *Journal of Public Economics* 47, 3-26.

Amiel, Y. and F. A. Cowell (1998). "Distributional orderings and the transfer principle: a re-examination," *Research on Economic Inequality* 8,195-215.

Amiel, Y. and F. A. Cowell (1999a). "Income transformations and income inequality." In D. Slottje (Ed.), *Advances in Econometrics, Income Distribution and Scientific Methodology*, pp. 209-232. Heidelberg: Physica Verlag.

Amiel, Y. and F. A. Cowell (1999b). *Thinking about Inequality*. Cambridge: Cambridge University Press.

Amiel, Y., F. A. Cowell, and A. Polovin (2001). "Risk perceptions, income transformations and inequality," *European Economic Review* 45, 964-976.

Amiel, Y., J. Creedy, and D. Hurn (1999). "Attitudes towards inequality," *The Scandinavian Journal of Economics* 101, 83-96.

Andersson, F. and C. H. Lyttkens (1999). "Preferences for equity in health beyond the veil of ignorance," *Health Economics* 8, 369-378.

Atkinson, A. B. (1970). "On the measurement of inequality," *Journal of Economic Theory* 2, 244-263.

Atkinson, A. B. and F. Bourguignon (1982). "The comparison of multidimensional distributions of economic status," *Review of Economic Studies* 49, 183-201.

Barsky, R. B., F. T. Juster, M. S. Kimball, and M. D. Shapiro (1997). "Preference parameters and behavioral heterogeneity: An experimental approach in the health and retirement survey," *Quarterly Journal of Economics* 112, 537-579.

Carlsson, F., D. Daruvala, and O. Johansson-Stenman (2000). "Are people inequality averse or just risk averse?," Working Paper, Department of Economics, Göteborg University, Box 640, SE-40530 Göteborg, Sweden.

Cowell, F. A. and K. A. Gardiner (2000). "Welfare weights," OFT Economic Research Paper 202, Office of Fair Training, Salisbury Square, London.

Cowell, F. A. and E. Schokkaert (2001). "Risk perceptions and distributional judgments," *European Economic Review* 42, 941-952.

Dalton, H. (1920). "Measurement of the inequality of incomes," *Economic Journal* 30 (9), 348-361.

Fischhoff, B. (1985). "Managing risk perceptions," *Issues in Science and Technology* 2, 83-96.

Fishburn, P. C. and R. D. Willig (1984). "Transfer principles in income redistribution," *Journal of Public Economics* 25, 323-328.

Frank, R. H., T. D. Gilovich, and D. T. Regan (1993). "Does studying economics inhibit cooperation?," *Journal of Economic Perspectives* 7 (2), 159-171.

Frey, B. S. and S. Meier (2001). "Political economists are neither selfish nor indoctrinated. Working paper, Institute for Empirical Economic Research, University of Zürich, Blmlisalpstrasse 10, 8006 Zürich.

Hadar, J. andW. R. Russell (1969). "Rules for ordering uncertain prospects," *American Economic Review* 79, 25-34.

Harsanyi, J. C. (1953). "Cardinal utility in welfare economics and in the theory of risk-taking," *Journal of Political Economy* 61, 434-435.

Harsanyi, J. C. (1955). "Cardinal welfare, individualistic ethics and interpersonal comparisons of utility," *Journal of Political Economy* 63, 309- 321.

Hirshleifer, J. (1970). *Investment, Interest and Capital*. Englewood Cliffs: Prentice Hall.

Kolm, S.-C. (1969). "The optimal production of social justice," In J. Margolis and H. Guitton (Eds.), *Public Economics*, pp. 145-200. London: Macmillan.

Kroll, Y. and L. Davidovitz (1999). "Choices in egalitarian distribution: Inequality aversion versus risk aversion," Distributional Analysis Research Programme Discussion Paper 43, STICERD, LSE, Houghton Street, London WC2A 2AE.

Laffont, J.-J. (1989). *The Economics of Uncertainty and Information*. Cambridge, Mass: MIT Press.

Marshall, A. W. and I. Olkin (1979). *Inequalities: Theory and Majorization*. New York: Academic Press.

Nermuth, M. (1993). "Different economic theories with the same formal structures: risk, income inequality, information structures, etc," In W. E. Diewert, K. Spremann, and F. Stehling (Eds.), *Mathematical Modelling in Economics - Essays in Honour of Wolfgang Eichhorn*, pp. 271-277. Heidelberg: Springer-Verlag.

Pass, C., B. Lowes, and L. Davies (1993). *A Dictionary of Economics*. London: Collins.

Pollak, R. (1973). "The risk independence axiom," *Econometrica* 41, 35-39.

Rawls, J. (1971). *A Theory of Justice*. Cambridge, Massachusetts: Harvard University Pres.

Rein, M. and S. M. Miller (1974, July/August). "Standards of income redistribution," *Challenge* , 20-26.

Rothschild, M. and J. E. Stiglitz (1970). "Increasing risk: I. A definition," *Journal of Economic Theory* 2, 225-243.

Rothschild, M. and J. E. Stiglitz (1971). "Increasing risk: II. Its economic consequences," *Journal of Economic Theory* 3, 66-84.

Rothschild, M. and J. E. Stiglitz (1973). "Some further results on the measurement of inequality," *Journal of Economic Theory* 6, 188-203.

Shorrocks, A. F. (1983). "Ranking income distributions," *Economica* 50, 3-17.

Shorrocks, A. F. (1988). "Aggregation issues in inequality measurement," In W. Eichhorn (Ed.), *Measurement in Economics*. Physica Verlag Heidelberg.

Theil, H. (1967). *Economics and Information Theory*. Amsterdam: North Holland.

Yates, J. F. (1992). *Risk-Taking Behavior*. John Wiley Ltd.

Chapter 10

PITFALLS IN EXPERIMENTAL ECONOMICS

Peter Bohm
Stockholm University
pb@ne.su.se

1. Introduction

Here, I would like to raise a couple of questions with respect to methods commonly used in Experimental Economics.

First, however, let me indicate briefly what my background is in terms of the experimental work I have been doing: it concerns primarily evaluations of policies and policy proposals, auctions, preference reversals, mechanisms for revelation of demand for public goods and recently, emissions trading. I have done several field tests, often using non-student subjects. So, if experimental economics is defined as standard lab experimental economics as often seems to be the case (see, e.g., Davis and Holt, 1993), I may not be much of an experimental economist - and when I am through with what I want to say here you may agree.

Charlie Plott noted in a paper from 1987 (Dimensions of Parallelism) that in the Samuelson-Nordhaus textbook it is stated that experiments in economics are impossible. He speculated that this statement probably was due to a belief that such experiments would have to be field studies. Plott goes on to say that "Economists should keep an open mind about experimental methodology and judge work by the statements of results rather than by methodological principles."

I could not agree more. But it seems that now a large group of experimentalists have established a rule book of methodological principles that seem to say that

- subject values should be induced, otherwise you lose control
- tests should deal with the bare bones of economic principles and not with particular contexts, since the latter might distort the behavior one wishes to observe

- students are acceptable subjects regardless of the test objective
- subjects should be repeatedly exposed to the same task in a given environment,

all of which obviously relate only to laboratory experimental economics.

These points relate more or less directly to what I'd like to discuss here, viz.

- incentive levels
- the choice of experimental subjects
- the attempt to use context-free experimental environments
- the use of stationary repetitions

2. Monetary Incentive Levels

All economist-experimentalists would agree that a 'low' level of monetary incentives jeopardizes the validity of a test. If we want to test theory, taking for granted that theory has been developed to cover non-trivial decisions, experimental payoffs must be large enough to clearly exceed likely decision costs. Still, I don't think this is always the case in actual practice. And this is no small problem, since, to attain payoff dominance, there are some further aspects that need to be taken into account:

First, the Hawthorne effect: subjects know they are observed, and this may affect their behavior, especially if such deviations do not cost them much. Hence, the reason for letting the relevant incentives talk loud and clear is reinforced.

Second, if we want to speak also to the large group of economists, policy makers, etc., who hesitate to take on board the evidence provided by experimental economics, it is particularly important that the stakes are convincingly high.

Third, people, who in real-world situations would prefer to be inactive and walk away from a certain market, cannot walk away from experiments that study similar situations and that they have agreed to participate in. As a consequence, they may end up being active in the experimental market. Two possible reasons for this behavior: They would be bored by doing nothing; hence, calculating something and reporting it may be more fun. Or they feel morally committed to participate actively, literally speaking - after all, they have been paid a show-up fee for participating and doing something. I have seen experiments, some concerning price bubbles, where I have wondered whether such counter-productive incentives may have distorted the observations. Making the monetary incentives strong enough might help.

We may not know exactly what minimum payoff levels are required for dominance with respect to a decision problem of given complexity, but I believe that most of us certainly can agree on levels that are clearly sufficient. I think experimental economists should be careful not to accept any compromises on this point. It is better with fewer experiments with clear payoff dominance than the opposite.

One reason for this concern is that astonishing results obtained from published studies using insignificant incentive payments might initiate replications, attempts to explain the findings by theoretical revisions and in general give rise to time- and resource-consuming research agendas with a number of new experiments that eventually lead to the insight that the phenomenon initially observed was due to lack of payoff dominance.

Preference reversal is an example of an experimental topic that might have received much less attention, if the incentive payments initially used had been more significant. Most preference-reversal experiments concern choice between, and reservation prices for, a certain kind of simple lotteries aimed at representing general risky options. An oft-quoted example is this pair of lotteries with two outcomes:

- 35/36 chance winning \$4 and 1/36 of losing \$1, called a Pbet
- 11/36 chance winning \$16 and 25/36 chance to lose \$1.50, a \$bet

Typical preference reversal behavior has been that subjects who choose the Pbet put a higher reservation price on the \$bet, so-called predicted preference reversal. Initially, high rates of preference reversal were observed for such pairs. But as shown, e.g., by Glenn Harrison (1992), the incentives for subjects to spend time and energy on calculating and reporting this rather than that reservation price were very small. Later tests with higher incentive levels (e.g. Bohm and Lind, 1993) revealed preference reversal rates much lower than the initial eye-catching ones.

To avoid the risks that I have mentioned here, one would hope that experimental results with trivial incentives would not be published. If this was transformed into a credible threat, it could make experimentalists consistently use more significant incentives. To that end, I think it might be valuable, if journals that publish experimental papers state among their rules for submission that authors should report the size of marginal payoffs and illustrate the complexity of the tasks their subjects are facing.

3. Subjects

A common critique from outsiders has concerned the use of students as subjects. The experimentalists' reply has essentially been that students are also people. I agree and, of course, access to this pool is easy and has low costs.

But can students or a particular type of students - or any other particular subject pool, for that matter - be fruitfully used for any kind of experimental topic?

Marwell and Ames gave experimentalists a warning to use economics students in tests of free-rider behavior. As you probably have seen, the telling title of their paper was "Economists Free Ride, Does Anyone Else?" (1981).

In Conlisk's (1989) study of possible explanations for the Allais paradox in lottery choice, students were used as experimental subjects. In an epilogue, he reported that a couple of the subjects in the experiments objected to the test they had been exposed to since they were opposed in principle to participating in lotteries. If there were many such subjects and their behavior differed from that of others, this may have significantly distorted the outcome of the experiments. After all, the economic theories of decision making that we test are about the behavior of decision-makers, not non-decision-makers.

So, perhaps, it matters what subjects we use. Two preference-reversal studies may be referred to for an illustration of how that can be tested:

Preference reversal experiments have often used students who volunteer for an 'experiment in decision making'. However, in one such experiment(Bohm and Lind, 1993), where we replaced the type of lotteries shown earlier by real-world multi-outcome state-lotteries, we used a design to enable us to check whether lottery consumers and non-lottery consumers behaved differently. The student subjects were allowed, in a first step, to choose one of the following three options:

- cash,
- Pbet-like state lottery tickets, and
- $bet-like state lottery tickets,

where the market prices for the lottery tickets equaled the cash amount. Subjects who chose a lottery instead of the cash amount, just as real-world lottery consumers do, were considered to be such consumers, the others not. After subjects had made their choice (for keeps), they were asked to choose between the remaining two options. Thus, we got each subject's ranking of the three options. After that, we went on to elicit ticket bids and asks for market transactions. In this way, preference-reversal rates for lottery and non-lottery consumers could be compared. Here the observed rates turned out to differ only to a very small extent.

Another preference-reversal experiment concerned choices between claims redeemed at different times in the future and the ranking of reservation prices for such claims; a typical pair of claims from the preceding experimental literature looked like this:

A: $1600 in 1.5 years time

B: $2500 in 5 years time

Earlier results (Tversky, Slovic and Kahneman, 1990) showed that more than 50 percent of subjects choosing claim A (redeemed sooner) reported a higher reservation price for claim B (with the higher amount of money), so-called predicted preference reversal. In these tests, questions were hypothetical - no wonder, given the money amounts involved! - and undergraduate students were used as subjects.

Bohm (1994) studied both hypothetical and non-hypothetical choices of this type - now with lower, but still non-trivial, amounts of money - using subjects who, in contrast to the typical undergraduate student, could have some experience with these pretty exotic options: one group of bank employees trained in giving loans to business and another with Ph.D. students in Finance. But, interestingly, subjects in the hypothetical case turned out to be at least as inclined to be choice/reservation-price inconsistent as the undergraduate students in the preceding study had been! (In passing, it may be noted that the non-hypothetical case revealed a preference-reversal rate of only 15 percent.)

The results of these two preference-reversal studies would suggest that we need not have worry about using consumers/experts or non-consumers/non-experts in these particular cases. There are studies by others who have made similar observations. Does that mean that we can stop worrying about whether or not decisions are tested on those who are familiar with making such decisions, for which the tested economic theories have been developed? I don't think so. Next time or for the next issue, we might get different responses from decision-makers and non-decision-makers, be they students or non-students. I think we should provide more often for that possibility. And there is a particular additional reason for doing so. Using more often a clearly relevant subject pool increases the probability that the results are taken in also by those who otherwise hesitate to do so because they tend not to believe in results from experimental studies.

4. Testing Theory in Context or Non-Context Environments

It is commonly argued that a specific context should not be used in experiments unless we know that the results can be generalized. Or as this recommendation was phrased somewhere, it is "better not to contaminate subjects with a specific field context". The idea is obviously that there are context-free alternatives that can be used.

I'd like to address this issue with respect to decision making concerning public goods. Knut Wicksell (1896, of Lund University!) and Paul Samuelson (1954) established a theory based on observations of real-world commodities that have a common element of non-rivalry in consumption. Therefore, in line with good theorizing, it was practical for them to isolate this element and analyze it with respect to an unspecified commodity. This led to the identification of the free-riding incentive. The theory said nothing about whether free-riding would be a dominant incentive for any particular decision procedure/mechanism employed with respect to a specific real-world good in a specific environment or if there could be procedures and circumstances that tended to neutralize this incentive. Indeed, the challenging question posed by this theoretical finding was whether any particular demand-revealing mechanism/procedure could be found, so that sufficiently close approximations to the consumers' true willingness to pay (WTP) could be elicited. If so, decision making in the real world could be based on this information instead of relying on decisions by imperfect representatives or inappropriate one-man-one-vote referenda.

A large number of experimental analyses during the last 20 years or so has been devoted to test the theoretical free-riding prediction in the context of a voluntary public exchange (VPE), where subjects are given tokens of a certain value that can either be kept or paid to the exchange, in return for an amount less than this value but then accruing to all participants. This elegant and inventive instrument was designed, and largely believed, I think, to test the context-free theory. (I leave aside here the claim implicit in some of this work that VPE experiments stand for the only truly scientific contributions to the experimental public-good literature, see e.g. Ledyard (1995).)

The findings of the VPE experiments are summarized in a paper by Elinor Ostrom (2000). Among them, we find that

- subjects contribute some 40-60% of their endowments in one-shot games or the first round of finitely repeated games,
- after a first round, contributions tend to drop but averages remain well above the theoretical prediction of zero,
- with a sufficient number of identical rounds, often more than 70% of the subjects contribute nothing in the last round.

These results are thought-provoking. But more exactly for what?

As a background to what I want to respond, I like to quote Graham Loomes' (1999) interpretation of Binmore (1999) and Loewenstein (1999):

"the dangers of constructing experimental environments ... [that are] stripped of context are that participants search desperately for cues about the kind of behavior that might seem sensible, or that they think the experimenters are looking for, with the result that they fail to process the tasks as they would do in the richer social environment we may be seeking to model." (p. F3)

I agree. Loewenstein goes one step further and argues quite convincingly, I think, that a "context-free experiment is an elusive goal". Specifically, the VPE approach hardly matches the context-free elementary public good used in the theory and therefore, strictly speaking, cannot be used to test it. It creates a particular context of its own, a kind of 'money-making game'. By contrast, a real public good is rarely, if ever, about money amounts for participants to pocket. And there are other differences that may play a role (see below). Thus, we cannot say for sure whether the choice between these two kinds of contexts really matters for ascertaining the responses to the pure free-rider incentives - the choice between an artificial, truly strange money-making game (where someone for some reason spends money to see you perform) vs. a real public good for which there may be a demand. Loewenstein seems to have made up his mind on this point when he says: "The goal of external validity is served by creating a context that is similar to the one in which economic agents will actually operate, not by engaging in futile attempts to eliminate context."

If we ask consumer subjects, what their non-hypothetical WTP is for a non-trivial real-world public good, they are likely to understand pretty fast what the issue is and why there is a reason for eliciting their WTP. By contrast, in the voluntary public exchange context, subjects are likely to wonder, for what purpose they are being exposed to this game, in line with what Binmore and Loewenstein suggest. Understanding or not understanding why you are confronted by a certain task may give rise to quite different thought processes.

The two different contexts, and the different understandings of why they are there, may make subjects invoke quite different parts of their personal experience and the social norms they may adhere to. This may affect subjects in different ways and even in opposite directions in the two cases, reinforcing or counteracting the effect of the free-rider incentive. (The Ostrom paper may be consulted on these points.) Thus, it is possible that the real public-good context invokes some instincts of cooperation, while the context of the money-making game raises primarily instincts of competition and rivalry - or perhaps, the other way round. Either way, the public exchange would poorly represent real-world public goods.

If I'm right in questioning the value of the insights we get from VPE experiments, the issue becomes what other types of public-good experiments would be more valuable to undertake. Identifying a practicable demand-revealing method remains a largely unsolved problem. A topic that I personally have found particularly interesting in that respect is to compare a mechanism that provide (hopefully, small) incentives to overstate but not to understate demand with a mechanism that have the opposite incentive structure, using representative samples of the consumer population for different real public goods. If the aggregate misrepresentation of a pair of such mechanisms was found to be robustly small, we would have an indication that any one of them could be used for close approximations of actual aggregate WTP; or we might still use the pair of the two mechanisms to avoid concealing the actual extent of misrepresentation in an individual application. For examples of this approach,

I refer to the tests reported in Bohm (1972 and 1984). At least in these two applications involving particularly context-rich cases, the extent of free-riding was small.

If robust findings are what we are after, we could contemplate testing potentially demand revealing mechanisms on a number of different, small but non-trivial, local public goods, as an alternative to tests replicating representative, maximally context-meager environments, whatever that would be. Examples of such local public goods feasible for simple experimentation may be access to service arrangements offered by the experimenter in student dormitories or student unions, department libraries etc., where students would be the relevant subjects. Or, for planting fish in a lake surrounded by private house owners. Or, for neighbors trying to reach a decision whether to build of commonly owned tennis court (access to which is a public good), a suggestion once made by Robert Solow.

Using approaches like this we would also contribute to meeting Vernon Smith's (1982) parallelism precept, perhaps already at an early stage of the research agenda, instead of constantly postponing that step which seems to be more or less common practice now.

5. Stationary Repetitions

Exactly what kind of useful information do we get from stationary repetitions, i.e. from having tests repeated identically one right after the other in a number of rounds? It seems pretty safe to say that this is a useful approach when analyzing the properties of real-world markets with traders engaged in continuing transactions. But what about the mechanical, as it often seems, use of this approach in other applications, e.g., in connection with tests of the voluntary public exchange (see the summary from Ostrom above). It is again primarily that case I'll have in mind here.

Stationary repetitions certainly add to the exotism of the voluntary public exchange context. If the activity mimicked by the exchange would occur at most very rarely in the real world, I'd not think of it as something that occurs 20, 40 to 60 times, especially not one right after the other. If, in a possible future, any real-world money voting on public goods would take place as seldom as at most once per year, it would seem that one-shot tests with different contexts, preceded by careful information and perhaps a trial round, would better represent the real issues here.

Stationary repetitions of experiments make subjects more familiar and experienced with the exercise they are asked to perform. In addition, they provide subjects with generic information about the properties of possible interactions among participants in money voting on real public goods. But this is done only for the very special case where these exercises are repeated identically. For decision making concerning public goods, my question is the following. Why would the information provided by stationary repetitions be more relevant than that obtained from subjects who have been told what voters/decision-makers are sure to have heard when a non-trivial public good issue has been set up for collective decision making? This would most likely include information, in particular, about any existing misrepresentation incentives.

The practice of using stationary repetitions introduces an arbitrariness of its own. We know from experience that the results after one repetition typically differs from those after five, etc. What is the relevant, if any, number of replications? I think it is necessary for the experimenter who wants to use stationary repetitions for a particular study to give a clear and hopefully convincing explanation exactly what insight this method is meant to provide. And more needs to be known about what goes on in the subjects' heads when they are exposed to stationary repetitions as compared to, e.g., series of periods under non-stationary conditions.

6. Concluding Remarks

I have argued here that certain steps need to be taken in Experimental Economics (a) to ensure that experiments are applicable to the real-world environment or otherwise relevant for a study of that environment - in particular, for those non-trivial real-world issues which theory is focused on - and hence, (b) to make experimental results more interesting also for those who are more hesitant believers in experimental methods.

At a minimum, there is a need for careful explanations of

- why the incentive levels used are deemed to be sufficient for the task to be analyzed;
- why, whenever that is the case, it is not necessary to use subjects who are decision makers of the type in focus;
- why exotic contexts such as that of the voluntary exchange mechanism, which result from futile attempts to find a context-free experimental environment, are relevant to study, and
- why - for a given type of issue - stationary repetitions are used.

References

Binmore, K., (1999). "Why Experiment in Economics," *Economic Journal* 109, February, F16-F24.

Bohm, P., (1972). "Estimating Demand for Public Goods: An Experiment," *European Economic Review* 3, 111-30.

Bohm, P., (1984). "Revealing Demand for An Actual Public Good," *Journal of Public Economics* 24, 135-51.

Bohm, P., (1994). "Time Preference and Preference Reversal among Experienced Subjects: The Effect of Real Payments," *Economic Journal* 104, November, 1370-78.

Bohm, P., and H. Lind, (1993). "Preference Reversal, Lottery-Interested Subjects and Real-World Lotteries," *Journal of Economic Behavior and Organization* 22, December, 327-48.

Conlisk, J., (1989). "Three Variants of the Allais Example," *American Economic Review* 79, 3, June, 392-407.

Davis, D., and C. Holt (1993). *Experimental Economics.* Princeton, N. J., Princeton University Press.

Harrison, G., (1992). "Theory and Misbehavior in First-Price Auctions: Reply," *American Economic Review* 82,5, June.

Ledyard, J., (1995). "Public Goods: A Survey of Experimental Research," in: The Handbook of Experimental Economics, (eds. J. Kagel and A. Roth), Princeton University Press, Princeton, N. J., 111-94.

Loewenstein, G., (1999). "Experimental Economics from the Vantage-Point of Behavioural Economics," *Economic Journal* 109, February, F25-F34.

Loomes, G., (1999). "Experimental Economics: Introduction," *Economic Journal* 109, February, F1-F4.

Marwell, G. and R. Ames, (1981). "Economists Free Ride, Does Anyone Else?," *Journal of Public Economics* 15, 295-310.

Ostrom, E., (2000). "Collective Action and the Evolution of Social Norms," *Journal of Economic Perspectives* 14, 3, Summer, 137-58.

Plott, C., (1987). "Dimensions of Parallelism: Some Policy Applications of Experimental Methods," in: Laboratory Experimentation in Economics (ed. A. Roth), Cambridge University Press, 193-219.

Samuelson, P. (1954). "The Pure Theory of Public Expenditure," *Review of Economics and Statistics*, 36, 387-389.

Smith, V., (1982). "Microeconomic Systems as an Experimental Science," *American Economic Review* 72, 5, December, 923-55.

Tversky, A. , P. Slovic and D. Kahneman, (1990). "The Causes of Preference Reversal," *American Economic Review* 80, 1, March, 204-17.

Wicksell, K., (1896). "Finanzteoretische Untersuchungen," Jena. English translation: Classics, in the Theory of Public Finance (eds. R. Musgrave and A. Peacock), International Economic Association, Macmillan, London, 1958.

Chapter 11

THE EFFECT OF TRADING PERIOD DURATION ON MARKET PERFORMANCE IN EXPERIMENTAL FINANCIAL MARKETS*

Darren Duxbury
International Institute for Banking and Financial Services
Leeds University.
dd@lubs.leeds.ac.uk

1. Introduction

The experimental asset market literature provides strong evidence concerning the robust convergence of transaction prices to the competitive equilibrium price and the high percentage of gains from trade exhausted in double auction (DA) markets. However, the designs of previous experimental asset market studies have incorporated trading period durations that are constant and known to the trading participants. Friedman (1984, p. 71) suggests that the predetermined, known time at which trade will cease is one of a number of institutional features of experimental DA markets that enhance the informational and competitive efficiency of observed outcomes. The intention here is to extend previous work (Duxbury, 1997) by conducting a series of experiments designed to determine the importance of trading period duration on observed market performance. To this end, markets are conducted with either constant and known (CK), variable and known (VK) or variable and unknown (VU) trading period durations. The VK treatment represents a novel feature of the experimental design, allowing the analysis to differentiate between the effects of variable

*The author acknowledges the helpful contributions of Professor Kevin Keasey, the editors and an anonymous referee, along with conference participants at the European Economic Science Association, October 2000 and the 20th Arne Ryde Symposium, November 2000. The programming support of Norman Spivey is gratefully acknowledged and thanks are also due to John Hey and Graham Loomes for permitting the use of EXEC's computer laboratory. This research has benefited from the financial support of The Nuffield Foundation's Social Science Small Grants Scheme (SOC/100-1353). All errors are the author's alone.

trading period duration and uncertain trading period duration. The few theoretical models of bid, ask and transaction price behavior in experimental DA markets developed to date rely on assumptions concerning the time remaining until the end of trade (see for example Friedman, 1991). Indication of the importance of these assumptions for the convergence behavior advocated by these theoretical models is necessary for future theoretical development. The issue is also of practical importance in the design of future auctions and institutional rules.

The structure of the paper is as follows. The subsequent section briefly reviews relevant theoretical literature and introduces the research hypotheses to be investigated. Section 3 discusses both general experimental design issues and the specific market designs adopted. Section 4 begins with a commentary on a number of data considerations and then reports the results of the study. Section 5 offers a summary of the results and draws conclusions from the research.

2. Relevant Literature and Research Hypotheses

The volume of experimental asset market literature is too large to review here, however, both Duxbury (1995) and Sunder (1995) contain extensive reviews. Sunder's (1995, p. 493) review concludes that the experimental asset market literature indicates both that markets are able to aggregate and disseminate information and that convergence to competitive equilibria is an observable and reproducible phenomena. In order to begin to understand why the DA institution is so efficient at pricing assets and exhausting gains from exchange, a dynamic theory of individual trading behavior is required. To date, however, only a few papers attempt to theoretically model trading behavior in DA markets (see for example, Friedman, 1984 and1991; Wilson, 1987; Easley and Ledyard, 1993).

Friedman (1991) proposes a model of the price formation process in DA markets that utilizes individuals' reservation prices to develop optimal trading strategies. The 'model generates specific predictions as to the time and nature of the next event in the Double Auction.' (p. 62). In the model trade is permissible over a finite time interval $[0, T]$ and it is assumed that new bid and ask prices are generated randomly and at random times within this interval. It is further assumed that agents have sufficient knowledge of the distribution of times to compute the expected number of new prices available to them before the end of the trading period. To achieve this traders require information regarding the time at which trade ceases in the period, thus there is implied knowledge of the trading period duration. It seems that this is a fundamental assumption if the model is to predict convergence of prices and allocations to almost Pareto optimal outcomes (see Proposition 3, op cit. p. 58). Easley and

Ledyard (1993) attempt a first pass at a positive theory of price formation in which individuals' reservation prices are assumed to be a function of time and are adjusted as individuals learn not to buy at too high a price (or sell for at low a price) and not to wait too long to trade such that they miss out on profitable opportunities.

Both Friedman (1991) and Easley and Ledyard (1993) offer insight into the modeling of trading behavior in DA markets. Considerably more research in this vein is required to provide a more thorough understanding of the dynamic price formation process in DA markets. Friedman (1984) concludes that the knowledge of the preset time at which trade will end is an important institutional feature that enhances the informational and competitive efficiency of experimental outcomes. Drawing on this conclusion Duxbury (1997) offers a preliminary investigation of the impact of trading period duration on market performance. The study reports that markets with unknown period duration exhibit a significantly higher volume of trade 'early' in a trading period than is observed otherwise and this causes a significant reduction in the level of informational efficiency obtained. The pilot study was limited in the scale of the investigation and so the current study provides a full-scale investigation of the impact of trading period duration on observed market performance.

In an attempt to overcome the potential bias of a known, artificial trading period deadline and evaluate the importance it plays in prior experimental results, trading period duration is incorporated in the current experimental design as a treatment variable. Markets are conducted with variable and known (VK) durations and variable and unknown (VU) durations. In the former markets individuals still know when the trading period will end, whilst in the latter markets individuals' knowledge of exactly when a trading period will end is removed. Markets with constant and known (CK) period duration form a control against which the trading behavior witnessed in VK and VU markets can be compared. Comparison of market behavior observed in VK and VU markets permits the impact of knowledge of period duration to be isolated and investigated. The hypotheses to be investigated are now introduced.

Early trading volume: The unknown period duration in VU markets may well result in a reduction in the length of time taken over bartering and thus an increase in the volume of trade early in the period as traders attempt to realize potential gains from trade before the trading period closes. A priori, it is not clear in which direction VK period duration will impact on the volume of trade. Therefore, for reasons of consistency, the alternative hypothesis will be two-sided for all comparisons.

1Ho: The period duration does not impact on the volume of trade early in a given period, as compared to that observed under a control market.

Informational efficiency: Following Friedman's (1984) line of reasoning, the introduction of unknown period duration (VU) may result in a decrease in the informational efficiency of the experimental markets, as measured by the convergence of prices to competitive equilibrium values. Non-convergence of prices could plausibly occur if the predicted higher volume of trade early in a period meant that, in their haste to trade, individuals imperfectly infer the underlying state of nature from the publicly available information. Alternatively, a priori, the predicted higher volume of trade may result in an increase in the speed of convergence to equilibrium values if the bids, asks and transaction prices correctly reveal the underlying state of nature. For the VK markets there is no a priori predicted directional change in volume and so consequently it is difficult to conjecture in what direction varying the period duration will impact on the informational efficiency of such markets.

2.1Ho: The deviation of transaction prices from theoretically predicted values in the treatment period duration market (VK or VU) does not differ from those observed in a control market.

2.2Ho: There is no correlation between the difference in the volume of trade, across the experimental markets, and the difference in the deviations from predicted transaction values, across the experimental markets, 'early' in a trading period.

Allocative efficiency: Friedman's (1984) line of reasoning further implies that the introduction of unknown period duration (VU) may result in a decrease in the allocative efficiency of the markets, as measured by the level of gains from trade to be exploited. Lower gains from trade could plausibly occur if the predicted higher volume of trade early in a period meant that, in their haste to trade, individuals imperfectly infer the underlying state of nature. Alternatively, allocative efficiency may be increased if, a priori, the predicted higher volume of trade resulted in the underlying state of nature being revealed earlier, providing more time for traders to position their portfolios efficiently. Once again, for the VK markets there is no a priori prediction.

3.1Ho: The percentage of gains from trade to be exhausted in the treatment period duration market (VK or VU) does not differ from those observed in a control market.

3.2Ho: There is no correlation between the difference in the volume of trade, across the experimental markets, and the difference in the percentage of gains from trade to be exhausted, across the experimental markets.

Collectively, the research hypotheses above allow an investigation of the impact of period duration on the volume of trade, and levels of informational and allocational efficiency observed in experimental asset markets. A discussion of the experimental design follows.

3. Experimental Design

The experimental design adopted here draws on the earlier design of Plott and Sunder (1982), as adapted by Banks (1985) and further developed by Sunder (1992). The novel feature of this experimental design is the introduction of variable, known and unknown period durations. The design extends significantly on that used in the Duxbury (1997) pilot study, with the inclusion of both perfect or imperfect information structures and costless or costly private information. Four groups of markets were conducted, resulting in a total of eighteen experimental asset markets.[1]

3.1 Overview of Experimental Procedures and Design

Participants are endowed with risky assets that pay an uncertain dividend at the end of each trading period and working capital in the form of a numeraire. Each trading period runs sequentially, thus removing the possibility of operating a futures market. Participants assume the dual role of being simultaneously buyers and sellers and trade is conducted under the following general rules of DA markets. New bid and ask prices are subject to the 'improvement rule'.[2] Within a trading period, the current bid and ask, and a history of transaction prices are publicly available. No queuing system for bid and ask prices is utilized and after each transaction the bidding process begins afresh. No short sales or borrowings were permitted. No payment of a commission on trade was adopted.

The numeraire is riskless, paying no return and the working capital endowments each period (in the form of an interest free loan of 50,000 experimental monetary units, emus) are sufficiently large so as never to be a binding constraint. The traded asset offers an uncertain payoff at the end of each trading period. Every period, each trader is endowed with two units of the risky asset. The dividend is conditional on the 'state of nature' prevailing throughout the period. Three possible states of nature exist, X, Y and Z, and all three are equally likely to occur in any given period (probability = 1/3). The sequence of states was randomly generated in advance by computer. The state of nature that exists in a particular period is revealed to all traders at the end of the period in question. Reinitialisation occurs at the end of each period prior to the start of the next.

In all the markets, six 'insiders' are provided with private information concerning the state of nature at the beginning of each trading period. Those individuals not so privileged (uninformed) only learn the identity of the state of nature with certainty at the end of the trading period. Their clues simply contained the word 'Blank'. The number and the manner in which insiders were determined each period were common knowledge in all markets. Also common knowledge was the fact that all traders would receive clues, even if they were 'Blank', so as to conceal the identity of insiders in all periods. The type of information (perfect and imperfect) given to insiders and the manner in which individuals were chosen to be insiders (exogenous and endogenous) differ between the four groups of experimental markets and are detailed below.

3.2 Experimental Markets

Markets were conducted with one of three different trading period duration types throughout (CK, VK or VU). The total number of periods in all markets is 15. In the CK markets the length of each of the 15 trading periods is held constant at 240 seconds.[3] The length of each trading period was common knowledge to all traders, who also had access to information concerning the time remaining in the prevailing trading period. In contrast, both the VK and VU markets incorporate differential period durations that permit the length of any period to vary between 120 and 360 seconds (integer values only). There may exist a minimum length of time that traders take to organize themselves and to evaluate the situation they are faced with, and it is for this reason that a minimum time limit is incorporated in the design. Participants did not know of the existence of a minimum trading duration. The actual duration of any period in the VK and VU markets was generated randomly by computer from a uniform distribution prior to the experiment.[4] In the interest of controlling for the experience gained by participants whilst actually taking part in the experiment the total trading time available in all the experimental markets was held constant at 3,600 seconds.

In VK markets participants know the duration of the trading periods, and they also have access to information concerning the time remaining in the current trading period. In VU markets participants do not know the duration of the trading periods and so they do not have access to information concerning the time remaining in the current trading period. Participants are simply informed that the trading period may close at any time. The fact that the actual duration of trade was drawn at random, with replacement, from a uniform distribution was common knowledge.

3.3 Participants and Motivation

The experimental markets were conducted during November 1996 through May 1997. The participants were a mixture of undergraduate and postgraduate students, drawn from the entire population of students at the University of York. Students were recruited via advertisement posters and mailing lists. Two further experimental markets were conducted using undergraduate students at the University of Leeds.

All markets comprise 12 participants divided equally among three trader type groups. These trader type groups differ with respect to the uncertain dividends payable to them at the end of each trading period. Traders in the same group receive the same uncertain dividend per asset held at the end of a trading period conditional upon the state of nature pertaining, whereas, across groups the state contingent dividend differs. An individual's distribution of returns is private, known only by themselves. Participants were instructed not to reveal this information to any other trader and were informed only that other trader's returns may differ from their own. They were not aware of the identity of the other traders in the same trader group. Table 11.1 illustrates the state contingent dividends paid to trader types. Two different parameter designs were used throughout the experiment, though only one parameter set was applicable for any given market. Note that whilst the expected emu dividend differs across trader types, the expected dividend in pound sterling terms is identical (expected emu dividend multiplied by the relevant conversion factor).

Table 11.1. State Contingent Dividend Distributions (emus).

Trader		*State*		*Conversion*
Type	*X*	*Y*	*Z*	*Factor*
1	350	200	200	0.000667
2	100	300	200	0.000883
3	300	200	700	0.000417

Panel A: Parameter set A

Trader		*State*		*Conversion*
Type	*X*	*Y*	*Z*	*Factor*
1	250	300	350	0.000833
2	200	350	950	0.000500
3	200	400	600	0.000625

Panel B: Parameter set B

The risky assets have no intrinsic value of their own and so preferences for them need to be induced via the procedures derived by Smith (1976). A redemption function, denominated in emus, is assigned to each trader of the form given in the equation below:

$$\text{Profit}_n = \sum_{j=1}^{15} [R_{j,n} - C_{j,n} + D_{j,i}(k) \cdot h_{j,n}]. \tag{11.1}$$

Where:

Profit_n = profit earned by trader n during the entire experiment,

$R_{j,n}$ = revenue of trader n from the sale of risky assets in period j,

$C_{j,n}$ = cost in period j of the purchase of risky assets for trader n,
$D_{j,i}(k)$ = dividend for trader type i in period j, given the state of nature k,
$h_{j,n}$ = number of assets held by trader n at the end of period j.

The loan of initial working capital of 50,000 emus is reclaimed each period and does not constitute profit, thus it is omitted from the redemption function. Each individual's redemption function is private information. Individuals' experimental currency profits where converted into 'domestic' currency and individuals were paid their earnings. To encourage volunteers in the first place, participants were also given a £ 2.00 attendance payment. Table 11.2 offers some descriptive statistics summarizing the payments made to participants across all eighteen experimental markets.[5] On average, participants received, in cash, £8.55 for 90 minutes of their time. This is equivalent to an hourly rate of £5.70, far more than would be available to students through part-time jobs such as bar work or waiting tables.

Table 11.2. Summary of Payment to Participants.

All Sessions	£
Mean	8.55
Median	8.40
Standard Deviation	1.62
Maximum	14.74
Minimum	3.15
5th Percentile	6.30
95th Percentile	11.52

Participants were issued the instructions prior to the beginning of an experimental session so they could familiarise themselves with the requirements. At the beginning of each experimental session the experimenter reviewed the instructions and answered any questions. Before each market commenced trading proper a nine minute practice period was played out so that individuals could familiarise themselves with the computer screen layout, the key strokes required to enter bids and asks and the whole process by which trade took place. After the practice session any further questions were addressed and the experimenter made sure that all participants appeared to understand the trading rules and the relationship between their trading performance and their ultimate payment for taking part in the experiment. All the markets were conducted using a computerised DA.[6]

3.4 Specific Market Designs

Table 11.3 illustrates the four different parameter sets employed,[7] whilst Table 11.4 provides a summary of the full experimental design. The main treatment variable, trading period duration, takes one of three levels, CK, VK and VU. The two other treatment variables both have two levels; the information structure is perfect (P) or imperfect (I) and there is either a pre-trade market for information (M) or no market (N). The labels used to identify a specific market reveal which treatment effects were in force for the duration of the market. For example, the CKPN1 market, governed by parameter set 1, had constant period durations and a perfect information structure.

Table 11.3. Summary of Parameter Designs.

Period	*Parameter set 1*		*Parameter set 2*		*Parameter set 3a*		*Parameter set 3b*	
	State	*Duration*	*State*	*Duration*	*State*	*Duration*	*State*	*Duration*
1	Z	186	X	178	Z	133	Y	133
2	X	251	Y	319	Y	249	Y	249
3	X	130	X	175	X	181	Z	181
4	Y	303	Z	138	X	129	Z	129
5	Z	319	Y	244	Z	360	X	360
6	Y	175	Y	351	Z	287	Y	287
7	Y	128	X	128	Y	327	X	327
8	Z	301	Z	213	Y	156	X	156
9	X	286	X	338	Y	226	Z	226
10	Z	140	X	182	X	349	X	349
11	Y	338	Z	350	X	328	Y	328
12	Y	197	X	327	Z	147	Y	147
13	X	347	X	130	X	129	Z	129
14	X	359	Y	355	Y	339	X	339
15	Y	140	Y	172	X	260	Y	260
Total	n/a	3600	n/a	3600	n/a	3600	n/a	3600

For Groups One and Two of the design two markets were conducted for each of the three period duration effects and all participants were inexperienced in so much as they had not taken part in a DA asset market previously.[8,9] In the Group One markets insiders received information that perfectly (P) revealed the state of nature for a given trading period, whilst in the Group Two markets insiders received imperfect information (I) that no longer identified the state of nature with certainty. Instead, the information allows insiders to eliminate one of the possible states of nature. The procedures are similar to Plott and Sunder (1988) with one slight modification. In order to maintain experimental control the design utilized here maintains the convention of including six uninformed

Table 11.4. Summary of Experimental Design.[a,b,c,d]

Exp. Group No.	*Information Structure*	*Cost of Information*	*Duration* Constant Known	Variable Known	Variable Unknown
1	Perfect	No market (free)	CKPN1[a] CKPN2[b]	VKPN1[a] VKPN2[b]	VUPN1[a] VUPN2[b]
2	Imperfect	No market (free)	CKIN1[a] CKIN2[b]	VKIN1[a] VKIN2[b]	VUIN1[a] VUIN2[b]
3	Perfect	Market	CKPM[c]	VKPM[c]	VUPM[c]
4	Imperfect	Market	CKIM[d]	VKIM[d]	VUIM[d]

[a] Parameter set 1. [b] Parameter set 2. [c] Parameter set 3a. [d] Parameter set 3b.

traders in all markets, whilst Plott and Sunder's (1988) design includes no uninformed traders. The six randomly chosen insiders receive clue cards that inform them of one of the three states of nature that will not occur in the coming trading period. For example, if the state of nature for the coming period was X then three insiders would receive the clue 'Not Y' and the other three insiders would receive the clue 'Not Z'. The information structure, therefore, provides for aggregate certainty. Two randomly determined insiders were chosen from each trader type group, with insiders in the same group never receiving the same clue. For example, assuming the sate of nature is X, if traders 1 and 2 are randomly chosen to be insiders from trader type 1 and trader 1 receives the clue 'Not Y' then trader 2 will receive the clue 'Not Z'. This feature ensures that the trader type group with the highest dividend payment given the state of nature receives both of the clues, permitting them to identify the state of nature in aggregate. In the Group One and Two markets insiders receive costless, private information and there is no pre-trade information auction (N).

4. Analysis and Results

4.1 Data Considerations

The main sources of data employed are the sequences of transaction prices generated each period, the volume of assets traded each period, and the end of period allocation of assets. The data sources are analyzed in either their raw form or as various measures of performance (such as measures of price convergence, gains from exchange realized, etc.). A number of general issues regarding the data require comment.

First, as is the convention, the measure of price convergence employed is the root mean squared deviation (RMSD) of transaction prices in a period from the predicted equilibrium values of the fully revealing rational expectations (FRE) model. To avoid any potential problems caused by outliers a more robust estimator than the simple mean is required. The method adopted here is to compute an M-estimator, $\overline{X}$, which allocates weights to the observations that decrease as the distance from the centre of the distribution increases.[10] Throughout the discussion the use of the acronym RMSD can be taken to mean the root mean squared deviation from predicted value where the 'mean' has been computed using the Andrew M-estimator.[11,12]

Secondly, in the discussion to follow, the data is analyzed on a period by period basis. This, however, introduces the problem of dependence in the data, due to a 'learning effect' as experience increases. The problem of dependence is remedied by employing a covariate adjustment technique (see Duxbury, 1997). In summary, the dependent variables, that is the various measures of performance employed (for example, RMSD), are adjusted in order to remove the influence of the covariate (the 'learning effect', as proxied by the trading period number).[13] The adjusted data was paired period by period across two markets at a time and compared using the nonparametric Wilcoxon signed-rank (WSR) test for matched pairs. The comparing of market performance across CK and VU markets permits a joint comparison of both varying period duration and knowledge of period duration. However, this joint comparison can be broken down to isolate the two component parts. Comparison of CK with VK markets isolates the impact of simply varying the period duration. More interestingly, comparison of market performance across VK and VU markets provides a strict evaluation of the knowledge of period duration to be isolated. The following sections discuss the main results from the PN and IN markets.[14]

4.2 Experimental Markets Group One (PN Markets)

The analysis proceeds with a preliminary investigation of observed market performance by way of graphical representation, utilizing the unadjusted data. This is followed by a direct evaluation of the stated hypotheses using the adjusted data.

First, the volume of trade per period was compared across markets to determine whether period duration would influence the overall volume of trade. So as to control for the disparate period durations across the six markets the absolute volume of trade each period was normalized by dividing the observed volume by the duration in seconds for each period in question, creating the measure NORMVOL. Figure 11.1 displays the normalized volume of trade per period for each of the three market types (the per period figures are averaged across the two parameter sets). The NORMVOL measure for CKPN markets is fairly erratic (mean of 0.0528), sometimes higher and sometimes lower than the measure for the other two market types. However, a comparison of the VKPN and VUPN markets is more informative, with the NORMVOL measure for VUPN exceeding that for VKPN in 14 of 15 periods. The mean NORMVOL of 0.0538 for VUPN markets convincingly exceeds that of 0.0431 for VKPN markets, indicating that knowledge of the period duration, when isolated from the effect of varying period durations, may be an important factor determining the volume of trade.

The deviation of transaction prices from the FRE predicted values (the FRE model predicts the price to be equal to the highest state contingent dividend value) were also considered. Figure 11.2 displays the RMSD of prices per period, computed using the Andrew M-estimator, for the three markets again averaged across the two alternative parameter sets. Whilst the high degree of variability makes it difficult to draw any conclusive inferences, the RMSD is highest for VUPN in 11 of the 15 periods, suggesting a potential effect of unknown period duration on transaction prices.

The trading efficiency across the three market types was also investigated. The measure %GAIN is based on the actual gains from trade realized expressed as a percentage of the maximum theoretical gains from trade possible (see for example Forsythe and Lundholm, 1990). This %GAIN measure also requires normalising to give NORM%GAIN, the %GAIN per period divided by the duration in seconds for the given period. Figure 11.3 contains the NORM%GAIN per period for each of the three market types averaged over the two alternative parameter sets. In 7 of the periods CKPN produces the highest NORM%GAIN, whilst the corresponding figures for VKPN and VUPN are 4 and 3, respectively. The mean NORM%GAIN for the CKPN, VKPN and VUPN markets are 0.1806, 0.1638 and 0.1574, respectively. Whilst it is not possible to draw any decisive conclusions, it seems that varying the period duration reduces trading efficiency and that removing knowledge of the period duration reduces the level of efficiency attained still further.

To directly address the predictions of 1Ho, 2.1Ho and 2.2Ho three measures of 'early' in a trading period were defined; the first 45, 60 and 90 seconds of trade in a period. The volume of trade (VOL45, VOL60 and VOL90) and the associated root mean (Andrew M-estimator) squared deviation of transaction prices from FRE values (RMSD45, RMSD60 and RMSD90) over these three time intervals were compared across the three market types. Figures 11.4-11.6 display the volume of trade in the first 45 seconds, 60 seconds and 90 seconds for the three market types. For all three measures VOL45, 60 and 90, the volume of trade is highest, or joint highest, in the VUPN market type in 12, 11 and 13 of the periods, respectively. This clearly supports the view that the volume of trade, early in a period, is dramatically influenced by the removal of knowledge of the trading period duration. Figures 11.7-11.9 graph the early RMSD for the three market types,[15] depicting values that are fairly erratic and exhibit little trend. It is difficult, therefore, to draw any firm conclusions

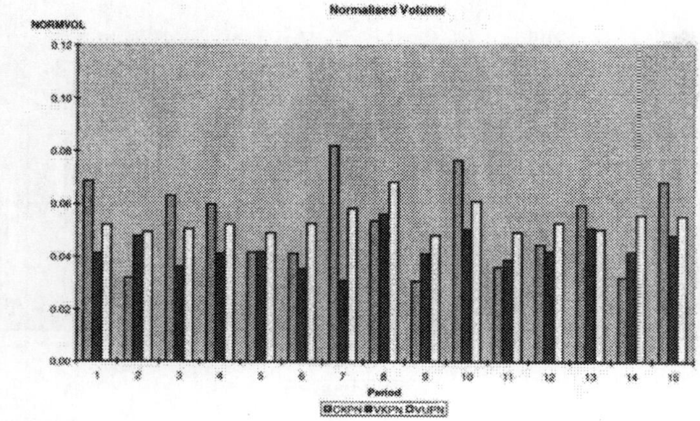

Figure 11.1. Normalised Volume of Trade per Period – Averaged Across PN Markets.

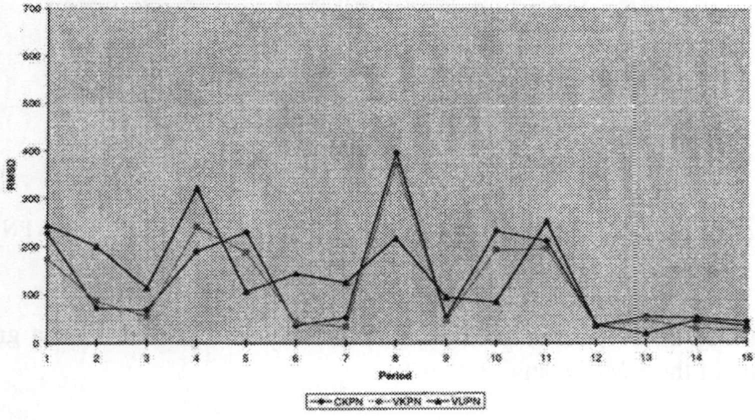

Figure 11.2. Root Mean (Andrew) Squared Deviation of Transaction Prices per Period – Averaged Across PN Markets.

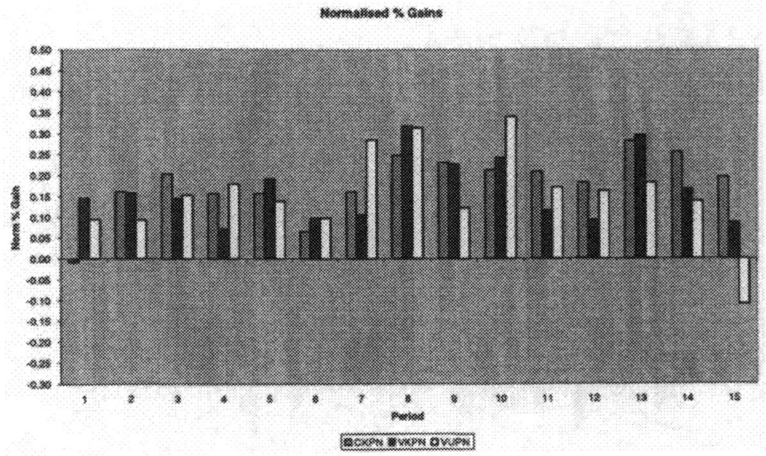

Figure 11.3. Normalised Percentage Gains from Trade – Averaged Across PN Markets.

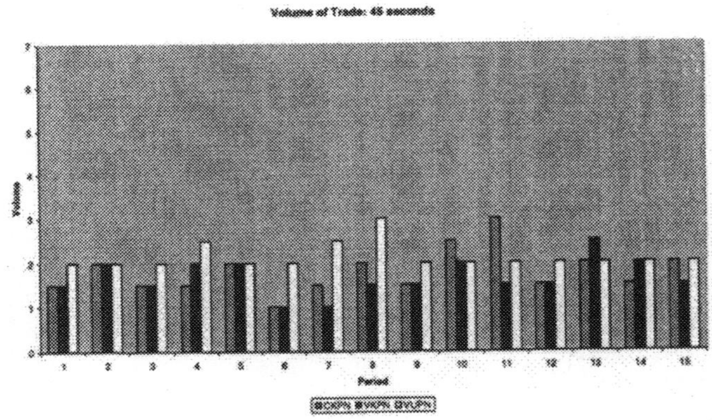

Figure 11.4. Volume of Trade in the First 45 Seconds of Trade – Averaged Across PN Markets.

concerning the impact of period duration early in a period from a graphical analysis of the RMSD data.[16]

Table 11.5 contains the results from the statistical analysis of the stated null hypotheses. For all measures, the main figures reported are the means of the unadjusted values across all trading periods, whilst the figures in parentheses report the means of the adjusted values. The Wilcoxon signed ranks test (WSR) was used to compute two-tail significance levels for the comparisons between the three market types.[17,18] The remainder of this section will consider

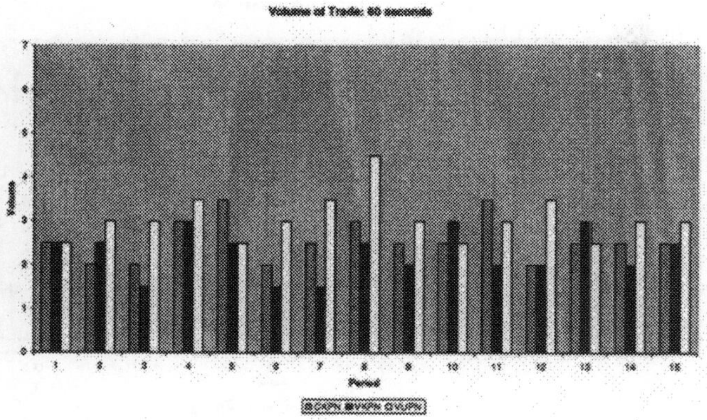

Figure 11.5. Volume of Trade in the First 60 Seconds of Trade – Averaged Across PN Markets.

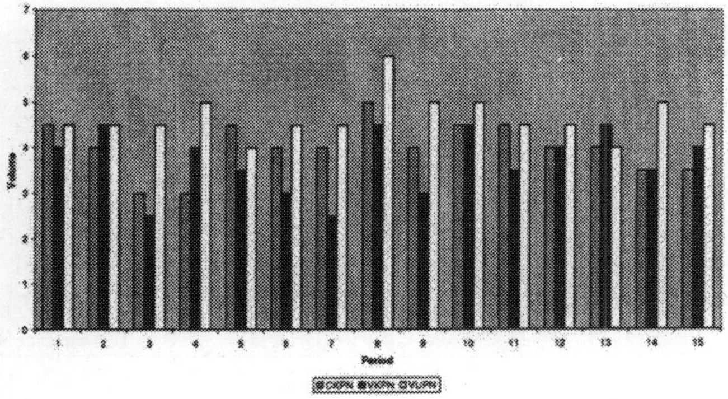

Figure 11.6. Volume of Trade in the First 90 Seconds of Trade – Averaged Across PN Markets.

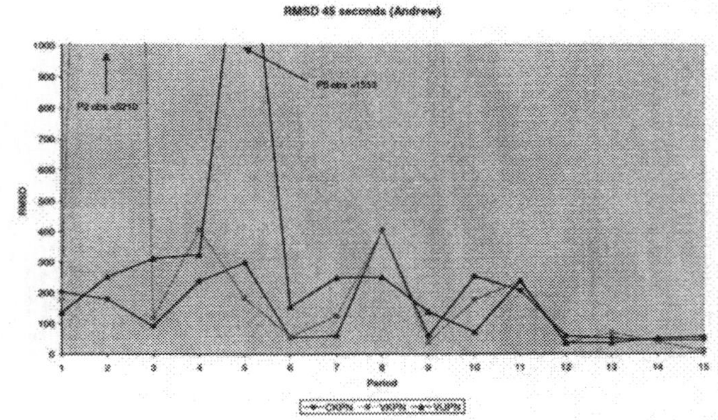

Figure 11.7. RMSD of Prices in the First 45 Seconds of Trade – Averaged Across PN Markets.

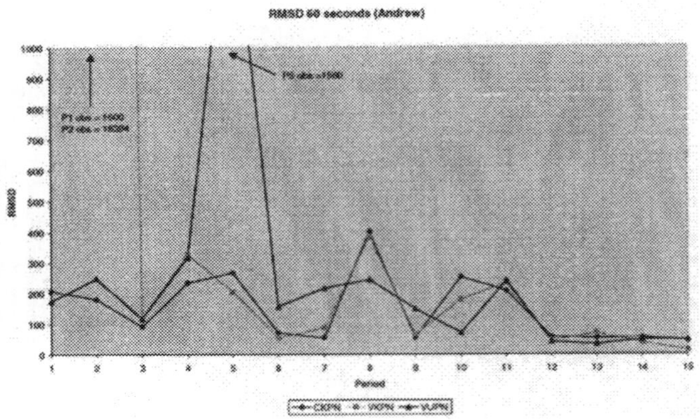

Figure 11.8. RMSD of Prices in the First 60 Seconds of Trade – Averaged Across PN Markets.

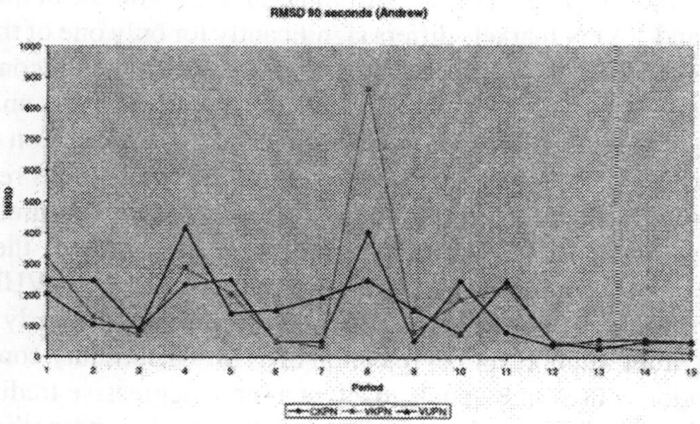

Figure 11.9. RMSD of Prices in the First 90 Seconds of Trade – Averaged Across PN Markets.

separately the impact of period duration on the volume of trade early in a period, and the levels of informational and allocational efficiency observed.

Table 11.5. Summary Table of Market Means (Adjusted Means) and Wilcoxon Signed Ranks Test Two-tail Significance Levels - PN Markets.

Variable	*Market Means (Adjusted Means)*			*WSR Two-tail α-values*		
	CKPN	VKPN	VUPN	CKPN: VKPN	CKPN: VUPN	VKPN: VUPN
VOL45	1.8000 (1.8858)	1.6667 (1.6876)	2.1333 (2.1577)	0.0034	0.3876	0.0104
VOL60	2.5667 (2.6225)	2.2667 (2.3456)	3.0667 (3.1468)	0.1499	0.0013	0.0022
VOL90	4.0000 (4.0112)	3.7000 (3.7007)	4.6667 (4.7334)	0.1414	0.0004	0.0001
NORMVOL	0.0528 (0.0514)	0.0431 (0.0445)	0.0539 (0.0551)	0.1254	0.2329	0.0000
RMSD45	150.1291 (146.8936)	486.0485 (174.2116)	257.4541 (281.3040)	0.0368	0.2289	0.1254
RMSD60	149.4388 (145.6553)	1321.64444 (148.7835)	244.8518 (265.8319)	0.0196	0.4779	0.0627
RMSD90	132.3513 (130.9472)	173.8193 (151.2606)	160.8230 (123.4888)	0.1779	0.9099	0.7189
RMSD	130.7098 (129.0361)	117.7417 (-237.9844)	136.2241 (89.1797)	0.0087	0.5170	0.0157
NORM%GAIN	0.1806 (0.2228)	0.1638 (0.1847)	0.1574 (0.1783)	0.0545	0.0495	0.7577

Volume of Trade. As can be seen in Table 11.5, the volume of trade between the CKPN and VKPN markets differs significantly for only one of the measures employed, with CKPN>VKPN for VOL45. After the first 45 seconds of trade, however, varying period duration no longer significantly impacts on the volume of trade observed in the CKPN and VKPN markets. Given that on average the duration per period is equal across the two market types, these results are to be expected. Of greater interest is the comparison of the measures of volume of trade across the VKPN:VUPN comparison, which isolates the impact of knowledge of period duration on the volume of trade observed. VUPN exhibits a significantly higher volume of trade for all three measures of early in a trading period, providing support for the rejection of 1Ho. Uncertainty concerning the period duration causes individuals to adopt a more aggressive trading strategy, with respect to the speed of trade. This result is further strengthened by the highly significant difference between the NORMVOL measures for the two market types, indicating that the rate of trade per period is, on average, far higher in VUPN markets than in VKPN markets.

Informational Efficiency. How the increased rate of trade early in a period due to unknown period duration impacts on the informational efficiency observed requires consideration. The investigation begins with an evaluation of hypothesis 2.1Ho. As reported in Table 11.5, for the three measures of early in a trading period, the mean RMSD does not differ statistically across the VKPN and VUPN market types. Thus, the higher early volume of trade in the VUPN markets does not impact on the level of informational efficiency attained early in a period. There is no need, therefore, to formally evaluate hypothesis 2.2Ho for trades early in a period. There was, however, a significantly higher RMSD measure over the entire trading period in the VUPN markets. Over an entire trading period, the level of informational efficiency attained is significantly reduced (relative to VKPN markets) as a result of the uncertainty over period duration.

It is possible that the faster rate of trade over an entire period may be the cause of the lower informational efficiency observed in the VUPN markets. To evaluate this possibility the degree of correlation between the difference in normalized volume of trade across the two market types and the difference in RMSD across the markets was computed. The correlation coefficient of 0.1684 computed using Spearman's rank correlation test was not statistically significant (α =0.374). It is not possible, therefore, to suggest that the higher rate of trade is the cause of the loss of informational efficiency observed over the entire period in VUPN markets. However, the ability to reject 2.1Ho for RMSD over the entire period still offers evidence in favor of Friedman's (1984) view that a predetermined, known trading period duration is one of a number of features that enhances the informational efficiency of experimental markets.

A comparison between the CKPN and VKPN markets offers insight into the influence of varying the period duration on the RMSD observed early in a trading period. For the RMSD45 and RMSD60 measures the VKPN markets generate significantly higher values than those in the CKPN markets. By the time 90 seconds of trade has elapsed there is no longer any significant difference and by the end of the period the trend has reversed with the CKPN markets generating significantly higher values. Initially, therefore, the relative level of informational efficiency early in a period is lower in VKPN markets. Over time, however, as the period proceeds the VKPN markets are able to correct themselves and end with a higher level of informational efficiency than the CKPN markets. This phenomenon is not due to any difference in early trading volume or overall rate of trade across the two market types. Only the VOL45 measure differed significantly between the two market types and the correlation coefficient between the difference in VOL45 and the difference in RMSD45 across the CKPN and VKPN markets is insignificant (α =0.566). It seems, therefore, that whilst varying the period duration does not have any major impact on the timing of transactions, it does impact on the relative informational efficiency attained both early in a period and over the entire trading period.

Allocational Efficiency. As is apparent from Table 11.5, an analysis of the level of allocational efficiency observed fails to reject the null hypothesis (3.1Ho, $\alpha = 0.7577$) of no statistical difference in the NORM%GAIN of 0.1638 for the VKPN and 0.1574 for the VUPN markets. Hypothesis 3.2Ho does not, therefore, require formal evaluation for the VKPN:VUPN comparison. In contrast, however, both the CKPN:VKPN and CKPN:VUPN comparisons provide significant results. The mean NORM%GAIN figure of 0.1806 for the CKPN markets significantly exceeds the corresponding figures for both the VKPN and VUPN markets. Once more it is not necessary to formally evaluate hypothesis 3.2Ho for either of these two comparisons, because in this case there is no statistically significant difference between the mean NORMVOL figure for the CKPN markets and the corresponding figures for the other two market types.

It can be concluded that varying the duration each period, with or without uncertainty concerning the actual period duration, has a negative impact on the level of allocational efficiency observed. In isolation, however, uncertainty over the actual period duration does not significantly influence the level of allocational efficiency observed.

4.3 Experimental Markets Group Two (IN Markets)

The analysis will continue with a discussion of the results from the markets where the information structure was imperfect, beginning with a graphical

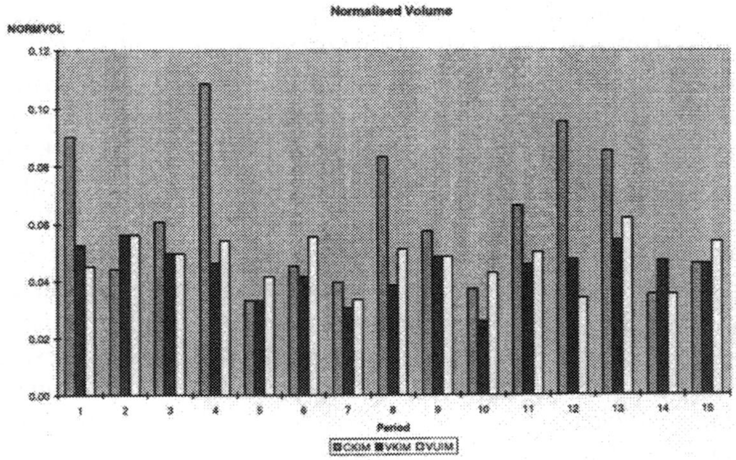

Figure 11.10. Normalised Volume of Trade per Period – Averaged Across IN Markets.

interpretation. Figure 11.10 displays the normalized volume of trade per period for the IN markets averaged across the parameter sets. For all three market types the NORMVOL measures are fairly erratic and there is little difference between the mean NORMVOL figures of 0.04666, 0.0450 and 0.04666 for CKIN, VKIN and VUIN, respectively. The informational efficiency was also compared across markets and Figure 11.11 illustrates the RMSD of prices per period, computed using the Andrew M-estimator, for the three markets averaged across parameter sets. Whilst the functions are fairly erratic, they follow very similar patterns and the differences in the RMSD measures across the three market types are small. It is not clear from this analysis how period duration impacts on informational efficiency in markets with imperfect information. The NORM%GAIN measure was used to compare the trading efficiency across markets, the figures for all three market types (see Figure 11.12) are very erratic and display no obvious pattern. The CKIN markets seem to generate a slightly higher level of NORM%GAIN than the VKIN markets and a much higher level compared to the VUIN markets. This is evidenced by the higher mean NORM%GAIN of 0.0700 for the CKIN markets compared to the values of 0.0671 and 0.0394 for the VKIN and VUIN markets, respectively. At this point, however, it is not possible to draw any decisive conclusions. An analysis of the stated hypotheses now follows, beginning with a graphical presentation of trade 'early' in a period and ending with a discussion of the statistical results.

Figures 11.13-11.15 depict the volume of trade for all three measures of 'early' in a period. In many of the periods the volume is highest, or joint highest,

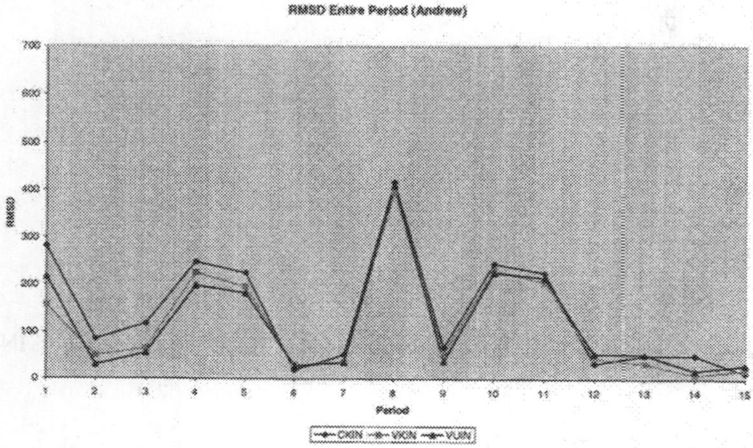

Figure 11.11. Root Mean (Andrew) Squared Deviation of Transaction Prices per Period – Averaged Across IN Markets.

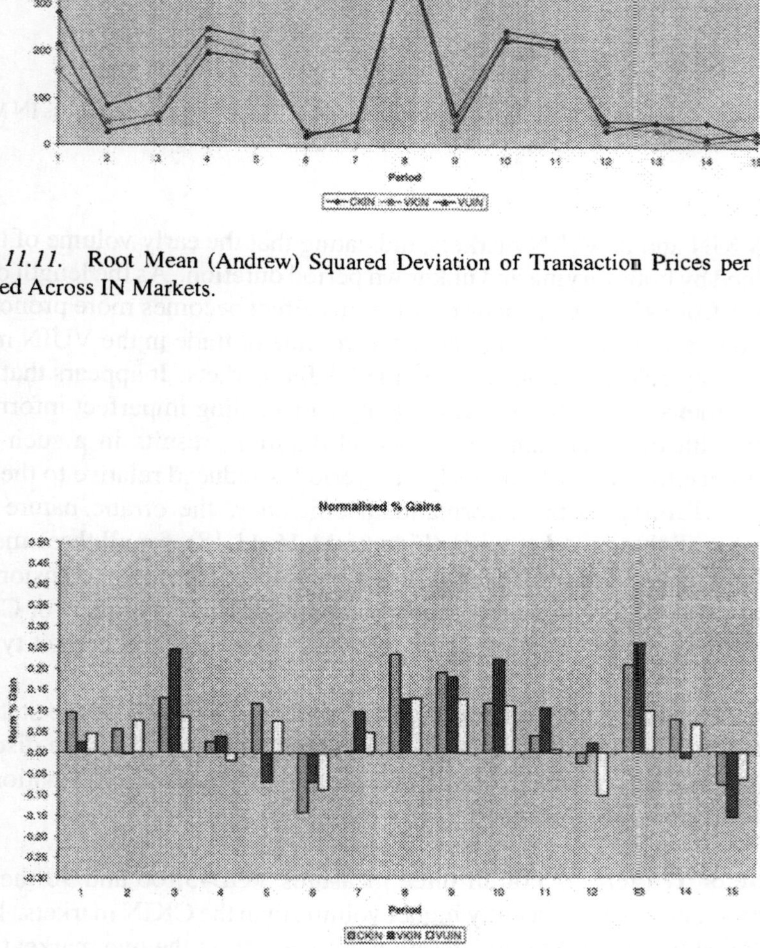

Figure 11.12. Normalised Percentage Gains from Trade – Averaged Across IN Markets.

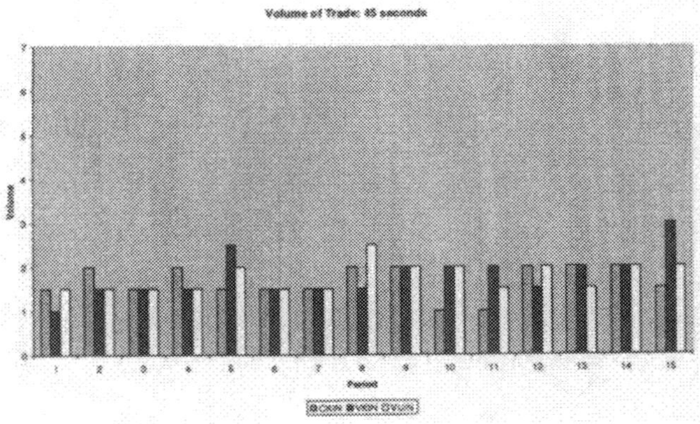

Figure 11.13. Volume of Trade in the First 45 Seconds of Trade – Averaged Across IN Markets.

in the VKIN and/or VUIN markets, indicating that the early volume of trade is influenced by both varying and unknown period duration. As the length of trade increases from 45 to 90 seconds of trade this effect becomes more pronounced. Unlike the results in the PN markets, the volume of trade in the VUIN markets appears to be below that observed in the VKIN markets. It appears that, in the VUIN markets, the additional uncertainty surrounding imperfect information, coupled with the uncertainty over period duration, results in a such a high level of uncertainty that trade early in a period is reduced relative to the VKIN markets. Turning to the informational efficiency, the erratic nature of the RMSD for all three market types (Figures 11.16-11.18), for all three measures of early in a period make it very difficult to draw any strong conclusions. The functions follow similar patterns and though the RMSD is higher for CKIN in the first five periods, the subsequent differences between the market types are slight.

Table 11.6 reports the results from the statistical analysis of the stated null hypotheses. The format of the table is identical to Table 11.5. The discussion to follow will report on the volume of trade and the levels of informational and allocational efficiency observed.

Volume of Trade. For all three measures VOL45, 60 and 90 the VKIN markets generate a significantly higher volume than the CKIN markets. Despite the fact that the average period duration is equal across the two market types, it appears that the short durations in some trading periods in the VKIN markets may have made traders more eager to trade early in a period to avoid the disappointment of missing out on profitable transactions. Over an entire trading period though, the mean rate of trade (NORMVOL) does not differ significantly

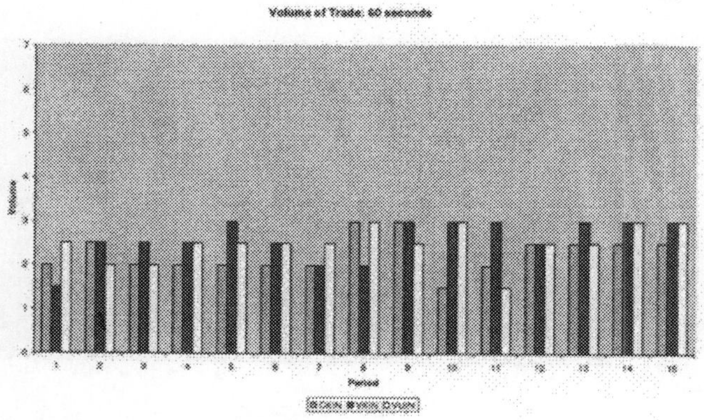

Figure 11.14. Volume of Trade in the First 60 Seconds of Trade – Averaged Across IN Markets.

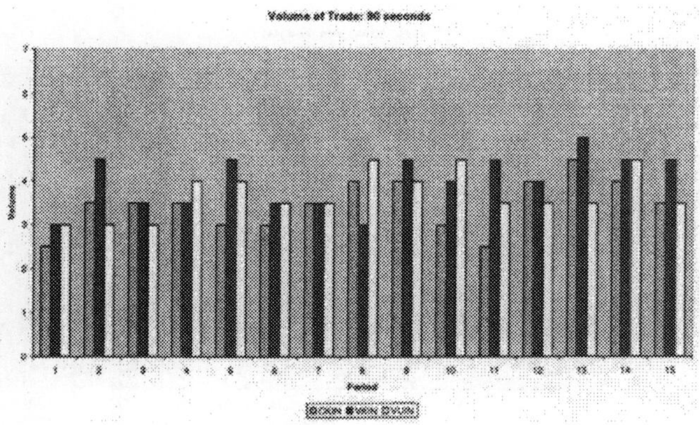

Figure 11.15. Volume of Trade in the First 90 Seconds of Trade – Averaged Across IN Markets.

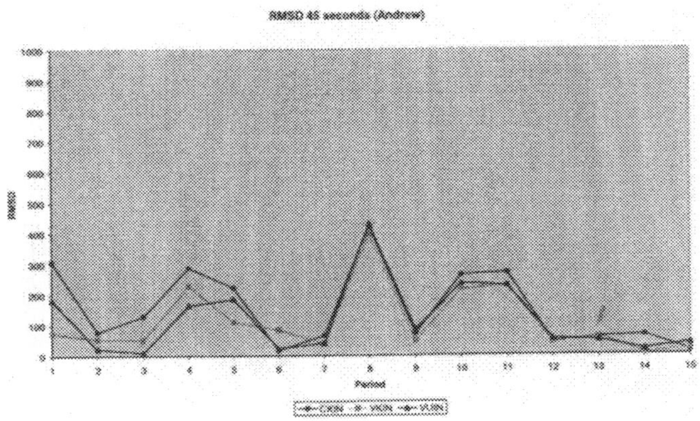

Figure 11.16. RMSD of Prices in the First 45 Seconds of Trade – Averaged Across IN Markets.

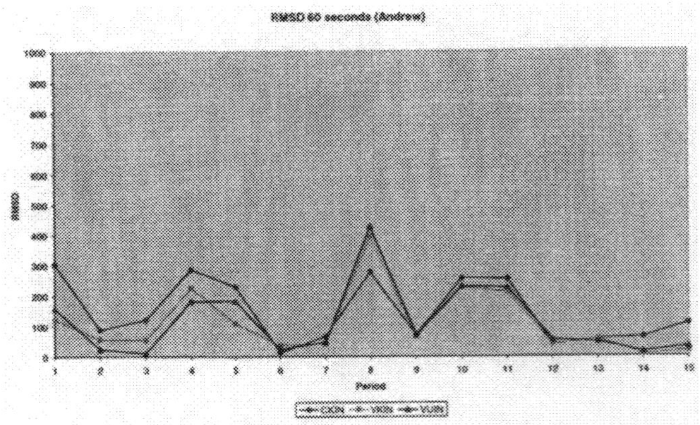

Figure 11.17. RMSD of Prices in the First 60 Seconds of Trade – Averaged Across IN Markets.

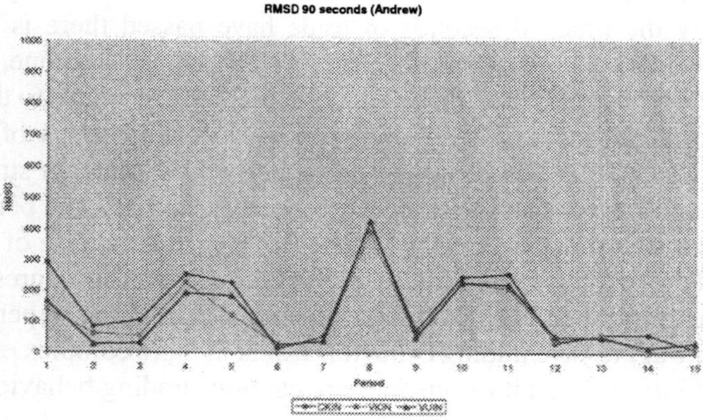

Figure 11.18. RMSD of Prices in the First 90 Seconds of Trade – Averaged Across IN Markets.

Table 11.6. Summary Table of Market Means (Adjusted Means) and Wilcoxon Signed Ranks Test Two-tail Significance Levels - IN Markets.

Variable	*Market Means (Adjusted Means)*			*WSR Two-tail α-values*		
	CKIN	VKIN	VUIN	CKIN: VKIN	CKIN: VUIN	VKIN: VUIN
VOL45	1.6667 (1.6511)	1.8000 (1.9715)	1.7667 (1.8664)	0.0117	0.0058	0.0207
VOL60	2.2667 (2.2332)	2.6000 (2.8193)	2.5000 (2.5925)	0.0002	0.0141	0.0062
VOL90	3.4667 (3.4589)	4.0000 (4.1870)	3.7000 (3.9186)	0.0053	0.0098	0.2655
NORMVOL	0.0466 (0.0478)	0.0450 (0.0475)	0.0420 (0.0434)	0.7971	0.4653	0.0645
RMSD45	154.4757 (144.7697)	110.7323 (125.0514)	117.8292 (126.5157)	0.0545	0.2059	0.7189
RMSD60	150.3773 (132.4749)	112.2919 (120.9447)	116.9566 (127.8973)	0.1204	0.5716	0.5038
RMSD90	146.8968 (136.9056)	111.3953 (117.2604)	117.4065 (125.6091)	0.0230	0.0822	0.2452
RMSD	142.7678 (132.6657)	117.3947 (124.8817)	119.9761 (124.7529)	0.1717	0.1156	0.8774
NORM%GAIN	0.0700 (0.0839)	0.0671 (0.0834)	0.0394 (0.0524)	0.9590	0.1180	0.3812

across the two market types, suggesting that, on average, the impact of short and long period durations in VKIN markets cancel out. Of greater interest is the comparison between the VKIN and VUIN markets. For VOL45 and VOL60, VUIN exhibits a significantly lower volume of trade than VKIN.

Thus, it is possible to reject 1Ho for these two measures of early in a trading period. By the time 90 seconds of trade have passed there is no longer a significant difference, though the mean VUIN figures continue to be lower than the VKIN figures.[19] It appears that the market's response to the increased uncertainty faced in the VUIN environment, in the presence of uncertainty regarding the state of nature due to the imperfect information structure, is to become more cautious and so trade less aggressively early in a period, relative to the less uncertain environment of VKIN. This is the reverse of the findings for the PN the markets incorporating perfect information structures. In simpler environments (perfect information) the uncertainty surrounding period duration causes more aggressive trading behavior, whilst in more complex environments (imperfect information) it results in more cautious trading behavior.

Informational Efficiency. The investigation of the impact of period duration begins with an evaluation of hypothesis 2.1Ho to determine the extent of any difference in transaction prices across the market types. As reported in Table 11.6, for the three measures of early in a trading period, the mean RMSD is higher in the VUIN markets than the VKIN markets, though there is no significant difference. Thus, the lower early volume of trade in the VUIN markets does not impact on the level of informational efficiency attained early in a period. Hypothesis 2.2Ho does not, therefore, require formal evaluation. The VKIN and VUIN markets were further compared to see if any difference existed between the RMSD of prices over an entire trading period. As reported in Table 11.6, the RMSD measure does not differ significantly across the two market types. Over an entire trading period, the level of informational efficiency observed in the VUIN markets relative to the VKIN markets is not influenced by uncertainty concerning period duration. These results, therefore, offer little support for Friedman's (1984) view that a predetermined, known trading period duration enhances the informational efficiency of experimental markets, when an imperfect information structure is present in the experimental design.

A comparison between the CKIN and VKIN markets offers insight into the influence of varying the period duration on the RMSD observed. The results are mixed. The RMSD45 and RMSD90 measures for the VKIN markets are significantly lower than the corresponding measures for the CKIN markets, whilst the RMSD60 and RMSD measures do not differ statistically.[20] The three measures of volume early in a period were all significantly higher under the VKIN markets than the CKIN markets. Thus to evaluate hypothesis 2.2Ho, the correlation coefficients between the differences in the early VOL measures and the differences in early RMSD measures were computed. The coefficients of 0.1804 for the first 45 seconds and 0.0884 for the first 90 seconds were not significant (α =0.520 and 0.754, respectively). It would be impossible to argue that the higher volume early in a period impacts in any comprehensive manner on the RMSD early in a period.

Allocational Efficiency. In considering the impact of the two treatments (VK and VU) on the level of allocational efficiency observed, the analysis fails to reject the null hypothesis 3.1Ho, for any of the paired comparisons of NORM%GAIN. It is, therefore, not necessary to formally evaluate hypothesis 3.2Ho for any of the comparisons. Whilst the increased uncertainty due to unknown period duration in VUIN markets results in a far lower mean NORM%GAIN figure than that observed in VKIN markets, this reduction is not significant. It is concluded that the treatment effects of varying period duration and unknown period duration neither separately, nor jointly, impact on the level of allocational efficiency observed in experimental asset markets with imperfect information structures.

4.4 Experimental Markets Groups Three and Four

Space limitations prevent the detailed discussion of the results from the markets where a pre-trade information auction was included (see Duxbury, 1998, for a detailed discussion), however, the results are reported in Tables 11.7 and 11.8. Where significant results where found, these were generally in line with the results reported above. For example, the significantly higher trade reported for all four volume measures in the VKIN markets compared to the CKIN markets is supported by the evidence from the comparison of the CKIM and VKIM markets. One result, however, is contradictory to the earlier evidence. The significantly higher trade reported for all four volume measures in the VUIM markets compared to the VKIM is the reverse of the findings in the VKIN and VUIN comparison. Indeed, the higher volume of trade is actually in line with the results reported from the VKPN and VUPN comparison. It is difficult to comment on why this is the case due to the confounded effects of costly information and increased experience, though it is more likely to be due to the influence of the latter.

5. Discussion and Conclusions

This paper has considered the importance of trading period duration on the convergence tendencies of experimental asset markets governed by the rules of the double auction. Experimental markets were conducted with either constant and known, variable and known or variable and unknown trading period durations. The results provide evidence of a significant impact of unknown period duration on observed market performance, in particular the volume of trade and informational efficiency. In markets with perfect information, unknown period durations result in an increase in the both the early volume and the rate of trade

Table 11.7. Summary Table of Market Means (Adjusted Means) and Wilcoxon Signed Ranks Test Two-tail Significance Levels - PM Markets.

Variable	*Market Means (Adjusted Means)*			*WSR Two-tail α-values*		
	CKPM	VKPM	VUPM	CKPM: VKPM	CKPM: VUPM	VKPM: VUPM
VOL45	1.6667 (1.8299)	1.7333 (1.6413)	1.800 (1.8959)	0.3343	0.5321	0.1556
VOL60	2.2000 (2.4743)	2.8000 (2.7330)	2.4667 (2.5420)	0.9096	0.9096	0.6909
VOL90	3.8667 (4.1440)	4.1333 (4.0030)	3.800 (3.8244)	0.4603	0.4265	1.0000
NORMVOL	0.0575 (0.0545)	0.0524 (0.0509)	0.0483 (0.0485)	0.4955	0.3635	0.2805
RMSD45	111.6958 (127.2370)	147.9507 (119.1727)	171.9100 (143.9317)	0.4603	0.7333	0.4603
RMSD60	119.4077 (131.1053)	133.4501 (105.6831)	170.6865 (142.4290)	0.2330	0.6496	0.3635
RMSD90	113.1627 (130.4018)	111.8327 (92.7783)	163.9640 (134.9071)	0.1118	0.5701	0.0995
RMSD	90.7525 (102.4972)	87.1397 (65.6754)	135.3720 (106.9726)	0.0268	0.6496	0.1728
NORM%GAIN	0.2455 (0.2678)	0.3032 (0.2891)	0.2145 (0.2577)	0.6092	0.7764	0.0884

observed, plus a reduction in the level of informational efficiency displayed over an entire trading period. This evidence directly supports Friedman's (1984) conjecture regarding the influence of predetermined, known period duration on the convergence tendency of transaction prices to competitive equilibrium outcomes in DA markets. The results suggest that the highly efficient outcomes in experimental asset markets from Plott and Sunder (1982) onwards, may partly be a product of the constant and known period durations employed in the experimental design of those markets. No evidence, however, is reported of a significant effect on the level of allocational efficiency generated in markets with unknown period durations. These results are generally in line with the results from the pilot analysis reported in Duxbury (1997). Contrary to the results reported for the perfect information markets, the coupling of increased state uncertainty (imperfect information) with period duration uncertainty resulted in a reduction in the volume of trade early in a period. There was little effect, however, on the level of informational or allocational efficiency.

Table 11.8. Summary Table of Market Means (Adjusted Means) and Wilcoxon Signed Ranks Test Two-tail Significance Levels - IM Markets.

Variable	*Market Means (Adjusted Means)*			*WSR Two-tail α-values*		
	CKIM	VKIM	VUIM	CKIM: VKIM	CKIM: VUIM	VIPM: VUIM
VOL45	2.0000 (2.0320)	1.2667 (1.1327)	2.0000 (1.9326)	0.0007	0.2330	0.0022
VOL60	2.7333 (2.6529)	2.0667 (1.8363)	2.5333 (2.3940)	0.0007	0.0609	0.0409
VOL90	4.4000 (4.4042)	3.4000 (3.0939)	4.1333 (4.1217)	0.0012	0.0995	0.0090
NORMVOL	0.0619 (0.0591)	0.0443 (0.0432)	0.0476 (0.0479)	0.0199	0.1556	0.0409
RMSD45	206.8142 (205.6309)	195.1038 (200.7549)	279.4136 (302.9129)	0.9096	0.2330	0.3066
RMSD60	205.4429 (203.9369)	197.4537 (202.5641)	198.3139 (190.5495)	0.8203	0.3066	0.6906
RMSD90	203.4377 (198.0157)	194.5666 (199.0151)	199.1760 (190.2554)	0.8203	0.3635	0.6496
RMSD	195.5250 (191.2118)	189.3137 (193.2263)	196.2242 (188.6278)	0.8203	0.7764	0.7764
NORM%GAIN	0.0673 (0.0083)	0.0784 (0.0820)	0.0950 (0.0927)	0.0268	0.0468	0.4265

Notes

1. Due to space constraints the discussion of the results will be limited to those markets where private information was free and no pre-trade auction for information was conducted. This represents twelve of the eighteen markets conducted.

2. New bids/asks must be higher/lower than outstanding bids/asks.

3. Plott and Gray (1990) suggest a rule of thumb of eight seconds per trade in a computerized double auction. With 24 assets in all markets, the period duration of 240 seconds should be sufficient to allow all assets to be traded at least once.

4. Traders are informed of the manner in which randomization of all such parameters occurs. To ensure they believe these parameters to be randomly determined, individuals are told they can inspect the random values used at the end of the experimental session.

5. To reduce the likelihood of bankruptcy, the parameter designs were chosen carefully so that the expected value of participating in the experiment, assuming the markets achieved 100% efficient allocations, was a minimum of £9.75. No individual went bankrupt in any of the markets.

6. Details of the instructions, illustrations of the computer screens and reviews of the process for trading are all available for download at http://lubswww.leeds.ac.uk/MKB/dd, as are additional figures relating to the PM and IM markets.

7. Participants were drawn from the entire population of both undergraduate and postgraduate students. Thus there was minimal contact and interaction between participants within a given market session, let alone across different sessions, which were conducted some months apart. There is little possibility, therefore, that participants could have known the pre-specified sequences of states of nature or period durations in advance.

8. The Group Three and Four markets replicate the Group One and Two markets, respectively, using participants from the Group One and Two markets and incorporating a pre-trade information auction (M). A more detailed description of the Group Three and Four designs is available upon request from the author.

9. Originally, it had not been the intention to use experienced participants in the Group Three and Four markets. Unfortunately, recruitment problems necessitated the use of experienced subjects. These problems also prevented cells in the experimental design from being repeated.

10. $\overline{X} = \sum w_i x_i / \sum w_i$, where $\overline{X}$ = the weighted mean, w_i = the weight applied to observation i, x_i = observation i.

11. Four commonly used M-estimators were considered; Huber's, Hampel's, Andrew's, and Tukey's (see Hoaglin, Mosteller and Tukey, 1983, for a detailed discussion). In the ensuing discussion of the results the values as computed using the Andrew M-estimator will be the only ones reported, however, the results are robust to the choice of, or even use of, M-estimator.

12. On a few occasions the M-estimators could not be computed because of the highly centralised distribution of observations around the median. On these occasions the mean was substituted in place of the M-estimator with out bias due to the highly centralized distribution and absence of outliers.

13. A discussion of this process is available upon request from the author. Note that in all graphical representation of the data and in the reporting of all preliminary descriptive statistics the unadjusted values are the figures utilized. It is only when statistical significance levels are reported that the adjusted data are used to control for dependence.

14. Two market specific data considerations also require comment. Firstly, given the three measures of early adopted throughout this study (the first 45, 60 and 90 seconds of trade within a period), it is conceivable that the first trade in a period could occur at a time in excess of either 45, 60 or 90 seconds and so consequently the three measures RMSD(45,60,90) would not be defined for that period. This occurred only on a few occasions and only in the markets with a pre-trade auction, the results of which are not discussed in detail here. However, when this did occur the mid-point of the bid-ask spread was used as a proxy for the transaction price. Secondly, for two of the markets, CKIM and VUIM, technical problems caused the computer programme to freeze during period 11 and the participants were unable to input any further bids or asks. After the period timed out the program reinitialised ready for period 12. Measures used to analyse the volume of trade and the level of allocational efficiency are normalised to control for disparate trading period durations and so are not affected by the programme freezing. In contrast, the RMSD measure over the entire trading period may have been influenced by the premature cessation of trade. Observation of the sequence of transaction prices in period 11 for both markets, however, revealed prices were stable, uniform and very close to the FRE price by the time the programme froze. It can be concluded, therefore, that the programme freezing did not introduce any bias into the results.

15. There are a few occasions where the RMSD values are exceptionally high. The low number of observations (transactions) for these early measures mean that any 'outliers' will have a strong influence even on the M-estimators.

16. Applying the three measures of early to NORM%GAIN is neither possible nor desirable. Any allocation of assets prior to the end of a trading period may be merely a temporary allocation. The FRE model makes no prediction about intra-period allocations, only end-period allocations.

17. The statistical tests paired observations period by period, across two market types at a time. For example, comparing the market performance across VKPN and VUPN, the observation from VKPN1 period 1 is paired with the observation from VUPN1 period 1 and so on until period 15. Then, the observation from VKPN2 period 1 is paired with the observation from VUPN2 period 1 and so on until period 15. Thus the total number of paired observations utilized in each statistical test is 30.

18. The CKPN:VUPN comparison confounds the effects of both varying period duration and uncertainty over when a trading period will end. The results of this comparison are reported for completeness, but are not discussed directly.

19. It is possible that the 90 second measure of early in a trading period does not in fact constitute 'early' in many of the trading periods. For example, the overall duration in some trading periods is as low as 128 seconds (Table 11.3) and so 90 seconds constitutes approximately 70% of the total time available to trade. This is clearly not early in such periods and so may explain the insignificant result. Consequently, greater emphasis is placed on the other two measures of early.

20. It is difficult to understand why there is no significant difference in the RMSD60 measure, the only explanation is due to noise in the data.

References

Banks, J.S. (1985). "Price-conveyed Information versus Observed Insider Behavior: A Note on Rational Expectations Convergence," *Journal of Political Economy* 93, 807-815.

Duxbury, D. (1995). "Experimental Asset Markets Within Finance," *Journal of Economic Surveys* 9, 331-371.

Duxbury, D. (1997). "A Pilot Exploration of Random Period Duration in Experimental Financial Markets: A Treatment Variable?" *Managerial and Decision Economics* 18, 309-327.

Duxbury, D, (1998). "Market Efficiency and the Role of Information: An Experimental Analysis", PhD dissertation, Leeds University Business School, University of Leeds.

Easley, D. and J. Ledyard, (1993). "Theories of Price Formation and Exchange in Double Oral Auctions," in The Double Auction Market: Institutions, Theories and Evidence, Eds. Friedman, D. and J. Rust, Addison Wesley, 63-97.

Forsythe, R. and R. Lundholm, (1990). "Information Aggregation in an Experimental Market," *Econometrica* 50, 537-567.

Friedman, D. (1984). "On the Efficiency of Experimental Double Auction Markets," *American Economic Review* 74, 60-72.

Friedman, D. (1991). "A Simple Testable Model of Double Auction Markets," *Journal of Economic Behavior and Organization* 15, 47-70.

Plott, C.R. and P. Gray, (1990). "The Multiple Unit Double Auction," *Journal of Economic Behavior and Organisation* 13, 245-258.

Plott, C.R. and S. Sunder, (1982). "Efficiency of Experimental Security Markets with Insider Information: An Application of Rational- Expectations Models," *Journal of Political Economy* 90, 663-698.

Plott, C.R. and S. Sunder (1988). "Rational Expectations and the Aggregation of Diverse Information in Laboratory Security Markets," *Econometrica* 56, 1085-118.

Smith, V.L. (1976). "Experimental Economics: Induced Value Theory," reproduced in Smith, V.L. (1991). Papers in Experimental Economics. Cambridge University Press.

Sunder, S. (1992). "Market for Information: Experimental Evidence," *Econometrica* 60, 667-695.

Sunder, S. (1995). "Experimental Asset Markets: A Survey," in The Handbook of Experimental Economics, Eds. Kagel, J.H. and A.E. Roth, Princeton University Press.

Wilson, R. (1987). "Equilibrium in Bid-Ask Markets," in Arrow and the Ascent of Economic Theory: Essays in Honor of Kenneth J. Arrow, Ed. by Feiwel, G., London: Macmillan, 375-414.

Chapter 12

ROBUST LEARNING EXPERIMENTS*

Werner Güth
Max Planck Institute, Jena
gueth@mpiew-jena.mpg.de

1. Introduction

The traditional assumption in economics is that decision makers are (perfectly) rational and that, at least when game theory is involved, this is commonly known. Rationality means to react optimally to one's decision environment. The orthodox interpretation assumes that material success is maximized an assumption that has been convincingly falsified, partly by experimental evidence. Recently more general notions of preferences are propagated which allow to capture non-material rewards like emotions, social concerns or intrinsic motivation. In any case decision alternatives are compared according to their present and future consequences. The past only plays a role in so far as it determines structural aspects, e.g. via state variables like in dynamic programming or in dynamic games. Thus rational decision making is purely forward looking.

Such forward looking deliberation requires well-behaved (intertemporal) preferences and unlimited cognitive abilities. But real decision makers meet neither of these requirements: When having to decide the first task is often to determine one's primary goals. Secondary goals may suggest themselves when actually predicting the consequences of certain decision alternatives. Although the human brain is quite a sophisticated problem solver, we are at best boundedly rational: Our capacity for processing and storing information and our analytic abilities are seriously limited.

In spite of long research traditions in cognitive, social, and economic psychology where such limitations were explicitly taken into account the rational choice approach has been justified by "as if"-arguments (only the rationally deciding firms will survive in competition); by the large variety of partly conflicting behavioral theories (by denying partly contradicting rational choice-

*I gratefully acknowledge the constructive comments of Fredrik Andersson and Håkan Holm.

explanations); or by the sometimes prevailing dominance of macro-economics (where individual deviations from rationality may be negligible).

The situation seems to have changed considerably: In experimental economics (see Roth, 1995a, for a selective historical survey) one designs laboratory experiments resembling as closely as possibly the formerly only (game) theoretically analyzed market models to explore actual decision behavior. At least the orthodox assumption that participants are guided purely by material incentives is, furthermore, convincingly rejected. Unlike the former empirical (and often experimental) findings in psychology this research (see, for instance Kagel and Roth, 1995) is now considered as a serious challenge of the prevailing rational choice approach. The reactions to these findings differ, however, in methodology.

One reaction (see e.g. Bolton, 1991; Bolton and Ockenfels, 2000; Fehr and Schmidt, 1999; Geneakopolous, Pearce, and Stacchetti, 1989; Rabin, 1993) is to maintain the rational choice-approach and to let the experimental results only question whether the (game) model is adequately representing the laboratory experiment. More generally: The rules, e.g. preferences, are "repaired" so that optimal behavior is in line with experimental observations. Güth (1995) therefore speaks of neoclassical repairs. Such attempts do not question rational forward looking deliberation but stress the imperfect control (e.g. by monetary incentives) of what determines experimental behavior. Of course, such repairs are not completely ad hoc but are suggested by naturally arising concerns.

A very different reaction is to substitute forward looking deliberation ("the shadow of the future") by pure adaptation to past results ("the shadow of the past"). Here the cognitive requirements are minor (in reinforcement learning whatever was good in the past is seen as good, in genetic evolution no cognition is needed). The possible adaptation dynamics depend, of course, on the information feedback (reinforcement learning relies on past own success, imitation, for instance, on comparing own and others' success). In our view, such denial of forward looking deliberation is empirically as false as perfect decision rationality: Human decision makers always try to cognitively perceive their decision environment so that they can relate likely consequences to behavior. This is not only true for mankind but also for the more developed species (e.g. mammals) in the animal kingdom (see, for instance, de Waal, 1982, and Flack and de Waal, 2000).

Theoretically it is quite understandable to confront the rational choice-approach with a purely adaptive one which is, furthermore, the orthodox assumption when analyzing animal behavior. There may even exist rare situations where homo sapiens knows so little about his decision environment that all what he can do is to repeat what has been better or good in the past. But such situations are typically not the ones for which decision (or game) theory has been developed. The true challenge is to describe how at best boundedly rational decision makers rely on past results in order to improve their cognitive representation of the decision problem and how they try to predict the likely consequences of certain decision alternatives based on such continuously updated mental models.

Earlier empirical studies suggest some ideas about how such decision making – combining path dependence and forward looking deliberation – could be organized (see Güth, 2000, for a discussion and a general framework). But any such attempt will have to rely heavily on speculation since too little is known to guide one's intuitions. To overcome this lack of facts the tradition of robust learning experiments has been initiated where, of course, other experimental studies should be considered too, especially those which confront their participants with many choice problems in the form of within-subjects designs.

Robust learning experiments provide evidence for both effects, namely for

- boundedly rational forward looking deliberation to predict the likely consequences of decision alternatives and
- adaptation to past experiences when feedback information is available.

In these experiments participants are confronted with several decision environments, e.g. with structurally different games, based on the same decision format. Forward looking deliberation is revealed by anticipation of changing rules (of the game) and by adaptation to past success since participants play the same game repeatedly. The evidence should make it clear that any reasonable behavioral decision or game theory should be based on a cognitive representation of the decision environment, which is continuously updated in the light of past experiences and which allows to assess the likely consequences of decision alternatives.

In the tradition of metastudies we review robust learning experiments of bidding behavior (section 2), repeated trust games (section 3), endogenous timing in bilateral negotiations (section 4), and alternative offer bargaining (section 5). Finally (section 6) we briefly discuss how to combine forward looking deliberation and adaptation to past success when modeling boundedly rational decision behavior.

2. Auctions and Fair Division Games

Bidding behavior is a favorite topic in experimental economics (see for a selective survey Kagel, 1995). We will focus here on sealed bid–experiments in which a single object is to be allocated and for which each potential buyer has an independent private value. Güth, Ivanova-Stenzel, Königstein, and Strobel (1999) investigate four different allocation rules or game types (see Table 12.1): First Price Auction (A1), Second Price Auction (A2), First Price Fair Division Game (F1) and Second Price Fair Division Game (F2). Fair division games differ from auctions since the price at which the object is sold is equally distributed among all bidders instead of being earned by an outside agent, the seller. Allocating inheritance is a real life situation which resembles a fair division game. The object is collectively owned by the heirs who, in many cases, are the only bidders. Similar problems result when a joint venture is terminated (for an experimental study on a related topic see Franciosi, Isaac, Pingry, and Reynolds, 1993).

Table 12.1. The four game types.

Price Rule	*Auction*	*Fair Division Game*
price = highest bid	A1	F1
price = 2nd highest bid	A2	F2

Table 12.2. Bidding function, expected price and expected payoff for risk neutral bidders.

Price	*Auction*	*Fair Division Game*
highest bid	$b_i^*(v_i) = \frac{n-1}{n} v_i$ $E(p^*) = \frac{n-1}{n+1}$ $E(\pi_i^*(v_i)) = \frac{v_i^n}{n}$	$b_i^*(v_i) = \frac{n}{n+1} v_i$ $E(p^*) = \left(\frac{n}{n+1}\right)^2$ $E(\pi_i^*(v_i)) = \frac{v_i^n}{n} + \frac{n-1}{n(n+1)}$
2nd highest bid	$b_i^*(v_i) = v_i$ $E(p^*) = \frac{n-1}{n+1}$ $E(\pi_i^*(v_i)) = \frac{v_i^n}{n}$	$b_i^*(v_i) = \frac{n}{n+1} v_i + \frac{1}{n+1}$ $E(p^*) = \frac{n^2+1}{(n+1)^2}$ $E(\pi_i^*(v_i)) = \frac{v_i^n}{n} + \frac{n-1}{n(n+1)}$

a) Design

Let v_i be a bidder's private value for the object to be sold, and suppose v_i is drawn for each player $i = 1, ..., n$ independently from a uniform distribution on the unit interval. For risk neutral bidders the equilibrium bid function $b_i^*(v_i)$, expected equilibrium price $E(p^*)$ and expected equilibrium payoff $E(\pi_i^*(v_i))$ are listed in Table 12.2 (see Güth and van Damme, 1986, for the derivation of results).

In the experiment the private values $\widetilde{v}_i$ did not vary continuously but were drawn from the set

$$\widetilde{V} = \{50, 60, 70, 80, 90, 100, 110, 120, 130, 140, 150\} \tag{12.1}$$

with all values $\widetilde{v}_i \in \widetilde{V}$ being equally likely. Transforming bids $\widetilde{b}_i$ and values $\widetilde{v}_i$ via

$$v_i = \frac{\widetilde{v}_i - 50}{100} \text{ and } b_i = \frac{\widetilde{b}_i - 50}{100}$$

(should) yield data in $[0, 1]$. Thus the theoretical benchmark in Table 12.2 neglects mainly discreteness.

Within a session each subject participated in 36 consecutive games of the four different types. 9 subjects formed a session group. In each of the 36 periods they were randomly partitioned into 3 groups of 3 bidders. The number of bidders involved in each game ($n = 3$) was commonly known but not their identity. All subjects in all sessions played the same sequence of games. In periods $t = 1$ to 3 they played A1, in $t = 4$ to 6 then A2, from $t = 7$ to 9 the game type was F2 and in $t = 9$ to 12 it was F1. This comprised the first block of 12 games. Then they played block 2 (periods 13 to 24) and 3 (periods 25 to 36) in the same sequence as block 1.

In each game participants had to submit a complete bidding strategy (bid vector), i.e. a bid $b_i(v_i)$ for each of the 11 values $v_i \in V$. The actual value v_i' was drawn thereafter. Payments were determined according to the game rules and the submitted bidding strategies. Subjects were informed on screen about v_i', whether or not they became the buyer, about the price p at which the object was sold and about their own payoff π_i. Then the next round started.

Each game type applied 9 times. In the first of these 9 plays the bid screen was blank and each subject had to enter a new vector of 11 bids (one for each $v_i \in V$). In later periods the last bid vector for the same game type was displayed as default. It could be revised or submitted as it is. Altogether we ran 6 sessions and collected 1944 bidding strategies (54 subjects times 36 games).

b) Results

If subjects learn something, their bid functions should approach some stable individual bid function. Each subject i played each type of game 9 times. For every type we will refer to the bid function in the 9th play as i's final bid function. Hence the final bid functions of game type A1, A2, F2, and F1 are $b_{i,27}(v_i)$, $b_{i,30}(v_i)$, $b_{i,33}(v_i)$, and $b_{i,36}(v_i)$, respectively. To measure bid function adjustments for game type A1 we calculated separately for each individual the Euclidean distance $D_i^{\text{A1}}(t) \equiv \|b_{it}(v_i) - b_{i,27}(v_i)\|$ between i's bid function $b_{it}(v_i)$ in period t and i's final bid function where $t \in \{1, 2, 3, 13, 14, 15, 25, 26\}$, i.e. t is a period in which game type A1 was played. Analogously we calculated $D_i^{\text{A2}}(t)$, $D_i^{\text{F2}}(t)$, and $D_i^{\text{F1}}(t)$. An adjustment process is monotone if $D_i^j(t)$ with $j \in \{\text{A1,A2,F2,F1}\}$ is decreasing in t. A monotone adjustment process is called 'convergent' if $D_i^j(t)$ decreases more rapidly in earlier than in later periods, i.e. if $D_i^j(t)$ is convex. Monotone and (even more) converging processes will be interpreted as evidence for learning.

Table 12.3. Classification of adjustment processes for different game types.

Adjustment Process	*Game Type* A1	A2	F2	F1
Monotone	92%	95%	96%	100%
Monotone and Convergent	61%	69%	74%	70%
Monotone and Not Convergent	31%	26%	22%	30%
Not Monotone	8%	5%	4%	0%
Sum (mon. and non–mon.)	100%	100%	100%	100%

For classification of the observed processes we used slightly weaker criteria than those described above to allow for some error. Specifically, we fitted a piecewise–linear regression to the data with $D_i^j(t)$ as dependent and t as independent variable, allowing for a kink after 4 (out of the 8) periods. Accordingly, a process is monotone if both slope coefficients are negative. If in addition the coefficient is smaller in absolute value for later periods, the process is convergent.

Table 12.3 displays the relative frequencies of monotone, respectively convergent adjustment processes. In between 61% and 74% of the adjustment processes one observes convergence; the corresponding interval for monotonicity is 92% to 100%. Although we do not know yet which behavior subjects learn, we know that they do learn something.

While in each game each subject had to enter a complete bid function, only one private value v_i' was actually drawn. So only the bid submitted for this value $b_i(v_i')$ was payoff relevant. Accordingly, the informational feedback received by individual i after each game — i.e., i's value v_i', the price p, whether or not i bought the object and i's profit — might suggest whether $b_i(v_i')$ should be adjusted in future periods. But it does not tell anything regarding bids $b_i(v_i'')$ for other values $v_i'' \neq v_i'$. A naturally arising question is therefore whether bid functions were adjusted only 'locally' at v_i' or rather 'globally' at all values.

Figure 12.1 shows frequency distributions for the number of bid function changes for the different game types. If the number of changes is 11, a bid vector is changed in each component. We observe that if a bid function is changed at all[1], it is simultaneously changed at all values in most cases. Thus bid functions are adjusted globally rather than locally.

While the game rules differed between the 4 game types, the format of subjects' decisions were the same. Figure 12.2 shows that decision time is first high and then decreases. If subjects followed a non–cognitive learning approach, we do not see why decisions should take less time in the end than in the middle of the sequence. Furthermore, Figure 12.2 shows that decision time 'jumps up' whenever the game type changes; i.e. at periods 1, 4, 7, 10, ...34.

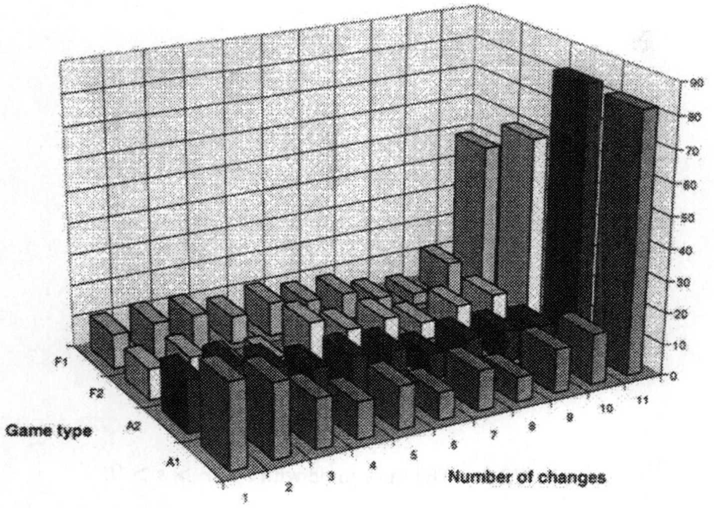

Figure 12.1. Frequency distributions for the number of bid function changes for the different game types.

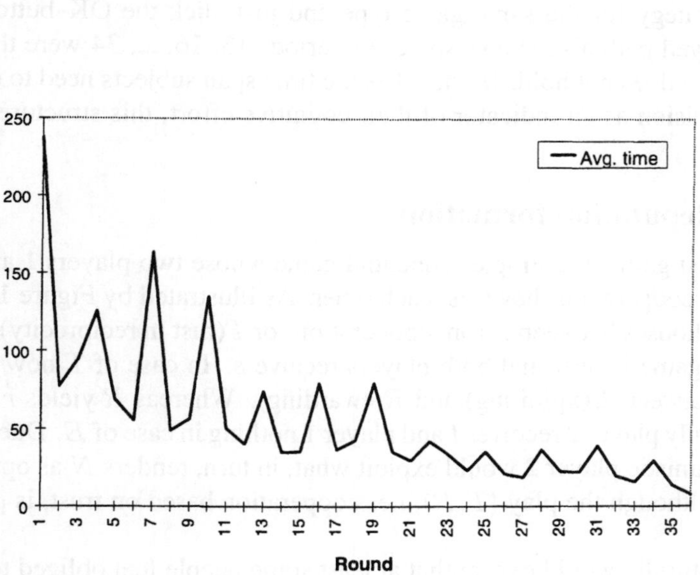

Figure 12.2. Average decision time by periods 1 to 36.

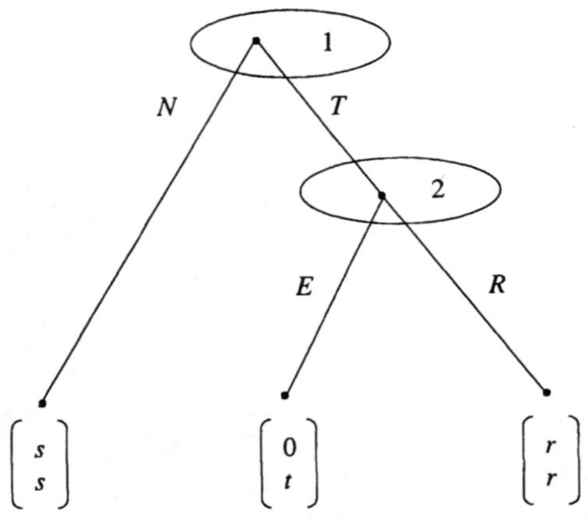

Figure 12.3. The trust game with $t > r > s > 0$.

Within the first block (periods 1, 4, 7, and 10) this is natural since subjects had to type in a new bid vector; in later periods, however, they could rely on their former strategy for the same game type and just click the OK–button. But, the displayed path also shows spikes in periods 13, 16, ..., 34 were the above explanation does not hold. If one takes the time span subjects need to come up with a decision as an indicator of their cognitive effort, this structure is quite plausible.

3. Reputation formation

The trust game is a simple sequential game whose two players 1 and 2 can profitably cooperate if they trust each other. As illustrated by Figure 12.3, first player 1 chooses between N(on–cooperation) or T(rust in reciprocity). In case of N the game is over and both players receive s. In case of T now player 2 decides between E(xploiting) and R(ewarding). Whereas R yields r for both players, only player 2 receives t and player 1 nothing in case of E. Due to $t > r$ an opportunistic player 2 would exploit what, in turn, renders N as optimal for player 1 although the play (T, R), i.e. cooperation based on trust, is preferred by both.

One naturally would expect that at least some people feel obliged to reward a trusting player 1. If such rewarding behavior by player 2 cannot be excluded, reputation equilibria (see Kreps, Milgrom, Roberts, and Wilson, 1982) predict that even an opportunistic player 2 will at least initially mimic such a rewarding player 2 when the trust game is played repeatedly by the same partners. By imitating an always rewarding player 2 such an opportunistic player 2 strategically manipulates the reputation (the conditional probability) of being of the always rewarding type. This may induce player 1 to continue initial cooperation in the course of the finitely repeated trust game.

a) Design

The main treatment of Anderhub, Engelmann, and Güth (forthcoming) explicitly introduces the possibility of a (second mover) type who always feels obliged to reward trust. Trust is automatically rewarded with probability p whereas with complimentary probability $1 - p$ player 2 is free to choose. Actually when trust was automatically rewarded, one did not encounter a human player 2 but a robot strategy. The instructions did not explicitly mention that the automatically rewarding player 2 is a robot (without indicating the presence of a real partner either). We conducted a control treatment with no automatically rewarding type of player 2, i.e. $p = 0$. Apart from this modification the design was the same. Participants choose mixed strategies to test the qualitative and quantitative predictions of reputation equilibria also on the individual level (and not just for the entire population).

The computerized experiment always relied on

$$s = \frac{1}{2}, r = \frac{3}{4}, t = 1, \text{ and } p = \begin{cases} \frac{1}{3} \text{ in the main treatment} \\ 0 \text{ in the control treatment.} \end{cases}$$

Robust learning concerns the number m of successive periods of play by the same two partners. Let y_t (x_t) denote the probability of reward R (trust T) in period t of the repeated game. The m periods of the basic trust game define one (repeated) game. Each participant played successively several repeated trust games with changing partners where the numbers of repetitions were

$$m = 3,\ 6,\ 2,\ 10,\ 3 \text{ and } 6.$$

To inspire learning a participant constantly assumed the role of player 1 or player 2. In each new repeated game of the main treatment it was again randomly decided whether or not a particular player 1 was matched with a real player 2 or not. A participant had to specify the probabilities in percent for his two decision alternatives.

Reputation equilibria are perfect or sequential equilibria, i.e. strategy vectors which prescribe locally optimal behavior for all choices of all players (Selten, 1975; Kreps and Wilson, 1982). Now a finitely repeated trust game usually has many possible choice situations (information sets) for which a reputation equilibrium has to specify unambiguously the decision behavior although most choice situations will be unreached by equilibrium play. To avoid the lengthy description of the unique reputation equilibria for the various numbers m of rounds only the plays, which they imply, are given. We do this by listing the action sequences $A_1 = (...,...)$ and $A_2 = (...,...)$ of players 1 and 2 in the form (A_1, A_2) for $m = 2$, 3, 6 and 10:

$$\begin{aligned}
m=2: &\quad ((N_1,N_2),(y_1=\tfrac{1}{4},E_2))\\
m=3: &\quad ((T_1,x_2=\tfrac{1}{2},x_3=\tfrac{1}{2}),(y_1=\tfrac{5}{8},y_2=\tfrac{2}{5},E_3))\\
m=6: &\quad ((T_1,T_2,T_3,T_4,x_5=\tfrac{1}{2},x_6=\tfrac{1}{2}),(R_1,R_2,R_3,y_4=\tfrac{5}{8},y_5=\tfrac{2}{5},E\\
m=10: &\quad ((T_1,T_2,T_3,T_4,T_5,T_6,T_7,T_8,x_9=\tfrac{1}{2},x_{10}=\tfrac{1}{2}),\\
&\quad (R_1,R_2,R_3,R_4,R_5,R_6,R_7,y_8=\frac{5}{8},y_9=\frac{2}{5},E_{10}))
\end{aligned}$$

Only when $y_t \in (0,1)$ player 2 is properly mixing between reward (R_t) and exploit (E_t). Similarly, only when $x_t \in (0,1)$ player 1 is truly randomizing between non-cooperation (N_t) or trust (T_t). Independent of m in the range $m \geq 3$ the mixing phase of both players extends over two periods, namely the last two periods for player 1 and the third and second to last period for player 2.

To exclude unwarranted repeated game effects resulting from playing repeatedly (the same) games, a participant confronted a new partner in each (repeated) game. Also indirect reputation effects were prevented by the matching procedure. More specifically, for each session 9 players 1 and 6 players 2 were invited and were matched accordingly. The 5 sessions of the main treatment thus provide data of altogether 45 players 1 and 30 players 2. Each of the $p = 0$ sessions of the control–treatment involved 6 players 1 and 6 players 2. Since the behavior of two participants cannot be regarded as independent, only the 5 sessions in the main treatment and the 3 sessions in the control treatment qualify as independent observations.

b) Results

With the help of $x_t(i)$ and $y_t(i)$ as a participant i's probability of trust (T_t), respectively of reward (R_t) in period t the mean probability of trust and reward in period t can be defined as

$$x_t = \sum_i x_t(i)/45 \text{ and } y_t = \sum_i y_t(i)/30,$$

where 45 and 30 are the numbers of participants playing the role of player 1 or player 2, respectively. How x_t and y_t develop over time is illustrated by Figure 12.4. Here only the x_t–choices of the players 1 confronted with real players 2 are considered. Since participants play successively repeated games with $m = 3$, 6, 2, 10, 3, and 6 periods, they play altogether 30 periods. A vertical dashed line in Figure 12.4 indicates the last period of a (repeated) game. The end or termination effect (x_t drops when the last period of the game is near) is minor only for the first two games. Afterwards there is always a sharp decline of x_t. A reason for this is suggested by the development of y_t. From the end of

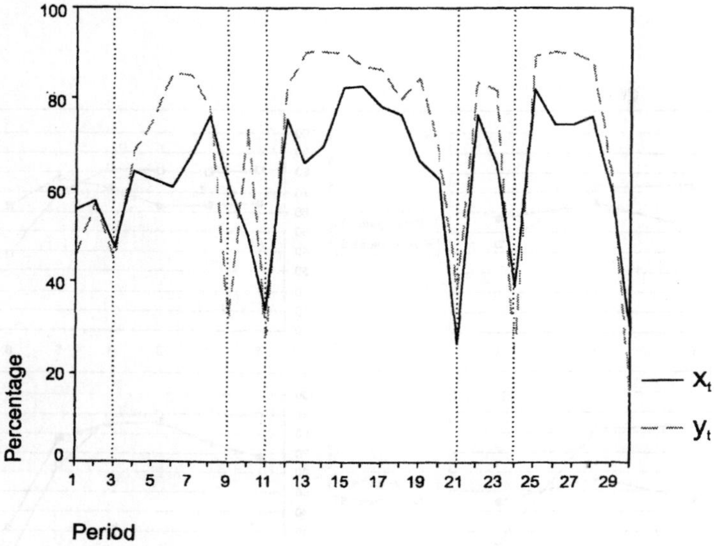

Figure 12.4. Average trust- and reward-probabilities per period.

the second game on (period 9) players 2 on average reward only rarely in the last period of a (repeated) game.

How did players 1 react to being exploited? 10 of the 45 players 1 were never exploited before the last period of a game. 10 of the remaining 35 players 1 never trusted again in the same game after being exploited, whereas 25 did. These 25 clearly violate a basic requirement of reputation equilibria.

To check for experience effects one can compare the 1st and the 5th as well as the 2nd and the 6th repeated game extending over 3 and 6 periods, respectively. In Figure 12.5 (left) we have confronted the x_t–development of the 1st game (solid squares) with the one of the 5th game (hollow squares) in the upper part and the y_t–development in the lower part. The analogous comparison of the 2nd and 6th game can be found in Figure 12.5 (right). While average trust– and reward rates hardly ever increase in the 5th and 6th game, this is not the case for the inexperienced participants in the 1st and 2nd game. For $m = 6$ the learning effects (players 1 learn to trust less and players 2 to exploit when the end is near) shift behavior into the direction of rational behavior. Average trust is initially nearly constant ($x_t \sim .8$ for $t = 1, 2, 3, 4$) before it drops to $x_6 \sim .4$. Similarly there is a sharp decline from $y_t \sim .9$ for $t = 1, 2, 3, 4$ to $y_6 < .2$.

Table 12.4 gives the results of a Wilcoxon–test comparing the individual decisions in corresponding periods for different games of equal length. The learning from earlier to later games towards the normative benchmark is sig-

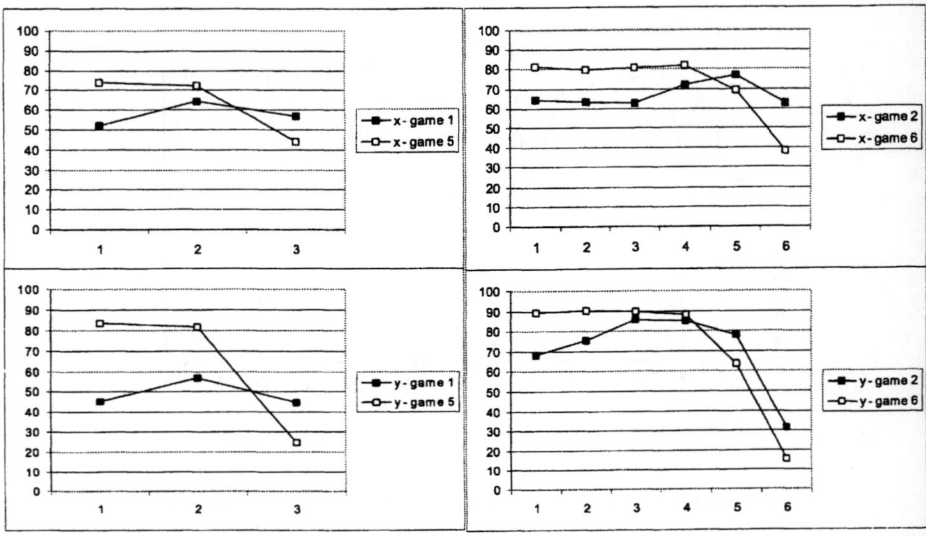

Figure 12.5. Average trust (top) and reward (bottom) rates for games with 3 (left) and 6 (right) periods.

Table 12.4. Wilcoxon–test for single periods in games of equal length.

player	*games*	*games 1 and 5*			*games 2 and 6*					
	period	1	2	3	1	2	3	4	5	6
1	*Z*	–2.750	–0.679	–1.391	–2.301	–2.159	–2.837	–1.426	–1.314	–2.626
	sign. *p*	.006*	.497	.164	.021*	.031*	.005*	.154	.189	.009*
2	*Z*	–3.158	–2.432	–1.862	–2.812	–1.869	–1.051	–0.406	–1.647	–2.014
	sign. *p*	.002*	.015*	.063	.005*	.062	.293	.684	.100	.044*

nificant (5%–level) for the first period and both types of players, i.e. trust and reward increase significantly from game 1 to game 5 and from game 2 to game 6. For the last period of the 6 period games the opposite effect is significant for both types of players.

4. Endogenous timing in bilateral negotiations

Endogenous timing makes it possible to reduce the wide variety of bargaining or, more generally, decision processes and thus to predict more precisely what will happen. Parties do not only negotiate but also determine the process of bargaining (for endogenous timing see, for instance, Spencer and Brandner, 1992, Sadanand and Sadanand, 1996, and van Damme and Hurkens, 1999; for our experimental situation Güth and Ritzberger, 1998).

a) Design

In the experiment (Güth, Marchand, Rulliere, Zeiliger, 2000) two parties, players 1 and 2, can share a randomly determined pie p with $0 \leq p \leq 1$. The distribution governing the random choice of the available monetary reward p is

$$F(p) = p^a \text{ with } a > 0.$$

The positive parameter a is the only treatment variable. If a is small, the expected pie is small; if a is large, also the expected pie is large. Both players $i = 1, 2$ have two choices, namely to decide early (the choice E_i), i.e. before p is randomly selected, or to wait (the choice W_i) till after p is chosen and commonly known. After both players $i = 1, 2$ have simultaneously decided for E_i or W_i, the chosen constellation is announced, i.e. when actually negotiating both timing dispositions are commonly known.

How then do players bargain knowing the timing dispositions? In case of (E_1, E_2) both players $i = 1, 2$ state their demand d_i with $0 \leq d_i \leq 1$ before p is randomly chosen. For (W_1, W_2) the order is reversed: First p is randomly chosen and publicly announced, then both players $i = 1, 2$ choose their demands d_i with $0 \leq d_i \leq 1$. If i has chosen E_i and j $(\neq i)$ the timing W_j, first i chooses d_i before p is randomly chosen; knowing d_i as well as p then j finally determines his demand d_j.

Regardless of the timing dispositions the monetary payoffs depend on d_1, d_2, and p as follows: If $d_1 + d_2 > p$, both players receive nothing; otherwise each player i gets his demand d_i, i.e. a positive residual $p - d_1 - d_2$ is lost for the two parties.

The experiment distinguishes three parameters a, $a = 3$ yielding (E_1, E_2), $a = .5$ with (W_1, W_2), and $a = 1.2$ where both, (E_1, W_2) and (W_1, E_2), are strict equilibria (of the early decision stage) according to the normative benchmark solution assuming commonly known risk neutrality (for more general results see Güth and Ritzberger, 2000). Participants played repeatedly each of the three treatments with randomly changing partners. Random matching was

Table 12.5. Average behavior.

		rounds 1-24 relative demands				rounds 25-48 relative demands				Theoretical predictions		
		d	σ^2	c	n	d	σ^2	c	n	D_E^*	d^*	c^*
E, E	$a = 3$	.533	.019	.60	40	.542	.022	.74	39	.37	.49	.41
	$a = 1.2$	.529	.032	.77	13	.467	.018	.77	13	.34	.62	.63
	$a = .5$	.955	.344	1	7	.464	.203	.88	8	.32	.96	.80
W, W	$a = 3$	.500	.004	.07	72	.500	.003	.04	72	$p/2$	.5	0
	$a = 1.2$	.684	1.216	.14	106	.483	.005	.06	110	$p/2$	.5	0
	$a = .5$	.492	.011	.08	118	.496	.006	.13	126	$p/2$	.5	0
		d_E ; A	σ_E^2	c	n	d_E ; A	σ_E^2	c	n	D_E^*	d_E^*	c^*
E, W	$a = 3$	.70;.94	.059	.30	76	.70;.78	.020	.59	81	.63	.84	.25
	$a = 1.2$	.72;.86	.083	.59	73	.62 ;.86	.037	.65	69	.52	.95	.46
	$a = .5$	.77;1	.282	.73	67	.56 ;.95	.290	.67	58	.44	1.33	.66

restricted to groups of eight participants. To limit repeated game effects 16 participants were invited without telling them how rematching was restricted. More specifically, participants played 4 rounds of $a = 3-$games, then 4 rounds of $a = 1.2-$games, and finally 4 rounds of $a = .5-$games. These 12 successive rounds establish one cycle which was repeated 3 times. Thus each group of 8 participants generates a data file of 48 successive rounds with 4 games per round.

b) Results

To describe how bargaining outcomes, i.e. demands and payoffs, depend on the timing of decisions, i.e. EE (both early), EW (one early, one late), or WW (both late), and on experience, i.e., the first 24 rounds are compared with the later ones. "D" stands for absolute and d for relative demands. The 'relative demands' "d" $= d_E$ in Table 12.5 for (E, E) and the first component in case of (E, W) measure what a party demands in proportion to the 'expected pie' which, of course, depends on the parameter a . For E, W the proportion of accepted $d = d_E-$offers by $W-$partners, denoted by A, is reported. In case of W, W the relative demand d is the share $d = D/p$ of the actually available pie. Further $\sigma^2 = \sigma_E^2$ denotes the variance of d_E and c the conflict ratio for the altogether n plays.

For all levels of parameter a the order of the conflict ratio c is

$$c(E, E) > c(E, W) > c(W, W)$$

and for all timing constellations $(t_1, t_2) = (E, E), (W, W), (E, W)$ one has:

$$c(a = .5) > c(a = 3) \text{ for rounds 1-24}$$
$$\text{and } c(a = .5) > c(a = 1.2) > c(a = 3) \text{for rounds 25-48.}$$

Table 12.6. Comparisons of the d_E-distributions for (E, E) and (E, W).

Kolmogorov Smirnov Test	*rounds 1-24*	*rounds 25-48*
$a = 3$	$p < .001$	$p < .001$
$a = 1.2$	$p < .001$	$p < .01$
$a = .5$	$p = ns$	$p = ns$

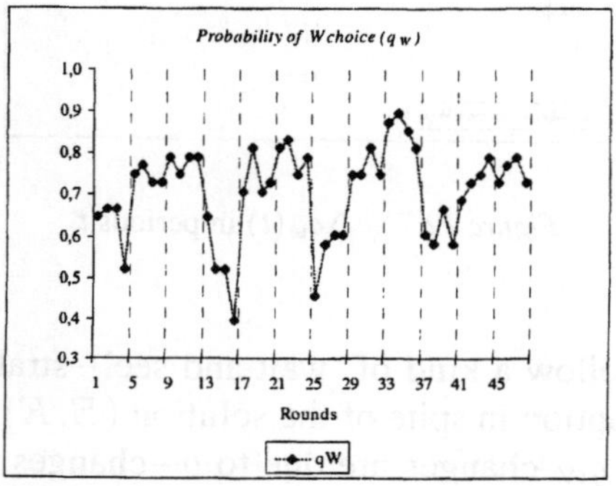

Figure 12.6. W-share in periods t.

How does a party react to being the (only) preemptor and how does this depend on the treatment variable a and on experience? To test this statistically the distribution of relative demands d_E for (E, E) is compared with the d_E distribution for (E, W) separately for each level a and early (rounds 1-24) and late (rounds 25-48) plays (see Table 12.6). Similar to the theoretical prediction the $E-$partners demand significantly more in case of $a = 3$ and $a = 1.2$ when they are the only preemptor in their group. There are two reasons for conflict in the $EW-$constellation, namely rejection by the $W-$partner or $d_E > p$. The majority of conflicts is caused by excessive demands ($d_E > p$). Rejections by $W-$partners are rare and irregular.

To illustrate the dynamics of timing decisions Figure 12.6 displays the relative frequency q_W of waiting (the $W-$choice) for all 48 successive rounds. The vertical dotted lines indicate a change of the treatment variable a where the order is always first $a = 3$, then $a = 1.2$, and finally $a = .5$. Figure 12.6 reveals that the major changes of q_W are caused by $a-$changes, especially when switching from $a = 3$ to $a = .5$.

Figure 12.7 illustrates the q_W-development by its deviation from the predicted timing disposition, i.e. $\Delta q_W(t) = q_W^{obs}(a) - q_W^*(a)$ where we set $q_W^*(a) = .5$ for $a = 1.2$. There are large deviations from the theoretical predictions, especially when $a = 3$ and $a = 1.2$. In the $a = 3-$situation 58%

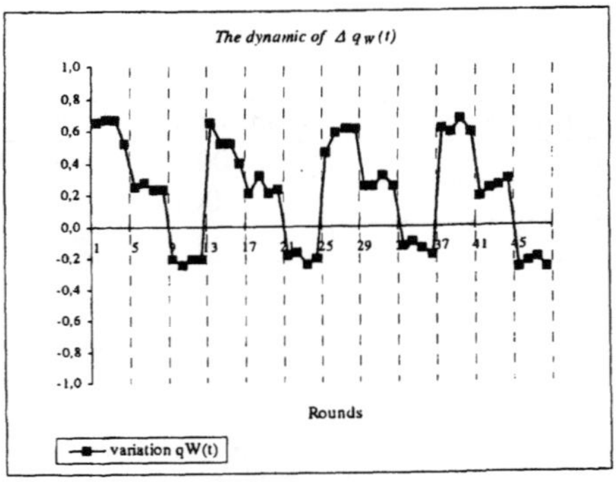

Figure 12.7. $\Delta q_w(t)$ in periods t.

of the participants' follow a kind of 'wait and see'—strategy, i.e. they prefer flexibility over preemption in spite of the solution (E, E).

How much of the q_W changes are due to a—changes is tested via a linear regression

$$q_W = \alpha + \underline{\alpha}_{I(a=.5)} + \overline{\alpha}_{I(a=3)} + \beta.t$$

with treatment dummies where $I(.)$ denotes the indicator function (assuming the value 1 for $a = .5$, respectively $a = 3$, and 0 otherwise) and with $a = 1.2$ as the base line. The result

$q_W =$	$.75+$	$.049_{I(a=.5)}-$	$.174_{I(a=3)}+$	$.0001\,t$,	$R^2 = .701$
	$t = 31.338$	$t = 2.09$	$t = 7.395$	$t = .019$	
	$p < .0001$	$p < .05$	$p < .0001$	$p = .828$	

reveals significant treatment dummies whereas the time coefficient β is insignificant (separate regressions $q_W = \alpha^a + \beta^a \cdot t$ for $a = .5$, 1.2, and 3 also yield insignificant time coefficients β^a).

How the payoff difference in E, W—groups feeds back on the timing disposition can be assessed by Figure 12.8 (for changes from W to E). The thin curves represent the average difference in earnings between the E— and the W—partner in period $t-1$ and the bold curves the proportion of participants who were the W—partner in (E, W)-pairs in period $t-1$ and decided to switch to E in t. According to Figure 12.8 most of the switches are driven by earning differentials (the two curves are rather parallel) whereas most (86%) of the changes from E to W cannot be explained by earning differentials.

5. Alternating offer bargaining

Alternating offer bargaining is a familiar topic in experimental economics. Starting with Binmore, Shaked, and Sutton (1985) it has been debated whether

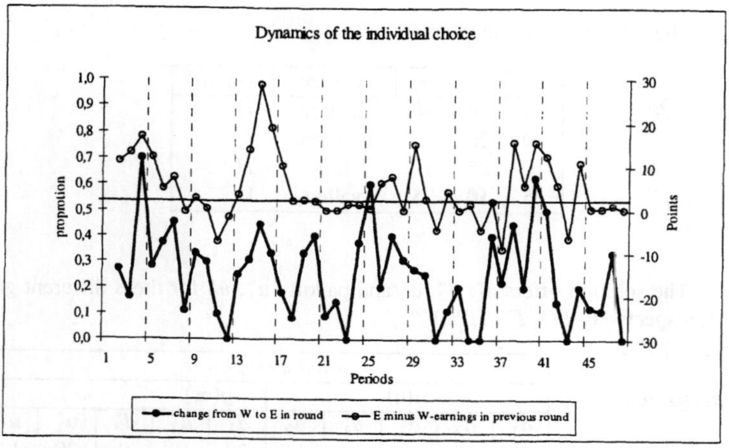

Figure 12.8. Changing from W to E after being in an $E, W-$pair.

and how actual bargaining behavior differs from game theoretic predictions (see Güth, 1995, and Roth, 1995b, for surveys).

a) Design

Let the maximal number of bargaining rounds be 3. Over time the "pie" p_t with $t = 1, 2, 3$ can either decrease or increase. Whereas a shrinking pie reflects the well-known costs of delaying an agreement like waste of time, starting too late cooperating etc., an increasing pie can be justified by the fact that later agreements are more adequate due to better information or superior incentives. Anderhub, Güth, and Marchand (2001) do not only rely on the two monotonic developments, but also allow for a "hill" (the "pie" is largest in round $t = 2$) and a "valley" (the "pie" is smallest in round $t = 2$). The vector (p_1, p_2, p_3) of pies p_t in periods $t = 1, 2, 3$ for each of these four different "pie"-developments is given in Table 12.7.

The four cases (p_1, p_2, p_3) are played as ordered in Table 12.7, first twice with and then twice without ultimatum power. Here (no) ultimatum power means that an offer can (not) be declared to be final (Güth, Ockenfels, and Wendel, 1993). Thus participants first learn to play a usual alternating offer game before commanding ultimatum power. We refer to the altogether 16 games (4 vectors $(p_1, p_2, p_3) \times 4$ successive plays) as a cycle. Participants play 3 such cycles, i.e. altogether 48 bargaining games.

Players 1 and 2 alternate in proposing an agreement which the other party can then accept or reject. Acceptance always ends the game with the proposed payoff distribution, a vector (u_1, u_2) with $p_t \geq u_1, u_2 \geq 0$ and $u_1 + u_2 = p_t$ where the pie p_t is what can be distributed in round $t = 1, 2, 3$. If $t < 3$ and the offer $p_t - d_t$ to the other party (d_t is what the proposer demands for himself)

Table 12.7. The four "pie"-developments.

p_1	p_2	p_3	*nickname*	*symbol*
30	20	10	decline	D
10	20	30	increase	I
10	25	10	hill	H
25	10	25	valley	V

Table 12.8. The solution offers d_1^*, d_2^*, d_3^* and payoffs u_1^*, u_2^* for the 8 different games D^y, I^y, H^y, V^y, respectively D^n, I^n, H^n, V^n.

(p_1, p_2, p_3)-type	*ultimatum power*									
	n(o)					y(es)				
	d_1^*	d_2^*	d_3^*	u_1^*	u_2^*	d_1^*	d_2^*	d_3^*	u_1^*	u_2^*
$D = (30, 20, 10)$	**19**	10	9	19	11	**29**	19	9	29	1
$I = (10, 20, 30)$	10	20	**29**	29	1	**9**	19	29	9	1
$H = (10, 25, 10)$	10	**15**	9	10	15	**9**	24	9	9	1
$V = (25, 10, 25)$	24	10	**24**	24	1	**24**	9	24	24	1

is not an ultimatum, rejection leads to round $t + 1$ where now p_{t+1} can be allocated by the rejecting party. If $t = 3$ or if for $t < 3$ the offer $p_t - d_t$ is an ultimatum, bargaining ends in conflict with each party receiving 0-payoff. In round

$t = 1$: player 1 chooses d_1, i.e. 1 proposes, 2 responds,
$t = 2$: player 2 chooses d_2, i.e. 2 proposes, 1 responds,
$t = 3$: player 1 chooses d_3, i.e. 1 proposes, 2 responds.

Each of the four developments D, I, H and V can be played with proposers having ultimatum power, the games D^y, I^y, H^y, and V^y, or not, the games D^n, I^n, H^n, and V^n. For each of the 4 developments D, I, H, and V the left column of Table 12.8 describes the solution demands (d_1^*, d_2^*, d_3^*) and their payoff implications u_1^* and u_2^* for player 1 and 2. If ultimatum power is available, it will always be used, i.e. each proposal d_t^* for $t = 1, 2, 3$ and the games D^y, I^y, H^y, and V^y is an ultimatum. Thus with ultimatum power bargaining always stops in round $t = 1$ whereas this is true only for D if no ultimatum power is available. The round t^* in which the agreement is reached is indicated in Table 12.8 by bf fat demands d_t^*.

The benchmark solution assumes that only integer offers are possible and that in case of indifference a responder always rejects. Whereas in the n-games D^n, I^n, H^n, and V^n the outcome is always efficient in the sense that u_1^* and u_2^* add up to the maximal "pie", this is only true for the y-games D^y and V^y when p_1 is largest. The computerized experiment involved 6 sessions with 12 participants each.

b) Results

Experience effects can be detected by comparing the average earnings of both players for the 3 cycles (the table in Figure 12.9 distinguishes by role, 1 or 2, by cycle (1st, 2nd, 3rd), game type (D, I, H, V, all games) and n(o) or y(es)-ultimatum power). According to the table in Figure 12.9 earnings are surprisingly constant over the three cycles when proposers command no ultimatum power. With ultimatum power average earnings increase significantly from the 1st to later cycles. It seems that the additional complexity due to ultimatum power of proposers (y) requires "learning to reach efficient agreements".

Average earnings are affected by

- the conflict rate
- the round of reaching an agreement
- the payoff distribution which is accepted.

The first aspect is illuminated by Table 12.9 listing the agreement, respectively conflict ratios as well as their absolute numbers (in the 3 cycles) for the 3 bargaining rounds separately for the n(o) and the y(es)-games. Most agreements occurred when the periodic pie is largest (in case of V this applies to the 1st and 3rd round) whereas game theory excludes conflict and predicts agreement for rounds with the largest periodic pie only in case of no ultimatum power (see Table 12.8). The fact that agreements are mostly achieved when the pie is largest partly (in case of no ultimatum power) confirms game theory and partly (with ultimatum power) rejects it.

The hypothesis that participants are simply efficiency-minded is questioned by the non-neglible numbers of conflict. Note that the data file consists of $6 \times 6 \times 6 = 216$ plays for each of the eight games types. Conflict frequency is 28 for D, 40 for I, 34 for H, and 45 for V when proposer have ultimatum power. For no ultimatum power the relative frequencies of conflict are .56 for D, .07 for I, .44 for H, and .25 for V. Only for game types D^y and V^y, when the 1st pie is largest, conflict occurs most frequently in the 1st round. Learning (measured by cycle) does not consistently reduce the frequency of conflict.

Since efficiency depends only weakly on the level of experience, Table 12.10 provides a fair impression of the overall efficiency

$$\delta = \frac{u_1 + u_2}{\max\{p_1, p_2, p_3\}}$$

for all eight game types. Only for the pie-dynamics I ultimatum power of proposers reduces efficiency. But none of the differences is significant. Also the differences between pie-dynamics are minor. As revealed by player 1's payoff shares

$$s = \frac{u_1}{u_1 + u_2},$$

Mean

		Role 1			Role 2			Both Roles		
		1st	2nd	3rd	1st	2nd	3rd	1st	2nd	3rd
Decrease	n	,47	,44	,49	,43	,40	,45	,45	,42	,47
	y	,41	,49	,49	,35	,41	,42	,38	,45	,45
Increase	n	,45	,49	,49	,41	,43	,43	,43	,46	,46
	y	,33	,45	,43	,29	,38	,37	,31	,41	,40
Hill	n	,42	,41	,41	,50	,49	,50	,46	,45	,46
	y	,34	,35	,36	,41	,47	,46	,38	,41	,41
Valley	n	,47	,48	,48	,40	,40	,41	,44	,44	,44
	y	,42	,40	,48	,34	,33	,39	,38	,36	,44
Total	n	,45	,45	,47	,43	,43	,45	,44	,44	,46
	y	,38	,42	,44	,35	,40	,41	,36	,41	,43

Figure 12.9. Average earnings as percentages of $\max\{p_1, p_2, p_3\}$ separated by game type, role and cycle.

Table 12.9. Conditional probability of reaching an agreement or conflict in round t (total numbers of 1st, 2nd, 3rd cycle in brackets).

	ultimatum power									
	$N(o)$				$Y(es)$					
	agreement				*agreement*			*conflict*		
	1	2	3 (agree. / conf.)		1	2	3	1	2	3
D	.80	.63	.44	.56	.82	.91	-	.13	.09	-
	(54,53,60)	(11,8,8)	(4,2,1)	(1,7,1)	(48,61,63)	(7,2,1)	(0,0,0)	(15,6,6)	(0,1,0)	(0,0,0)
I	.03	.06	.93	.07	.05	.08	.92	.01	.12	.08
	(4,1,1)	(7,4,1)	(54,61,63)	(5,4,5)	(5,6,0)	(6,3,6)	(38,54,52)	(3,0,0)	(10,5,9)	(8,2,3)
H	.04	.91	.56	.44	.06	.84	.50	.01	.15	.50
	(2,2,4)	(62,61,61)	(4,3,3)	(2,4,2)	(6,4,2)	(50,56,57)	(1,0,0)	(1,1,1)	(12,9,9)	(0,0,1)
V	.50	-	.75	.25	.68	-	.65	.22	.09	.35
	(38,34,32)	(0,0,0)	(23,27,30)	(9,9,8)	(49,45,49)	(0,0,0)	(4,6,12)	(11,15,7)	(1,2,0)	(5,2,2)

Table 12.10. Efficiency and relative payoff distribution δ and s.

	$N(o)$	$Y(es)$
	(δ, s)	(δ, s)
D	(.93,.52)	(.98,.54)
I	(.96,.53)	(.93,.54)
H	(.95,.46)	(.96,.45)
V	(1,.54)	(1,.55)

listed in Table 12.10, the proposer for the largest pie is always slightly favored. Altogether average payoff distributions are very fair (in the sense of $.45 \leq s \leq .55$).

6. Discussion

Each of the individual experiments, reviewed here, investigates already a broader spectrum of games:

- In section 2 bidding behavior is explored for the two most prominent price rules as well as for auctions and fair division tasks.
- Section 3 studies different numbers of repeating the basic trust game.
- Different random moves, determining the size of the pie, are examined in section 4.
- Section 5 considers structurally different (deterministic) pie developments as well as proposers with and without ultimatum power.

As such each individual study reveals that participants anticipate rule changes and that they are guided by earlier experiences. The two basic determinants of behavior, based on the situations studied in section 2, are illustrated by Figure 12.10: It shows for each of the 11 possible true values how bids are adjusted. Initially bids are often adjusted even when confronting the same game type repeatedly. But later major adjustments occur only when facing a new game. Evidently learning slows down rather soon (see the evidence for "convergence" in Table 12.3) whereas anticipation of new rules persists and becomes even stronger with experience. For the other studies a comprehensive illustration like in Figure 12.10 is less obvious.

All four studies support the major claim that human decision behavior is influenced by both, the shadow of the past (path dependence) as well as by the shadow of the future (forward looking deliberation): For section 2 this is illustrated by Figure 12.10. The claim is, however, also supported

- in section 3 by the more reasonable behavior when playing the same game again as well as by the systematic end effects,
- in section 4 by reacting to the differential payoffs in mixed pairs as well as by the different timing decisions for a large, medium, or small expected pie, and
- in section 5 where participants pay attention to ultimatum power and focus on the largest pie.

For the theory of boundedly rational decision making this means that one has to combine ideas

- how decision makers cognitively perceive their decision environment and update their cognitive model in the light of new information and

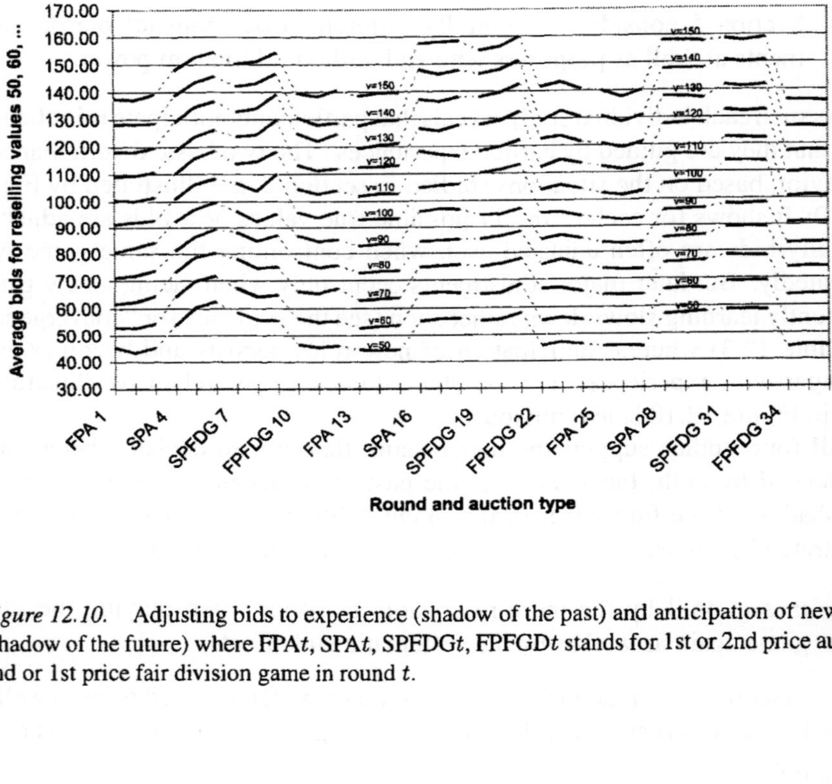

Figure 12.10. Adjusting bids to experience (shadow of the past) and anticipation of new rules (shadow of the future) where FPAt, SPAt, SPFDGt, FPFGDt stands for 1st or 2nd price auction, 2nd or 1st price fair division game in round t.

- how previous own and others' success (provided that such information feedback is available) will lead to behavioral adaptation.

Any comprehensive concept of bounded rationality has to rely on both aspects. Thus no simple learning or evolutionary dynamics will do. Similarly, no rational choice-approach which does not pay attention to the limited cognitive abilities of human decision makers meets both requirements. As the most developed species in the animal kingdom humans still rely on animal-like learning like reinforcement dynamics but also continuously try to develop causal models (of the world) allowing to predict the likely consequences of alternative ways of behavior.

Simple concepts of bounded rationality like satisfying (Simon, 1976, and Selten, 1998) do not yet meet such requirements. One would have to specify how aspirations are formed in the light of past experiences as well as of forward looking deliberations. This requires ideas like a "behavioral repertoire", e.g. in the form of managerial experiences and skills for qualitatively and quantitatively different decision environments, and a "hierarchy of decision considerations" progressing from simple (for less relevant decisions) to more demanding (for important decisions) types of deliberation (early and preliminary approaches are Güth, 2000, and Neisser, 1987).

What else can be learned by comparing the results of the different studies reviewed here? In highly complex situations like in sections 2 and 3, where incomplete information is crucial, learning seems to be more important at least initially. Only after experiencing previous plays participants seem to become aware of crucial (strategic) considerations like over-, respectively underbidding incentives or the risks and chances of (initial) trust.

Compared to this the bargaining games of section 4 and 5 require less learning since common norms, e.g. to aim at (efficient and) fair agreements, provide reliable guidance already for inexperienced participants although these bargaining games are partly more complex than those usually studied (see Roth, 1995b). In even simpler bargaining problems learning should matter even less (see Prasnikar and Roth, 1992, and Roth et al., 1991, for results supporting this conjecture).

There are other experiments which confront participants with more or less similar decision problems like robust learning experiments. Often the main attempt is to study how a certain structural aspect, e.g. a payoff or probability parameter, affects behavior. This is partly studied by confronting different groups of participants with the various decision problems (between subjects-designs) and partly by always relying on the same participants (within subjects-designs). The latter approach is closely related to robust learning experiments provided that participants decide often enough for observing learning effects. It is, however, hardly possible to review all such studies in addition to the more narrowly defined robust learning experiments, reported here.

Notes

1. A single subject plays each game type 9 times. The subject can thus change its bid function for each game in at most 8 periods (change periods). The maximal number of change periods per subject is therefore 32 and the maximal number of change periods per game type is 432 (54 subjects times 8). The percentages of change periods (observed change periods divided by maximal change periods times 100) are 54% in A1, 48% in A2, 34% in F2 and 33% in F1.

References

Anderhub, V., D. Engelmann, and W. Güth (forthcoming): An experimental study of the repeated trust game with incomplete information, *Journal of Economic Behavior and Organization*.

Anderhub, V., W. Güth, and N. Marchand (2001): Alternating offer bargaining experiments with varying institutional details, *Discussion Paper* 180, Humboldt-University of Berlin.

Binmore, K., A. Shaked, and J. Sutton (1985): Testing noncooperative bargaining theory: A preliminary study, *American Economic Review* 75 (5), 1178-1180.

Bolton, G. (1991): A comparative model of bargaining: Theory and evidence, *American Economic Review* 81, 1096-1136.

Bolton, G. and A. Ockenfels (2000): ERC - A theory of equity, reciprocity and competition, *American Economic Review* 90(1), 166-193.

de Wall, F. B. M. (1982): *Chimpanzee politics*, London.

Fehr, E. and K. M. Schmidt (1999): A theory of fairness, competition and cooperation, *Quarterly Journal of Economics* CXIV, 817-868.

Flack, J. C. and F. B. M. de Waal (2000): Any animal whatever: Darwinian building blocks of morality in monkeys and apes, *Journal of Consciousness Studies* 7 (1-2), 1-29.

Franciosi, R., R. M. Isaac, D. E. Pingry, S. S. Reynolds (1993): An Experimental Investigation of the Hahn-Noll Revenue Neutral Auction for Emmissions Licences, *Journal of Environmental Economics and Management* 24, 1-24.

Geanakoplos, J., D. Pearce, and E. Stacchetti (1989): Psychological games and sequential rationality, *Games and Economic Behavior* 1 (1), 60-79.

Güth, W. (1995): On ultimatum bargaining - A personal review, *Journal of Economic Behavior and Organization* 27, 329-344.

Güth, W. (2000): Boundedly rational decision emergence - A general perspective and some selective illustrations, *Journal of Economic Psychology* 21, 433-458.

Güth, W., P. Ockenfels, and M. Wendel (1993): Efficiency by trust in fairness? - Multiperiod ultimatum bargaining experiments with an increasing cake, *International Journal of Game Theory* 22, 51-73.

Güth, W. and E. van Damme (1986): A comparison of pricing rules for auctions and fair division games, *Social Choice and Welfare* 3, 177-198.

Güth, W. and R. Ritzberger (1998): Preemption or wait-and-see? - Endogenous timing in bargaining, *Working Paper*, Humboldt-University of Berlin.

Güth, W., R. Ivanova-Stenzel, M. Königstein, M. Strobel (1999): Learning to bid - An experimental study of bid function adjustments in auctions and fair division games, SFB *Discussion Paper* 70, Humboldt-University of Berlin.

Güth, W., N. Marchand, J.-L. Rulliere, and R. Zeiliger (2000): Preempt or wait! An experimental study of endogenous timing in bargaining, *Discussion Paper* 160, Humboldt-University of Berlin.

Kagel, J. H. (1995), Auctions: A Survey of Experimental Research, in: J. H. Kagel and A. E. Roth (eds.), *The Handbook of Experimental Economics*, Princeton (N.J.): Princeton University Press, 501-585.

Kagel, J. H. and A. E. Roth (1995): *The Handbook of Experimental Economics*, Princeton (N.J.): Princeton University Press.

Kreps, D., Milgrom, P., Roberts, J., and Wilson, R. (1982): Rational Cooperation in the Finitely Repeated Prisoner's Dilemma, *Journal of Economic Theory* 27, 245–252.

Neisser, U. (1987): *Concepts and conceptual development: Ecological and intellectual factors in categorization*, Cambridge/MA: Cambridge University Press.

Prasnikar, V. and A. E. Roth (1992): Considerations of fairness and strategy: Experimental data from sequential games, *Quarterly Journal of Economics* 107(3), 865-888.

Rabin, M. (1993). Incorporating fairness into game theory and economics, *American Economic Review* 83(5), 1281-1302.

Roth, A. E. (1995a). Introduction to experimental economics, in: *Handbook of Experimental Economics*, J. H. Kagel and A. E. Roth (eds.), Princeton, N.J.: Princeton University Press, 3-109.

Roth, A. E. (1995b): Bargaining experiments, in: *Handbook of Experimental Economics*, J. H. Kagel and A. E. Roth (eds.), Princeton, N.J.: Princeton University Press, 253-348.

Roth, A. E., V. Prasnikar, M. Okuno-Fujiwara, and S. Zamir (1991): Bargaining and market behavior in Jerusalem, Ljubljana, Pittsburgh, and Tokyo: An experimental study, *American Economic Review* 81, 1068-1095.

Sadanand, A. and V. Sadanand (1996): Firm scale and the endogenous timing of entry: A choice between commitment and flexibility, *Journal of Economic Theory* 70, 516-530.

Spencer, B. J. and J. A. Brandner (1992): Pre-commitment and flexibility - Applications to oligopoly theory, *European Economic Review* 36, 1601-1626.

Selten, R. (1998): Aspiration adaption theory, *Journal of Mathematical Psychology* 42, 191-214.

Simon, H. (1976): From substantive to procedural rationality, in: *Method and Appraisal in Economics*, S. J. Latsis (ed.), Cambridge/MA: Cambridge University Press; reprinted in: *Models of Bounded Rationality*, Boston/MA: MIT Press, 1982.
Van Damme, E. and S. Hurkens (1999): Endogenous Stackelberg Leadership, *Games and Economic Behavior* 28, 105-129.

Chapter 13

THE IMPACT OF FAIRNESS ON DECISION MAKING - AN ANALYSIS OF DIFFERENT VIDEO EXPERIMENTS*

Heike Hennig-Schmidt
Laboratorium für experimentelle Wirtschaftsforschung
Bonn University
hschmidt@wiwi.uni-bonn.de

1. Introduction

It has been standard in economic theory that agents are modeled as self-centered individuals pursuing their own material interest only. In recent years increasing evidence, however, from economic experiments in particular, suggests that subjects are also motivated by concerns for others. Although fairness has been taken to be a main explanatory variable for certain observed deviations of behavior from game theoretic predictions (cf. Fehr and Schmidt, 2001), fairness is not defined in a consistent way in the economics literature. Fehr and Schmidt (1999) modeling fairness as self-centered inequity aversion assume inequality to be the relevant notion of inequity. Rabin (1993), in turn, employs beliefs about opponents' intentions in characterizing fairness, extending the notion of fair behavior to include reciprocal fairness (Camerer, forthcoming; Fehr et al. 1996, 2000). Many authors, on the other hand, fail to specify how fairness is defined. Equality is often implicitly assumed to be the reference point for fairness judgments (cf. the survey by Fehr and Schmidt, 2001). Sometimes, however, determining a reference point is regarded as more complicated, and

*I thank Thorsten Chmura, Markus Graf, Stefan Graubner for their assistance in evaluating the transcripts, Simon Gächter as well as participants of the 25th IAREP/SABE Annual Meeting on Fairness and Cooperation in Baden/Vienna, the 20th Arne Ryde Symposium on Experimental Economics, Lund, Sweden, and the Annual Meeting of the German Association for Experimental Economics (GEW) for helpful comments and suggestions. I am indebted to an anonymous referee and the editors of this volume for their valuable advice. Any remaining errors are, of course, my own. Financial support by Deutsche Forschungsgemeinschaft, Sonderforschungsbereich 303, and the European Union, TMR-research-network ENDEAR (FMRX-CT98-0238) is gratefully acknowledged.

authors ask their experimental subjects to state their perception of fairness (e.g. Gächter and Riedl, 2001; Babcock at al., 1995; Kahneman et al., 1986 a,b; Yaari and Bar-Hillel, 1984).

The aim of this paper is to achieve greater clarity concerning the important question of what fairness involves. Specifically, I am concerned with the fairness perceptions experimental subjects have in distributive tasks. However, I neither infer what conceptions of fairness subjects have on the basis of experimental results, nor do I query subjects how fairness is conceived. Rather, I use a completely different approach, one that does not draw subjects' attention to my research intentions. The approach involves replacing single players by groups of players, having them discuss within the groups and decide jointly how money should be distributed between them and another group of players, the discussions being videotaped. I investigate then to what extent fairness becomes an issue in the course of argumentation[1]. My specific interest is in the question of whether some allocations are indicated as being fair more frequently than others. Further research questions are: Are some allocations perceived as fair despite their not being egalitarian ones? If several different allocations are considered fair, is there a common principle characterizing all of them? Do subjects exhibit a self-serving bias in their fairness judgments? How is actual behavior influenced by considerations of fairness?

I found that equality is not the only type of allocation perceived as fair. Fairness is also attributed to allocations involving inequality of payoffs. Since fair but inequitable payoff allocations are advantageous for the one player and disadvantageous for the other, subjects may fall prey to a self-serving bias in their fairness perceptions (cf. Babcock and Loewenstein, 1997). Opponents may adhere to different conceptions of fairness making agreement impossible. Strategic asymmetries may induce players in the weaker position to show aversion to *inequality* as Fehr and Schmidt (1999) have assumed, whereas players in the stronger position may exhibit an aversion towards *equality*. Experimental results obtained using the strategy method (Selten, Mitzkewitz and Uhlig, 1997) or the video method (Hennig-Schmidt, 1999) indicate behavior to be goal-oriented, fairness criteria based on equity norms serving as reference points that influence the decision process which leads to the outcomes observed.

In the present paper I analyze three experiments in which there may be one or more fair allocations. These experiments are the ultimatum game - UG in the following - (Güth et al., 1982; Sadrieh and Osterholt, 1998); the tripled take game - TTG - (Sadrieh and Hennig-Schmidt, 1999); and an alternating-offer bargaining game - BG - (Selten, 1981; Hennig-Schmidt, 1999). In each case, the subjects' task is to agree on the allocation of a sum of money.

The paper is organized as follows: Section 2 reviews some of the literature of relevance. Sections 3 and 4 provide a detailed account of the video method employed and of the experimental design. Section 5 presents results concerning the different fairness norms and their influence on decision behavior. The conclusions drawn are taken up in section 6.

2. Relevant Literature

Fairness in the sense of equality has become an important element in economic models. Two recent examples of theories which take interpersonal motivations into account are those of Fehr and Schmidt (1999) and of Bolton and Ockenfels (2000). Fehr and Schmidt's model rests on the assumption of inequity aversion. The authors assume outcomes to be perceived as fair if they are equitable. This assumption requires a reference point according to which individuals measure the fairness of an outcome. Since Fehr and Schmidt restrict their attention to individual behavior in economic experiments, they regard the egalitarian outcome as the natural reference point. Deviations from equality play a crucial role in this model since players' utility is dependent on their own payoff and on the payoff difference towards the other players.

A premise in the Bolton and Ockenfels (2000) model is that people are motivated both by the absolute and by the relative payoffs involved. The authors emphasize the collective significance of an equal division of payoffs, thus referring to equality as the social reference point.

Both models neglect the possibility that asymmetries, whether perceived or real, may exist, also in an experimental situation. Such asymmetries could lead to players' reference point for fairness judgments deviating from equality. Asymmetry can easily be created in UG if players are endowed with positive but divergent outside options. In the standard UG, a proposer can decide how to split a given amount of money (the cake) between himself and a receiver. The receiver can either accept or reject the division proposed. If the receiver accepts, both receive the amounts as allocated, whereas in case of rejection both receive nothing. In analyzing an asymmetric UG, Knez and Camerer (1995) found that the presence of divergent outside options led to subjects' computing a fair offer in either of two ways: as an equal split of the whole cake or as an equal split of the surplus above the outside options. Both ways of computing a fair allocation seem plausible (cf. Binmore et al., 1989, 1991). Knez and Camerer attribute the extremely high rejection rate in their experiments to the possibility that proposers and responders adhere to the definition of fairness that benefits them most.

There is considerable evidence from the psychological literature (cf. Babcock et al., 1995; Babcock and Loewenstein, 1997, as well as the literature cited there) and from the economics literature (cf. Konow, 2000; Gächter and Riedl, 2001) of a self-serving bias in fairness judgments that has been found both in controlled laboratory experiments and in field studies. According to Dahl and Ransom (1999, p. 703), a "... self-serving bias occurs when individuals subconsciously alter their fundamental views about what is fair or right in a way that benefits their interests". Important for a self-serving bias to prevail is that there be some form of asymmetry, such as outside options or the roles being different, making the parties interpret the situation differently. Babcock and associates indicate that in negotiations a self-serving bias can impede a settlement. Even if each party endeavors to achieve a fair outcome, the views of the two parties on what is fair tend to differ considerably reducing their readiness to make concessions and thus the prospects for reaching agreement.

The literature on fairness judgments and on self-serving bias to date pertains to individual behavior. In our experiment, subjects instead decide together in groups. It is possible that the behavior evoked in a group setting may be different and that this influences judgments of fairness. One can hypothesize that group members tend to show a more "politically correct" behavior than individuals do in perceiving an egalitarian division as fair[2]. A possible motive for this could be that group members want to avoid being viewed as greedy, both by the other group members and by those viewing the video. We know of no other studies that have examined fairness judgments made by groups. There is, however, an extensive literature on group decision making in social psychology which indicates that groups are likely to behave in a more competitive or less cooperative way than individuals do (Insko et al., 1988; Schopler et al., 1993). This tendency, which has been termed the *discontinuity effect* has been found in 2-person prisoner's dilemma games, in multiperson as well as in intergroup public good (IPG) and prisoner's dilemma games (IPD) (Insko et al., 1994), in ultimatum games for senders (Robert and Carnevale, 1997; Bornstein and Yaniv, 1998) and in negotiations (Polzer, 1996).

Two explanations for the discontinuity effect have been proposed (Insko et al., 1994). One of these, the *fear hypothesis* assumes there to be expectations that other groups, as opposed to other individuals, are more competitive. These expectations lead to competition, which is the only way to prevent one's own group from being exploited. According to another hypothesis, the *greed hypothesis*, groups are more competitive than individuals due to their being able to provide their members social support when acting in a selfish and self-interested manner, whereas individuals have no such support.

This section I close with a brief discussion of how notions and perceptions of fairness relate to fairness norms. According to Schlicht (1998), fairness, like other social norms, represents a generally accepted standard, one that biases behavior and thinking in the direction of it. The transcripts obtained in the present investigation show the existence of a number of different fairness perceptions, each of them shared by a non-negligible fraction of the players. In the following , these perceptions will be termed 'fairness norms'. It will be shown that, with very few exceptions, fairness norms involve equitable allocations. Accordingly, the terms fairness norm and equity norm will be used synonymously.

3. Method

Questionnaire studies, computer and paper-and-pencil experiments concerned with decision making often simply document the decisions made. If a researcher is interested in the decision *process*, however, and wants subjects to spontaneously verbalize their thinking, it may be of importance to also observe subjects during the decision making process. One approach is to let several subjects act together in a group and have them solve a *common* decision task, discussions within the groups being recorded for further evaluation.

In social psychology experiments, groups of subjects have frequently been used as decision making units many of such experiments having been documented by tape recording (e.g. Orbell et al., 1988; Rapoport and Bornstein, 1989; Insko et al., 1994; Bornstein et al., 1996; Goren and Bornstein, 2000; see also Klemisch-Ahlert, 1996). Tape recording has a marked advantage as compared with note taking. One drawback is that speakers can often not be identified, making it impossible to attribute individual characteristics or arguments to specific individuals (Orbell et al., 1988). There is no record of non-verbal articulations either. Video recording overcomes these limitations in that speakers can be identified and non-verbal forms of expressions are documented. Speech there is often much easier to understand as well, especially in heated debates, due to the possibility of observing gestures, facial expressions and lip movements. The video technology also makes it feasible to focus on particular aspects or combinations of observable behavior (Kerr et al., 2000). These advantages led to the video method being introduced into experimental economics (Hennig-Schmidt, 1996; 1999)[3].

In the experiments reported here, the video method was applied within the framework of the following design. Three subjects acted together as a group in arriving at a consensus decision. They played against another group of three persons, the two groups together forming a dyad. The intra-group discussions were video taped, whereas the inter-group contacts were anonymous, the experimenter transmitting each of the decisions made to the other group. The two groups in the dyad will be termed A and B players. The video taped discussions were transcribed word for word by graduate students specially trained and instructed in this task. The transcripts were then used for content analysis[4].

Although the reliability of verbal data has been questioned (cf. Nisbett and DeCamp Wilson, 1977) there appears to be broad consensus within social psychology regarding video recordings and content analysis being important research methods (Smith, 2000; Bakeman, 2000) that provide information often not available or going unnoticed by other methods. Recently, economists have also noted the advantages of the video methodology. According to Loomes (1999) the use of audio and video recording represents a real challenge for experimental economics in the future. Loomes acknowledges, however, that it may not be easy to analyze the qualitative data obtained or to "... present such data to audiences skeptical of anything other than (supposedly) 'hard' numbers" (p. F44). He nevertheless believes that these techniques will provide greater insights into human behavior and how subjects arrive at their decisions than the more conventional methods used in experimental economics do.

The video method also has a number of drawbacks, however. For one thing, experiments are costly since the same number of independent observations in group experiments requires three times as many participants as in individual experiments. Thus, as in group experiments generally, the number of sessions is usually less than in the case of individual experiments (see also Kerr et al., 1996, regarding the effects this has on statistical significance). Also, even a few observations yield a large amount of material to be evaluated, especially in experiments with repeated interaction between opponent groups. In the present case, there were 3 hours of video recordings of UG, 4 hours of TTG and 45 hours of BG. Transcribing and evaluating such transcripts can be extremely time-consuming. There is a tradeoff between statistical requirements and the need of handling such a profusion of material. For this reason, the number of independent observations was limited to 9 for UG, to 12 for TTG, and to 6 for each of two treatments in BG, there being an additional 8 observations involving experienced subjects. These frequencies are sufficient for the use of non-parametric statistical tests, and are in line with those in other group experiments (see e.g. Bornstein and Yaniv, 1998; Goren and Bornstein, 2000). For still another reason I regard this restriction in the number of observations to be justified. This is that my main interest is not in statistical investigation of the 'hard' numbers the final decisions provided but rather in analyzing the discussions. The 52 hours of video material is an extremely rich source of information and reveals regularities that analyzing the choices alone would not have revealed.

Since the video method generates a rich set of data, a problem arises regarding selection of the data from the transcripts to be taken for further analysis. Since the present study focuses on the different notions of fairness that exists, extracting these from the transcripts was of primary interest. The coding scheme for "fairness" that was employed involved two different content categories: (a) allocations that participants characterized by the words "fair" or "just" in all combinations, (as e.g. fairness, justice) and (b) allocations that participants regarded as "equal". Two independent coders analyzed the transcripts and recorded all the allocations in line with this scheme. The allocations were then classified according to the different equity norms. Finally, the number of A and B players who discussed these norms at least once was determined. These frequencies and the classifications made are the data used in the analysis that followed.

It could be argued that the effect of video recording itself could have had an impact on behavior. No support for such an objection was found in the discussion data obtained, however. Nearly all the subjects appeared to feel quite comfortable about the camera being present and appeared to forget after a few minutes that they were being video recorded. Participants often discussed very private matters and showed a remarkable frankness in expressing not only their positive but also their negative views regarding their professors. Although no systematic study of the effect of video recording on behavior has been carried out in economics, a psychological investigation by Endres et al. (1999) failed to show any effect of it on the performance of preschool children who answered suggestive questions either with or without being video recorded.

4. Experimental design

The video experiments analyzed in this paper - a one-shot UG, a one-shot TTG, and an alternating offer BG - are two-player games between A and B players. Except for the bargaining experiment, the strategy method (Selten, 1967) was applied where players had to report a decision for every possible allocation. We forced players to discuss all possible allocations in order to have a chance of finding characterizations of different fairness notions.

4.1 The Ultimatum Game

In the UG video experiment, player A is endowed with 10 Taler (the experimental money unit) which he can allocate between himself, and player B who has an endowment of 0. A decides on the amount $x \in \{0, ..., 10\}$ to be sent to player B. Simultaneously and independently player B decides on an acceptance limit $y \in \{0, ..., 10\}$ for the amount x she is willing to accept. For $x \geq y$ A receives the payoff $10 - x$, and B receives x. For $x < y$ both receive nothing.

The sub-game perfect equilibrium of this game is $x = 0$ and $y = 0$ if money is infinitely divisible. A will keep the whole endowment which B will accept. With a smallest money unit of 1 Taler, a second sub-game perfect equilibrium exists, namely $x = 1$ and $y = 1$. A will send an amount equal to the smallest money unit which B will accept since she is better off than when rejecting.

4.2 The Tripled Take Game

In the TTG video experiment, player B is endowed with 12 Taler, and player A has an endowment of 0. B decides on an acceptance limit $y \in \{0, ..., 12\}$ for the amount x which A can take away from her. Simultaneously and independently player A is deciding on the amount $x \in \{0, ..., 12\}$ he is taking away from B. For $x \leq y$ B receives the payoff $12 - x$, and A receives $3x$. For $x > y$ both receive nothing.

The sub-game perfect equilibrium of this game is $y = 12$ and $x = 12$ if money is infinitely divisible, and $y = 11$ and $x = 11$ with a smallest money unit of 1 Taler. The reasoning is as above. A will take away all the money but one Taler which B will accept since she is better off than when rejecting.

4.3 An Alternating Offer Bargaining Game

The game played in this video experiment is a two-person characteristic function game. It comprises a situation where two players, A and B, anonymously bargain on the distribution of a given amount of money, the coalition value $v(\mathrm{AB})$, by alternating offers. The number of offers is not restricted, and no bargaining costs (e.g. discount factor) are assumed. If players agree on an allocation they receive the amounts they agreed upon. If they do not reach an agreement they receive a conflict payoff $v(\mathrm{A})$, $v(\mathrm{B})$, respectively, with $v(\mathrm{A}) > v(\mathrm{B})$, and $v(\mathrm{A}) + v(\mathrm{B}) = v(\mathrm{AB})/2$. In our experiment, $v(\mathrm{AB}) = 320$. We had two variations of conflict payoffs, (i) $v(\mathrm{A}) = 128$, $v(\mathrm{B}) = 32$, $v(\mathrm{A})/v(\mathrm{B}) = 4/1$; (ii) $v(\mathrm{A}) = 96$, $v(\mathrm{B}) = 64$, $v(\mathrm{A})/v(\mathrm{B}) = 3/2$. Another treatment variable was experience. Inexperienced subjects did not play this game before, experienced subjects played either in condition (i) or in condition (ii). Sessions with inexperienced subjects under condition (i) are termed IH-sessions, those under condition (ii) are denoted IL-sessions (with H(igh) and L(ow) referring to the ratio $v(\mathrm{A})/v(\mathrm{B})$). Experienced sessions are played under condition (i) only and are termed EH-sessions.

4.4 Procedure

Experiments have been run in the Laboratory of Experimental Economics, Bonn University. 186 students participated in all three experiments, most of them majoring in law and economics. Subjects were recruited by campus advertisements promising monetary reward for participation in a video decision-making task. Upon registering, participants signed an agreement that video tapes could be used for scientific purposes. They were assigned to rooms separate from each other such that participants of different groups did not meet. Although registration was arranged that three subjects played together in a group, due to now-show ups several groups consisted of only 2 people (see Table 13.1). Groups were assigned randomly to be A or B players. For each point retained by his/her group, each group member was paid DM 3 in UG, DM 1 in TTG and DM 0.10 in BG. In addition, a show up fee of DM 5 was paid in UG and TTG. The monetary reward was calculated to equal the hourly wage in a typical students' job, ranging from DM 15 to DM 20. Average payments varied between experiments, approximating DM 13 ($7) in UG, DM 14.5 ($8) in BG and DM 17 ($9.5) in TTG. For further characteristics of the experimental design see Table 13.1.

Table 13.1. Characteristics of experimental design and subject pool.

Game	*Dates of experi-ments*	*Number of partici-pants*	*Average length of session*	*Payment range (average pay-ment) in DM*	*Subject pool*	*Number of groups (group size)*
Ultimatum	Oct. 1997	48	30 min	5-29 (16.88)	law and	12(3), 6(2)
Tripled	Nov. 1999	65	40 min	5-38 (12.65)	econo-	17(3), 7(2)
Bargaining	Dec. 1991	73	71 min	3.20-21.50	mics, hu-	29(3), 11(2)
	Feb. 1992			(14.45)	manities	

Upon arrival, participants were seated in front of the video camera such that all verbal and nonverbal expressions could be recorded. The video camera was switched on when the session started. All students were handed the introduction which was read loudly by the experimenter. They were requested to carefully read it again and to ask questions which were answered. Subjects were fully informed on all features of the experimental design. There was no face-to-face contact between A and B players, decisions being transmitted via the experimenter.

5. Results

A first result of the video experiments is that behavior does not correspond to the game theoretic solutions of section 4. Table 13.2 shows the average x of A players and the average y of B players to be far from game theoretic predictions. Moreover, there is a considerable percentage of disagreements.

Our findings in the UG group experiment are in line with results in UG played by individuals[5]. Individual A players typically offer 40-50 percent of the cake, the equal split often being the modal offer. Proposals offering responders less than 30 percent of the available sum are rejected with very high probability. These findings have been replicated across different populations of subjects, with different monetary stakes and different experimental procedures (see e.g. Fehr and Gächter, 2000; Camerer, 1997; Camerer and Thaler, 1995; Roth, 1995).

Session outcomes are shown in Figures 13.1-13.3

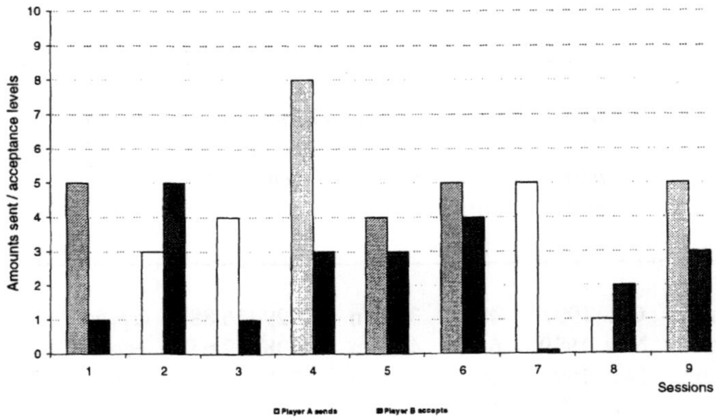

Figure 13.1. Amounts sent and acceptance levels in the Ultimatum Game.

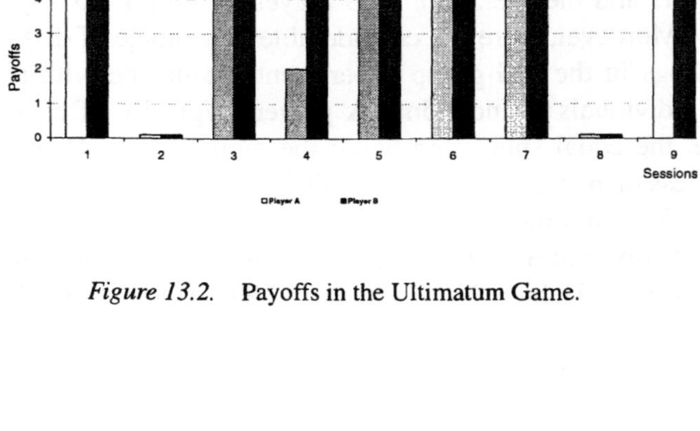

Figure 13.2. Payoffs in the Ultimatum Game.

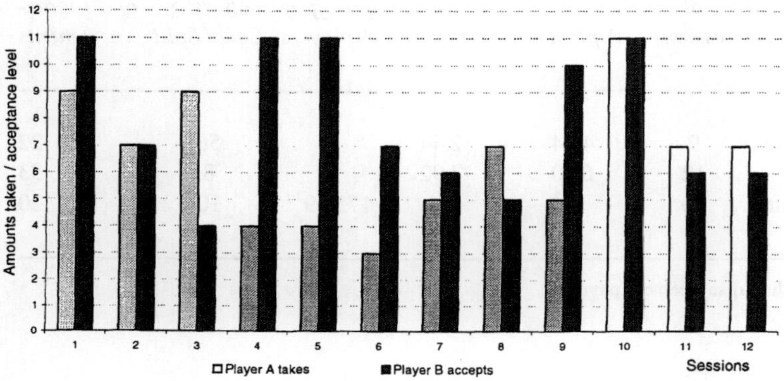

Figure 13.3. Amounts taken and acceptance levels in the Triple Take Game.

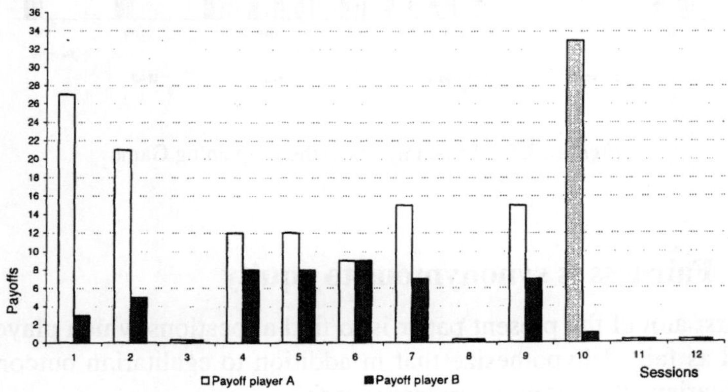

Figure 13.4. Payoffs in the Triple Take Game

Table 13.2. Outcomes in the different video experiments.

Game	*Number of sessions*	*Average x of A players*	*Average y of B players*	*Average payoff of A players*	*Percentage of offers $\geq$ Equal Split*	*Percentage of disagreements*
Ultimatum	9	4.44	2.44		56	22
Tripled	12	6.50	7.92		8	33
Bargaining	20			175.89[1)]	10	20

[1)] Including disagreement payoffs.

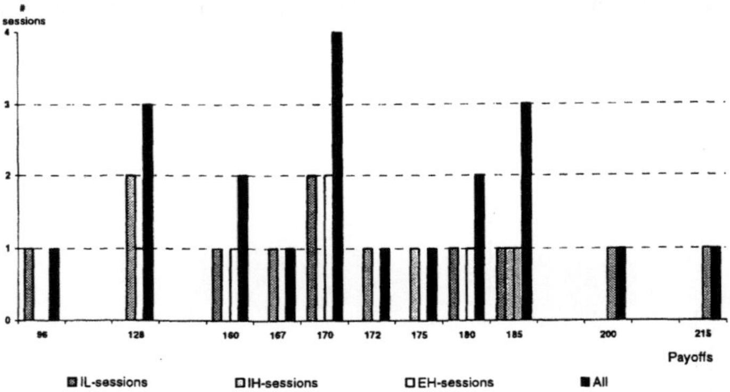

Figure 13.5. Final Payoffs in the Bargaining Game

5.1 Fairness is synonymous to equity

The first aim of the present paper is to find allocations which players characterized as fair. I hypothesize that in addition to egalitarian outcomes also non-egalitarian allocations are perceive as fair.

Table 13.3 shows the allocations participants stated as fair at least once in a session. With very few exceptions, *fairness* is attributed to *equitable* allocations, the common property of which being the *equity principle* (Selten, 1978; 1987). This principle comprises the equal division of an amount of money

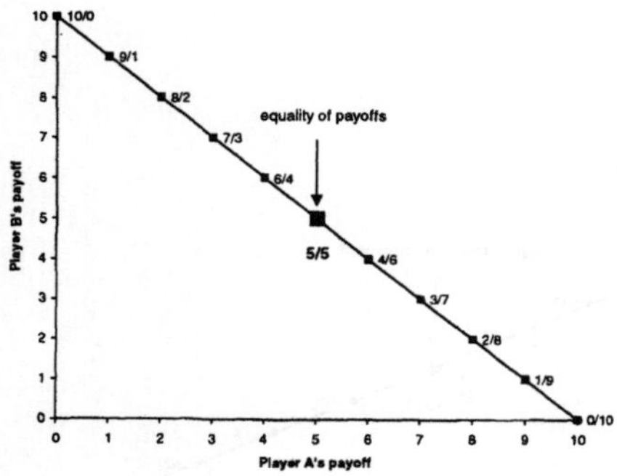

Figure 13.6. *One* fair allocation in the Ultimatum Game

(e.g. rewards or costs) and is a concept of great importance in distributive negotiations. Realization of the equity principle seems to be rather obvious, yet, defining the amount to be distributed and reaching consensus on the notion of equality is frequently at dispute between negotiators. In BG, for instance, player A may consider the surplus above conflict payoffs to be at stake and, in contrast, player B may want to base the division on the total cake. In addition, player A may define equality proportional to conflict payoffs, whereas player B defines equality in terms of egalitarian outcomes. Both players will arrive at rather divergent payoffs which may render an agreement impossible.

In the following, I use the terms introduced by Selten (1978). He termed the amount to be distributed *standard of distribution*. The quota that is applied to the standard of distribution to arrive at the final outcome is called *standard of comparison*.

The allocations in Table 13.3 differ with respect to the standard of distribution and/or the standard of comparison. They are not only termed fair, but are also indicated by their equality characteristic[6]. Apart from UG, *more than one* norm has been identified as fair. Depending on the norm, rather unequal payoffs for both players result (cf. Table 13.3 and Figures 13.4 - 13.6).

In addition to knowing which fairness norms were identified, it is also important to know how frequently these norms were brought up. Table 13.4

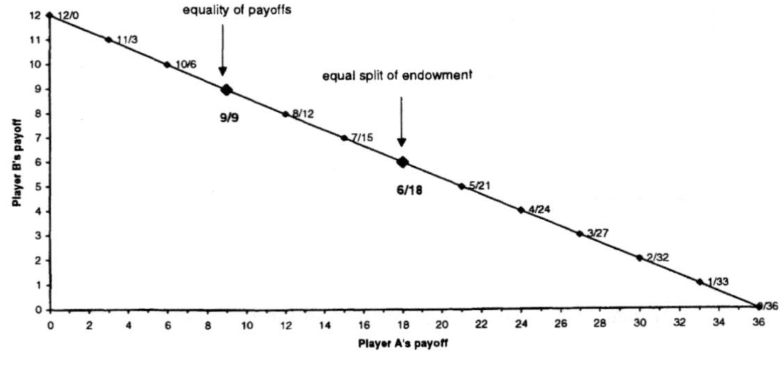

Figure 13.7. *Two* fair allocations in the Tripled Take Game.

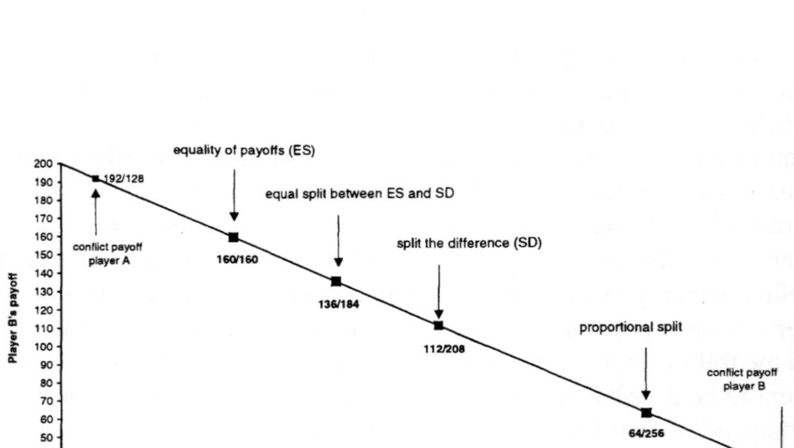

Figure 13.8. *Multiple* fair allocations in the Bargaining Game (H-sessions).

Table 13.3. Allocations characterized as fair in different video experiments.

Game	*Equity norm*	*Standard of distribution*	*Standard of comparison*	*Payoff Player A*	*Payoff Player B*
Ultimatum	-Equal Split of endowment	-endowment	-egalitarian	5	5
Tripled	-Equality of payoffs	-joint payoff	-egalitarian	9	9
	-Equal split of endowment player B	-endowment player B	-egalitarian	18	6
Bargaining	-Equal Split (ES)	-coalition value	-egalitarian	160	160
	-Proportional split (P)	-coalition value	-proportional to conflict payoff	256(192)	64(128)
	-Split the Difference (SD)	-coalition value minus sum of conflict payoffs	-egalitarian	208(176)	112(144)
	-Equal Split of difference between SD and and ES (ESSD)	-(SD-ES)	-egalitarian	184(168)	136(152)
	-Equal Split of difference between proposals of bargainers	-difference between proposals of bargainers	-egalitarian	depending on proposals	depending on proposals

Note: Numbers in parentheses are those for L-sessions.

shows two regularities: the existence of a self-serving bias with regard to equity norms and a seeming preference for the equal split over other equity norms.

a) Self-serving bias

The existence of a self-serving bias with regard to fairness was already shown in early experiments. The perception of fairness seems to be role-specific. If multiple rules of fairness are available subjects do utilize them to their benefit (cf. Komorita and Kravitz, 1979; McClintock et al., 1984). This view is confirmed in later research (Babcock et al., 1995; Babcock and Loewenstein, 1997; Hennig-Schmidt, 1999; Gächter and Riedl, 2001).

A clear pattern of self-serving bias in our experiments is displayed in Table 13.4 although the differences between A and B players are not significant[7]. The more profitable equity norm is mentioned more often by the advantaged player than by the disadvantaged one. For instance in TTG, 83% of B players term equality of payoffs fair against only 75% of A players. For equitable payoffs giving *more* to A players than to B players the opposite holds. In TTG only 17% of B players identify these allocations as fair against 50% of A players, the same tendency holding for BG. And even in UG with just one fairness norm, only 78% of A players call the equal split a fair division against 100% of B players

Subjects extensively discussed this point as the following quotes from BG show. One B player group reasoned that "the proportional split might be the 'equal split' for the A group as the equal split is the 'equal split' for us". An A group debated the different equity norms in the following way: "Split the difference is one fairness definition, equal split is another. The proportional split is a third one to be included as well. Our perception of fairness is split the difference, their idea of fairness is the equal split. This would also be ours if we were in a B group position".

There is an interesting further observation from BG concerning the prevalence of the self-serving bias. Remember that in BG we had sessions with experienced players, as well. We arranged groups to change their roles, either from A to B players or vice versa. Several groups in EH-sessions explicitly state their perception of an acceptable offer to self-servingly depend on their player type. Thus, players might not have reached an agreement had they played against themselves.

b) Is the equal split the social reference point?

The equal split is characterized as fair most frequently by B *and* A players. This result apparently supports the aforementioned models claiming equal division to be *the* social reference point and *both* players being inequity averse. Having analyzed the video transcripts, I argue that two kinds of aversion exist, B players exhibit *inequality* aversion, whereas most A players exhibit an aversion against *equality*. Using the language of Fehr and Schmidt (1999), A players may *dislike* egalitarian outcomes and may *not* suffer from inequity being to their material advantage.

All players, A as well as B, are aware that equal division is a very strong fairness norm, yet, possibly one among others. A players know the equal split most likely to be *the* fairness norm for B players, discussing this frequently (see the quotation above). According to our coding scheme, these discussions are included in the percentages of Table 13.4. The transcripts clearly reveal nearly all A players' wanting *more* than the equal split. This is also confirmed

Table 13.4. Frequency of fairness characterizations.

Game	*Equity norm*	*A Players (percentage)*	*B Players (percentage)*
Ultimatum	-Equal Split of endowment	78	100
Tripled	-Equality of payoffs	75	83
	-Equal Split of endowment player B	50	17
Bargaining	-Equal Split (ES)	65	75
	-Proportional Split (P)	15	5
	-Split the Difference (SD)	25	15
	-Equal Split of difference between SD and ES (ESSD)	10	5
	-Equal Split of difference between proposals of bargainers	35	30

by Table 13.2 and Figures 13.1 - 13.3. The percentage of A players finally offering less than the equal split is substantial: in TTG 92%, (11 out of 12), in BG 90% (18 out of 20) and even in UG - where only one equity norm exists - 44% (4 out of 9). In BG, players could make more than one offer, and here aversion against equality is even more obvious: less than 1% of all A players' proposals was the equal split. In fact, only two A players agreed on equality of payoffs who were the same group of participants playing in the inexperienced and experienced treatment.

B players exhibit inequality aversion from a fairness point of view. Even though with one exception *acceptance levels* in UG and TTG involve payoffs less than the equal split *fairness statements* are clearly in favor of payoff equality (cf. Table 13.4). Moreover, in BG B players offered the equal split or even less in 49% of all proposals showing B players to be tough negotiators in order to avoid unequal payoffs.

The impact of the multiplicity of fairness norms on decision making is important in two respects: First, in games with one equity norm only, A players offer the equal split significantly more often than in games with several fairness norms (Fisher exact test, $p < 0.05$, one sided). This result suggests that we have to account for the multiplicity of fairness norms when analyzing distributive tasks. Second, the rather small percentage of players perceiving non-equal payoffs as fair (cf. Table 13.4) may nevertheless be important with respect to bargaining impasse. As was shown by Babcock and co-authors (1995, 1997), the self-serving bias in fairness judgments may prevent agreement when players adhere to different fairness norms. The transcripts clearly show that disagreements occur because of incompatibility of opponents' aspirations. Since they are anchored at different equity norms, players are not willing to make sufficient concessions. I will discuss this point further in section 5.2.

I conclude this section by formulating the following result:

A multiplicity of fairness norms spontaneously evolve resulting in equitable allocations; fairness judgments are self-serving.

5.2 The influence of fairness on decision making

In the remainder of the paper I will investigate how actual behavior is influenced by fairness norms. I analyze the transcripts of BG, *the alternating offer bargaining game.*

According to the transcripts, subjects' decision behavior is clearly *goal-oriented.* Very early in the bargaining process they formulate aspirations on the final payoff they want to achieve. These initial *aspiration levels* are adapted during the bargaining process.

There was no evidence in the transcripts that subjects use an optimization approach to solve the bargaining task[8]. If they did, they should verbalize this during discussions. Players should form beliefs about their opponents' behavior and formulate strategies according to these expectations. If behavior is preference-based subjects should refer to substitution and substitution rates, for instance between money and fairness. There were no indications for such a behavior. Neither did subjects characterize their own behavior in terms of optimization or maximization nor did they refer to substitution. Forming expectations on opponents' behavior and formulating expectation-based strategies for even the next round proved to be too complicated. Rather, players tended to react ex-post to their opponents' decisions.

Do fairness norms have an impact on the initial formulation – i.e. the formation – of *aspiration levels*? Do they also influence adjustment of these levels? Thess questions can usually not be answered by computer experiments since aspiration levels are not directly observable from decisions. The video taped discussions, however, show a surprising fact: the *equity principle* and the *prominence principle*[9] can explain formations and adaptations of aspiration levels in all groups except in 6 cases (cf. Table 13.5). Since it was shown before that fairness is attributed to equitable allocations I will neglect prominence and concentrate on the influence of the equity principle on the decision-making process.

Table 13.5. Principles of formation and adaptation of aspiration levels in BG.

Aspiration levels	*Number of A players (Total = 20)*	*Number of B players (Total = 20)*
Formation of aspiration levels		
Equity Principle	*16*	*16*
Equal Split	3	12
>Equal Split	8	2
Split the Difference	2	1
Proportional Split(P);<P	1	1
Middle between demands/ingroup-porposals	2	
Prominence Principle	*2*	*1*
Equity and *Prominence Principle*	*2*	*2*
Other		*1*
Adaptation of aspiration levels		
Equity Principle	*12*	*15*
Prominence Principle	*15*	*16*
Equity and *Prominence Principle*	*8*	*5*
Other	*4*	*1*

How do subjects form the first aspiration level in BG? Table 13.5 shows that 36 out of 40 player groups are influenced by the equity principle and that A and B players behave differently. 75% of the B players focusing on the equity principle only, base their initial aspiration level on the equal split, against only 19% of A players. Aspiration adaptation is guided by the equity principle, too (cf. Table 13.5). Aspiration levels are adapted to another social norm, or they are adjusted to a value being the midpoint between A and B players' aspiration levels or demands.

I now return to the multiplicity of fairness norms and the impact of the self-serving bias on disagreements in BG. In 4 sessions no agreement is reached (payoffs < 160 in Figure 13.3). All A players' aspiration levels are guided by a fairness norm resulting in highly unequal payoffs - proportional split and split the difference (cf. Table 13.6). B players start the negotiation with an

Table 13.6. Diverging aspirations of A and B players in disagreement sessions of BG.

	Player A		*Player B*	
Dis-agreement session	*Fairness norm guiding final aspiration level*	*Payoff*	*Fairness norm guiding lowest (initial) aspiration level*	*Highest (intended) offer*
1	*Split the Difference*	208	(*Equal Split*)	(190)
2	*Proportional Split* and prominence principle	240	(>*Equal Split*)	200
3	*Proportional Split* and prominence principle	200	>*Equal Split*	160
4	*Proportional Split* and prominence principle	259	*Split the Difference*	(208)

initial aspiration level attached to the equal split or split the difference. In the final stage of the negotiation, they favor allocations much lower than A players' equitable aspirations. Although two B players offer a fair distribution, opponents' fairness notions do not match. Since both sides are not ready to make any further concessions, a break-down of the negotiation results.

Our result on the self-serving bias of fairness norms is not as clear-cut as in Loewenstein et al. (1989) who report negotiators to be strongly adverse to settling even slightly below the point they view as fair. One possible reason for the difference in results may be that we did not ask subjects on their fairness notion beforehand and thus did not attract their attention to this point. Participants could not stick to a previously declared fairness statement which may have resulted in some groups being willing to make concessions far below their initial aspiration level. In the disagreement groups, we nevertheless find considerable divergence between fairness norms, demands and offers.

I conclude this section with the following result:

Aspiration formation and adaptation are determined by fairness norms; self-serving bias in fairness perceptions may cause conflict.

6. Conclusion

In the present paper I showed that different fairness norms exist even in one game, and that fairness norms differ across games. Fairness perceptions coincide with the different appearances of the equity principle. When explaining behavior, it seems problematic to base general models on one specific fairness concept only. The self-serving bias in fairness perceptions causes players to stick to opposed fairness norms, and thus may impede agreement.

The impact of fairness on decision making was demonstrated in the case of an alternating offer bargaining game (BG). Subjects exhibit goal-directed behavior. Equity norms guide aspiration formation and aspiration adaptation. There is evidence in UG and TTG for fairness norms to serve as points of orientation when players estimate the opponent's acceptance limit. Further analyses of the transcripts are necessary to clarify this phenomenon.

Notes

1. In employing this procedure, I did not ask subjects their perception of fairness as such, since there is evidence in the literature that statements regarding fairness have a strong impact on behavior (see e.g. Loewenstein et al., 1989; Gächter and Riedl, 2001). This was an effect I wanted to avoid.
2. A point the editors of this volume drew to my attention.
3. Recently video recording has been increasingly used (e.g. Artale, 1996; Jacobsen and Sadrieh, 1996; Kuon et al., 1999; Brosig et al., 1999, 2001; Ockenfels and Selten, 1999; Bosman et al., 2001, and Brosig (forthcoming).
4. According to Smith (2000, p. 314), content analysis is "... a technique used to extract the desired information from a body of material (usually verbal) by systematically and objectively identifying specified characteristics of the material".
5. In a study comparing groups and individuals, Bornstein and Yaniv (1998) found, however, that groups propose less but also accept less than individuals.
6. They are also characterized as " appropriate, best, equilibrium allocations, ideal, logical, normal, optimal, rational, reasonable, social". See also Königstein (2000) and Gantner et al. (forthcoming) for studies on equitable choices in bargaining games with joint production.
7. A caveat with regard to statistical tests of our data is appropriate. Independence is violated in 2 respects. (i) Fairness characterizations are not independent observations because many groups stated more than one fairness norm which might be interrelated. (ii) In BG, persons are included in our analysis playing as inexperienced *and* experienced players.
8. This finding is in accordance with the results of Selten et al. (1997) who in a strategy experiment found no optimizing behavior either.
9. The prominence principle refers to the fact that people tend to choose round numbers.

References

Artale, A. (1996). *Rings in Auctions: An Experimental Approach*, Lecture Notes in Economics and Mathematical Systems, 447, Berlin, Heidelberg, New York, London, Paris, Tokyo et. al.: Springer Verlag.

Babcock, L., and G. Loewenstein (1997). "Explaining Bargaining Impasse: The Role of Self-Serving Bias," *Journal of Economic Perspectives* 11, 109-126.

Babcock, L., G. Loewenstein, S. Issacharoff and C. Camerer (1995). "Biased Judgments of Fairness in Bargaining," *American Economic Review* 85, 1337-1343.

Bakeman, R. (2000). "Behavioral Observation and Coding," in: Reis, H.T., and Charles M Judd (eds.), *Handbook of Research Methods in Social and*

Personality Psychology. Cambridge, UK: Cambridge University Press, 138-159.

Berg, J., J. Dickhaut and K. McCabe (1995). "Trust, Reciprocity and Social History," *Games and Economic Behavior* 10, 122-142.

Binmore, K., A. Shaked and J. Sutton (1989). "An Outside Option Experiment", *The Quarterly Journal of Economics* 104, 753-770.

Binmore, K., P. Morgan, A. Shaked and J. Sutton (1991). "Do People Exploit Their Bargaining Power? An Experimental Study," *Games and Economic Behavior* 3, 295-322.

Bolton, G., and A. Ockenfels (2000). "A Theory of Equity, Reciprocity and Competition," *American Economic Review* 90, 166-193.

Bornstein, G., and I. Yaniv (1998). "Individual and Group Behavior in the Ultimatum Game: Are Groups More Rational Players?," *Experimental Economics* 1, 101-108.

Bornstein, G., D. Mingelgrin and Ch. Rutte (1996). "The Effects of Within-Group Communication on Group Decision and Individual Choice in the Assurance and Chicken Team Games," *Journal of Conflict Resolution* 40, 486-501.

Bosman, R., H. Hennig-Schmidt and F. van Winden (2001). "Emotions in the Power to Take Game Played by Groups - A Video Experimental Study," University of Amsterdam/University of Bonn Working Paper.

Brosig, J. (forthcoming). "Identifying Cooperative Behavior. Some Experimental Results in a Prisoner's Dilemma Game," *Journal of Economic Behavior and Organization*.

Brosig, J., A. Ockenfels and J. Weimann (1999). "Why Communication Enhances Cooperation," Fakultät für Wirtschaftswissenschaft, University of Magdeburg Working Paper 23.

Brosig, J., A. Ockenfels and J. Weimann (2001). "The Effect of Communication Media on Cooperation," University of Magdeburg Working Paper.

Camerer, C.F. (forthcoming). *Behavioral Game Theory*. Princeton: Princeton University Press.

Camerer, C. (1997). "Progress in Behavioral Game Theory," *Journal of Economic Perspectives* 11, 167-188.

Camerer, C., and R.H. Thaler (1995). "Anomalies - Ultimatums, Dictators and Manners," *Journal of Economic Perspectives* 9, 209-219.

Dahl, G.B., and M.R. Ransom (1999). "Does Where You Stand Depend on Where You Sit? Tithing Donations and Self-Serving Bias," *American Economic Review* 89, 703-727.

Endres, J., C. Poggenpohl and C. Erben (1999). "Repetitions, Warnings and Video: Cognitive and Motivational Components in Preschool Children's Suggestibility," *Legal and Criminological Psychology* 4, 129-146.

Fehr, E., and S. Gächter (2000). "Fairness and Retaliation: The Economics of Reciprocity," *Journal of Economic Perspectives* 14, 159-181.

Fehr, E., and K. M. Schmidt (forthcoming). "Theories of Fairness and Reciprocity - Evidence and Economic Applications," in: Dewatripont, M., et. al. (eds.), *Advances in Economic Theory*, Eighth World Congress of the Econometric Society.

Fehr, E., and K. M. Schmidt (1999). "A Theory of Fairness, Competition and Cooperation," *Quarterly Journal of Economics* 14, 815-868.

Fehr, E., S. Gächter and G. Kirchsteiger (1996). "Reciprocal Fairness and Noncompensating Wage Differentals," *Journal of Institutional and Theoretical Economics*, JITE 152, 608-640.

Fehr, E., A. Klein and K. M. Schmidt (2001). "Fairness, Incentives, and Contractual Incompleteness", mimeo, University of Munich.

Gächter, S. and A. Riedl (2001). Moral Property Rights in Bargaining, mimeo, University of Amsterdam.

Gantner, A., W. Güth and M. Königstein (forthcoming). "Equitable Choices in Bargaining Games with Joint Production," *Journal of Economic Behavior and Organization*

Goren, H., and G. Bornstein (2000). "The Effects of Intragroup Communication on Intergroup Cooperation in the Repeated Intergroup Prisoner's Dilemma (IPD) Game," *Journal of Conflict Resolution* 44, 700-719.

Güth, W., R. Schmittberger and B. Schwarze (1982). "An Experimental Analysis of Ultimatum Bargaining," *Journal of Economic Behavior and Organization* 3, 367-388.

Hennig-Schmidt, H. (1999): *Bargaining in a Video Experiment - Determinants of Boundedly Rational Behavior*. Lecture Notes in Economics and Mathematical Systems, 467, Berlin, Heidelberg, New York, London, Paris, Tokyo et. al.: Springer Verlag.

Hennig-Schmidt, H. (1996): Bargaining between Groups as Players - Textprotocols of a Video Experiment. Sonderforschungsbereich 303, University of Bonn, Experimental Data Documentation Series 1.96.

Insko, C.A., R.L. Hoyle, R.L. Pinkley, G. Hong, R. Slim, G. Dalton, Y. Lin, P.P. Ruffin, G.J. Dardis, P.R. Bernthal and J. Schopler (1988). "Individual-group Discontinuity: The Role of a Consensus Rule," *Journal of Experimental Social Psychology* 24, 505-519.

Insko, C.A., J. Schopler, K.A. Graetz, S.M. Drigotas, D.P. Currey, S.L. Smith and D. Brazil (1994). "Interindividual-Intergroup Discontinuity in the Prisoner's Dilemma Game," *Journal of Conflict Resolution*, 38, 87-116.

Jacobsen, E. and A. Sadrieh (1996). "Experimental Proof for the Motivational Importance of Reciprocity," Sonderforschungsbereich 303, University of Bonn, Discussion Paper B-386.

Kahneman, D.L., J.L. Knetsch and R. Thaler (1986a). "Fairness as a Constraint on Profit Seeking: Entitlements in the Market," American Economic Review 76, 728-741.

Kahneman, D., J.L. Knetsch and R. Thaler, R. (1986b). "Fairness and the Assumptions of Economics," *Journal of Business* 59, 285-300.

Kerr, N.L., J. Aronoff and L.A. Mess, (2000). "Methods of Small Group Research," in: Reis, H.T., and Charles M Judd (eds.), *Handbook of Research Methods in Social and Personality Psychology*. Cambridge, UK: Cambridge University Press,160-189.

Kerr, N.L., Kramer, G.P., and R.J. MacCoun (1996). "Bias in Judgment: Comparing Individuals and Groups," *Psychological Review*, 103, 687-719.

Klemisch-Ahlert, M. (1996): *Bargaining in Economics and Ethical Environments. An Experimental Study and Normative Solution Concepts*. Lecture Notes in Economics and Mathematical Systems, 436, Berlin, Heidelberg, New York, London, Paris, Tokyo et. al.: Springer Verlag.

Knez. M.J. and C.F. Camerer (1995). "Outside Options and Social Comparison in Three-Player Ultimatum Game Experiments," *Games and Economic Behavior* 10, 65-94.

Konow, J. (2000). "Fair Shares: Accountability and Cognitive Dissonance in Allocation Decisions." *American Economic Review* 90, 1072-1091.

Königstein, M. (2000). *Equity, Efficiency and Evolutionary Stability in Bargaining Games with Joint Production*. Lecture Notes in Economics and Mathematical Systems, 483, Berlin, Heidelberg, New York, London, Paris, Tokyo et. al.: Springer Verlag.

Komorita, S. S. and D.A. Kravitz (1979). "The Effects of Alternatives in Bargaining, *Journal of Experimental Social Psychology* 15, 147-159.

Kuon, B., B. Mathauschek and A. Sadrieh (1999). "Teams Take the Better Risk," Sonderforschungsbereich 303, University of Bonn, Discussion Paper B-452.

Loewenstein, G., L. Thompson and M. Bazerman (1989). "Social Utility and Decision Making in Interpersonal Context," *Journal of Personality and Social Psychology* 57, 426-441.

Loomes, G. (1999). "Some Lessons from Past Experiments and Some Challenges for the Future," *The Economic Journal* 109, F35-F45.

McClintock, Ch. G., R.M. Kramer and L.J. Keil (1984). "Equity and Social Change in Human Relationships," in: Berkowitz, L. (ed.), *Advances in Experimental Social Psychology*, 17, New York, London: Academic Press, 184-228.

Nisbett, R.E., and T. DeCamp Wilson (1977). "Telling More than We Can Know: Verbal Reports on Mental Processes," *Psychological Review*, 84, 231-259.

Ockenfels, A., and R. Selten (1999). "An Experiment on the Hypothesis of Involuntary Truth-Signaling in Bargaining," *Games and Economic Behavior* 33, 90-116.

Orbell, J.M., R.M. Dawes and A.J.C. van de Kragt (1988). "Explaining Discussion-Induced Cooperation," *Journal of Personality and Social Psychology* 5, 811-819.

Polzer, J.-T. (1996). "Intergroup Negotiations: The Effects of Negotiating Teams," *Journal of Conflict Resolution* 40, 678-98.

Rabin, M. (1993). "Incorporating Fairness into Game Theory and Economics," *American Economic Review* 83, 1281-1302.

Rapoport, A., and G. Bornstein (1989). "Solving Public Good Problems in Competition between Equal and Unequal Size Groups," *Journal of Conflict Resolution* 33, 460-79.

Robert, C., and P.J. Carnevale (1997). "Group Choice in Ultimatum Bargaining," *Organizational Behavior and Human Decision Processes* 72, 256-279.

Roth, A. E. (1995). "Bargaining Experiments," in: Kagel, J. H. and A.E. Roth (ed.), *The Handbook of Experimental Economics*. Princeton, N.J.: Princeton University Press, 253-348.

Sadrieh, A., and H. Hennig-Schmidt (1999). "The Tripled Take Game - Textprotocols of a Video Experiment," Sonderforschungsbereich 303, University of Bonn, Experimental Data Documentation Series 6.99.

Sadrieh, A., and S. Osterholt (1998). "Gruppen- und Einzelentscheidungen in einem Videoexperiment zum Ultimatumspiel - Textprotokolle," Sonderforschungsbereich 303, University of Bonn, Experimental Data Documentation Series 4.98.

Sadrieh, A., and V. Pückhoff (1998). "Gruppen- und Einzelentscheidungen in einem Videoexperiment zum Investitionsspiel - Textprotokolle," Sonderforschungsbereich 303, University of Bonn, Experimental Data Documentation Series 5.98.

Schlicht, E. (1998). *On Custom in the Economy*. Oxford: Clarendon Press.

Schopler, J., C.A. Insko, K.A. Graetz, S.M. Drigotas, V.L. Smith and K. Dahl (1993). "Individual-group Discontinuity: Further Evidence for Mediation by Fear and Greed," *Personality and Social Psychology Bulletin* 19, 419-431.

Selten, R. (1967). "Die Strategiemethode zur Erforschung des eingeschränkt rationalen Verhaltens im Rahmen eines Oligopolexperimentes," in: Sauermann, H. (ed.), *Beiträge zur experimentellen Wirtschaftsforschung*. Tübingen: J.C.B. Mohr (Paul Siebeck), 136-168.

Selten, R. (1978). "The Equity Principle in Economic Behavior," in: Gottinger, H.W. and W. Leinfellner, W. (eds.), *Decision Theory, Social Ethics, Issues in Social Choice*. Dordrecht: D. Reidel Publishing Company, 289-301.

Selten, R. (1981). "A Non-cooperative Model of Characteristic-function Bargaining," in: Aumann, R. J., et al. (eds.), *Essays in Game Theory and Math-*

ematical Economics. Mannheim et al: Bibliographisches Institut AG, 131-151.

Selten, R. (1987). "Equity and Coalition Bargaining in Experimental Three-person Games," in: Roth, A. E. (ed), *Laboratory Experimentation in Economics*, New York et al.: Cambridge University Press, 42-98.

Selten, R. (2000). "Eingeschränkte Rationalität und ökonomische Motivation," *Schriften des Vereins für Socialpolitik*, N.F. 274, 129-157.

Selten, R., M. Mitzkewitz and Uhlich, G. R. (1997). "Duopoly Strategies Programmed by Experienced Players," *Econometrica* 65, 517-555.

Smith, Charles P. (2000). "Content Analysis and Narrative Analysis," in: Reis, H.T., and Charles M Judd (eds.), *Handbook of Research Methods in Social and Personality Psychology*. Cambridge, UK: Cambridge University Press, 313-335.

Yaari, M. E., and M. Bar-Hillel (1984). "On Dividing Justly," *Social Choice and Welfare* 1, 1-24.

Chapter 14

THE SEQUENTIAL PRISONERS' DILEMMA: RECIPROCITY AND GROUP SIZE EFFECTS*

Carles Solà
Departament d'Economia i Empresa
Universitat de les Illes Balears
carles.sola@uib.es

1. Introduction

Sequential prisoners' dilemma games can be regarded as formalizations of many everyday situations involving trade-offs between private and collective interest. Examples of such situations are donating to fund-raising campaigns in which donors can observe what others have donated earlier; efforts to provide collective goods of society by listing volunteers, or team production where workers observe their co-workers' efforts.

There is large body of experimental evidence showing that behavior in such situations is not consistent with standard economic predictions. Ledyard (1995) discusses a variety of results of this sort and the explanations economists can provide for some of them. In recent years, efforts have been directed at developing different models for behavior. Two such approaches are the analysis of limited rationality and the analysis of different forms of preferences.

In considering this last approach, a specific type of situation, little investigated experimentally, will be examined in terms of two separate issues, those of strategic sensitivity and the impact of group size on behavior.

According to Bolton et al. (2000), agents are strategy-sensitive in reacting to their expectations of the actions other players will take. Inequality aversion models, such as those of Bolton and Ockenfels (2000) and Fehr and Schmidt (1999), as well as pure reciprocity models like those of Rabin (1993) and Dufwenberg and Kirchsteiger (1998), are examples of models dealing with

*I gratefully acknowledge comments and suggestions from the editors, an anonymous referee and Jordi Brandts, Enrique Fatás, Arthur Schram, Rosemarie Nagel, Klaus Abbink, Aleix Calveras and Daniel Cardona.

different levels of strategy-sensitive behavior. In contrast to such models, a linear altruism model such as that presented originally by Ledyard (1995) and later modified by Anderson, Goeree and Holt (1998) is strategy-insensitive in the type of situations of present interest.

There has been controversy regarding the effect of the size of a group involved in collective action. At the same time, there appears to be no direct experimental evidence concerning this for the type of games considered here. An initial conjecture by Olson (1971) was that larger collective-action groups would be less efficient in providing the public good. On the other hand, if altruism is involved, free riding can be predicted to diminish as group size increases, which contrasts with what inequality aversion models predict. Group size may also be important if reciprocity drives certain behaviors, the propensity to reciprocate some previous action differing with the size of the group. According to Elster (1989), the perceived obligation to reciprocate is greater in a large group.

Through experimental analysis of sequential prisoners' dilemma games of differing size, one can address issues both of strategic sensitivity and of group size effects. Specific predictions are derived from two models for interdependent preferences, those of altruism and of inequality aversion. The models address these two issues differently providing testable predictions about them. Note that reciprocity, which can contribute to strategy sensitivity and explains positive effects of group size, can be a useful conjecture here, although such reciprocity models as those of Rabin (1993) and Dufwenberg and Kirchsteiger (1998) are not tested in this context due to their failure to provide distinguishable predictions.

The paper is organized as follows. Section 2 summarizes earlier experimental evidence that served as an starting point. Section 3 takes up the theoretical framework of the paper and derives predictions from the models of behavior just referred to. Section 4 describes the experimental design. In Section 5 the empirical results are presented and the validity of the predictions derived from the models is discussed. Section 6, finally, presents the conclusions drawn.

2. Previous Experiments

There has been extensive research on prisoners' dilemma situations and on public-good games. Ledyard (1995) reports substantial evidence of splitting in public-good games and also of cooperation in one-shot simultaneous prisoners' dilemma games. He refers to relevant communication, MPCR (Marginal Per Capita Return) and repetition as being factors that strongly affect behavior here. The literature in this area has been mainly concerned, however with simultaneous type situations.

A considerable amount of research has dealt with the contradiction between results for the initial period and the standard prediction of no cooperation occurring. A possible explanation of this apparent contradiction may be that individuals are altruistic. Andreoni (1995) designed an experiment aimed at distinghishing between altruism and errors as explanations for splitting, doing so by paying each player according to the rank of the player's earnings. He found that about 50% of the contributions observed could be explained by altruism or kindness.

Evidence for reciprocal behavior also appears in the experimental literature on games of different types. Fehr, Gächter and Kirchsteiger (1997) explored reciprocal behavior in experimental labor markets; Berg, Dickhaut and McCabe (1995) in a trust game; and Croson (1998) in simultaneous public-good games. Croson (1998) tested the explanatory power of altruism versus reciprocity in simultaneous public-good games. She designed several experiments for studying the relationship between an individual's contribution in each round and his/her expectations concerning the contributions of the other agents, as well as between an individual's contribution and the actual contributions of the other agents. The positive correlations for most of the players between the variables mentioned show that the subjects' behavior could be interpreted as their behaving in terms of a matching rule rather than of a model of altruism, also when reputation effects were removed. The proportion of players who appeared to follow a reciprocity rule was about 70%.

For sequential public-good games the experimental literature is less extensive. Dorsey (1992) and Kurzban, McCabe and Smith (1999) explored public-good games with real-time revisions of the contribution decisions. Kurzban, McCabe and Smith (1999) found that full information about the proposals of the other players and a use of increase-only mechanism in making revisions increased the contributions to the public good, and also that the mean of the contributions of the other players was a better predictor of individual contributions than other measures were.

In studying simultaneous public-good games, Isaac and Walker (1988) and Isaac, Walker and Williams (1994) explored group size effects by manipulating both group size and MPCR. In the Isaac and Walker (1988) experiment there were four treatment cells, MPCR being equal to either 0.3 or 0.75, and group size to either 4 or 10. There was a clear MPCR effect but the effect of group size was ambiguous in that at low MPCR the 10-person group was more successful in providing for the public good, whereas at a high MPCR there was scarcely any difference based on group size. On the other hand, the general assumption Olson (1971) made of lesser contributions was supported since low MPCR generated lower contributions. Isaac, Walker and Williams (1994) used much larger groups, of 40 and of 100 subjects. They found that at low MPCR levels groups of 40 and of 100 persons provided for the public good with greater efficiency than groups of 4 and of 10 persons did. On the other hand, the MPCR level as such had no effect in either of the two larger groups.

In summary, the experimental evidence that has accumulated provides substantial support for the occurrence of strategy-sensitive behavior in different games, as Bolton et al. (2001) have shown in a direct test of different behavioral models. There is also support for a number of recent experimentally based theories that appear able to explain a wide variety of findings from experiments of different kinds by including a relative payoff component in the utility function. Bolton (1991) initially introduced a model of complete information that took relative payoffs into consideration. Fehr and Schmidt (1999) presented a model of inequality aversion. Bolton and Ockenfels (2000), in turn introduced a model, termed ERC, generalizing the relative payoff considerations of the individual in an incomplete information setting. This model can accommodate different patterns of behavior, including what has been interpreted as reciprocal behavior. For the games considered here, this model does not differ from that of Fehr and Schmidt (1999). Altruism, one should note, may be able to explain the ambiguous experimental evidence for a group size effect obtained in simultaneous games, as Anderson, Goeree and Holt (1998) have indicated.

3. Models and Predictions

A basic sequential prisoners' dilemma game in which each subject decides whether or not to contribute to a public-good project is studied here. Consider the situation in which N individuals are each endowed with z monetary units. Each individual decides sequentially whether or not to invest one's entire endowment in the public good, so as provide for each individual in the group a return of mz whereas keeping the endowment for oneself would yield a return per unit that is normalized to 1. Setting $m \in \left(\frac{1}{N}, 1\right)$ yields the standard parameterization of the problem. The payoff to each individual i is expressed by the following payoff function.

$$\pi_i(x_i, x_{-i}) = (z - x_i) + m(x_i + x_{-i}). \tag{14.1}$$

The determination by agent i of the contribution to the public good, x_i, is a binary decision $x_i \in \{0, z\} \, \forall i$ and $x_{-i} = \sum_{j \neq i} x_j$ is denoted as the contribution of the rest of the group. If each individual knows the structure of the problem and the decisions of the previous players, there is a unique SPE (Subgame Perfect Equilibrium) which involves the decision of each player to keep her/his endowment. This result is clearly inefficient (recall that $m \cdot N > 1$).

In this paper, both a two-person and a three-person sequential game in which $m = 0.6$ and $z = 1500$ will be considered. These games are depicted in Figure 14.1.

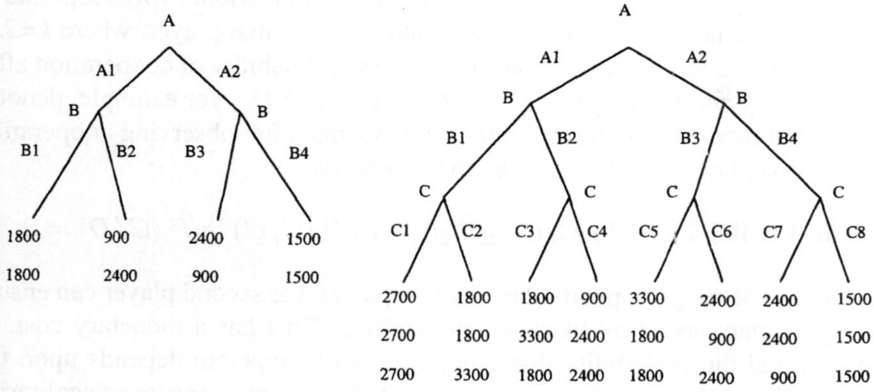

Game 1: Two-person sequential prisoner's dilemma game.

Game 2: Three-person sequential prisoner's dilemma game.

Figure 14.1. Two-person and three-person games.

3.1 Inequality Aversion

Bolton and Ockenfels (2000) present a general motivation function describing the characteristics mentioned above. A more specific motivation function they propose, one which simplifies the analysis and the intuitions involved while at the same time retaining the qualitative characteristics of the general motivation function, will be used to compare predictions across different models. The reason for selecting this particular motivation function is that it is consistent with reciprocal behavior in a two-person sequential prisoners' dilemma game. The function has been adapted to the notation introduced above, such that the motivation function v for individual i is:

$$v_i\left(\pi_i, \pi_{-i}\right) = a_i\pi_i - \frac{b_i}{2}\left(\frac{\pi_i}{\left(\pi_i + \pi_{-i}\right)} - \frac{1}{N}\right)^2, a_i \geq 0, b_i \geq 0, \forall_i. \quad (14.2)$$

Observe that this motivation function is sensitive to the scale of the payoffs involved, an assumption meaning that, as the payoffs increase, the relative component of the motivation function decreases.[1]. This allows each agent to be characterized by the ratio $\frac{a_i}{b_i}$ and ERC assumes there to be a distribution $F\left(\frac{a}{b}\right)$ which is known to all agents. Equilibrium analysis is used to obtain the probabilities of cooperation for each game and position. Since players observe the decisions of the previous players, conditional probabilities are obtained. The following claims refer to the probability that an individual will cooperate under the circumstances in question, given the values of the parameters specified before.[2] $P_k(C/C)$ denotes the probability that an individual will cooperate in a *k*-player game after observing cooperation by the first player, where *k*=*2,3*. Statements are also provided concerning to the probability of cooperation after defection by another player, $P_k(C/D)$. $P_3(C/C \cap D)$, for example, denotes the probability that the third player will cooperate after observing cooperation by the first player and defection by the second player.

Claim 1 (ERC-2): *a)* $P_2(C/C) \geq P_2(C)$. *b)* $P_2(C/C) \geq P_2(C/D) = 0$.

After observing cooperation by the first player, the second player can ensure an egalitarian payoff by likewise cooperating. This has a monetary cost, of course, and the probability that this player will cooperate depends upon the type of player she/he is. In contrast, the first player cannot ensure an egalitarian payoff by cooperating because the second player can defect, and there are monetary costs in cooperating. Accordingly, the first player has less incentive to cooperate, since doing so can be followed by the second player's defecting and thus generating inequality. The second player, in turn, would never cooperate after defection by the first player, since this would result in both the monetary and the relative payoff components of the utility function driving the second player to defect.

Claim 2 (ERC-3): *a)* $P_3(C/C \cap C) \geq P_3(C/C) \geq P_3(C)$. *b)* $P_3(C/C \cap D) \leq P_3(C/C)$. *c)* $P_3(C/C \cap C) \geq P_3(C/D \cap D) = 0$. *d)* $P_3(C/C \cap D) = P_3(C/D \cap C)$.

Part a) of this claim follows from the line of argumentation presented for the two-player case. Part b) follows because if the second player cooperated after defection by the first player, this would introduce inequality into the distribution of payoffs, whereas cooperation by the second player after cooperation by the first can be followed by cooperation by the third player, producing an egalitarian payoff. c) The third player, after observing two choices of defection would never cooperate since this would reduce both the monetary and the relative payoff she/he would receive. Part d) of the claim expresses the fact ERC is insensitive to some aspects of the choice process. For example, the sequence of decisions is irrelevant for player 3 if all sequences result in the same trade-off between the monetary payoff and the relative payoff component of the utility function.

Claim 3 (ERC 2-3): *a)* $P_2(C/C) \geq P_3(C/C \cap C)$. *b)* $P_2(C/C) \geq P_3(C/C)$.

Note that since MPCR is constant across the two games, the private incentive of the last player remains constant across games. The predictions involved here come from the self-centered inequality-aversion component of the utility function. The inequality generated in the two-player game by defection following cooperation by the previous player is greater than the inequality that would be generated by a third player defecting after the two preceding players had cooperated. The propensity to cooperate is thus greater because of the comparatively greater inequality that failure of the second player to cooperate would result in. Concerning part b), comparing the 2-person with the 3-person game in terms of the results of actions by the second player after cooperation by the first player shows the arguments just made to be valid here too. This is because, after defection by the second player in a 3-player game, cooperative action by the third player is still possible whereas in a 2-person game such possibility is lacking. This is the case even if player 3 should defect. Thus, player 2 has stronger incentives in the 2-person than in the 3-person game so as to prevent a high degree of inequality from developing.

3.2 Altruism

As already noted, altruism has been the object of considerable debate concerning the motivations behind the behavior observed in public-good games. Altruism can be defined as a concern for the welfare or payoff of the other players. A simple utility function will be employed involving linearly pure altruism and individual degrees of altruism. This function is one adapted from Ledyard (1995).

$$u_i(\pi_i, \pi_{-i}) = \pi_i + \alpha_i \pi_{-i}\ ,\ \alpha_i \in (0,1]\ , \forall_i. \tag{14.3}$$

As can be seen, altruism here represents a concern for the payoff of the other members. The parameter α denotes the weight agents give to other agents' payoffs. It is ruled out that $\alpha = 0$, since this represents strict egoism, the standard assumption mentioned above. It is assumed that α_i represents private information but that there is a distribution function $G(\alpha_i)$, commonly known to all the agents. The following claim is derived from an equilibrium analysis of the various games.

Claim 4 (Altruism): *a)*$P_2(C) = P_2(C/C) = P_2(C/D) \leq P_3(C)$ $= P_3(C/C) = P_3(C/D) = P_3(C/C \cap C) = P_3(C/C \cap D) = P_3(C/D \cap C) = P_3(C/D \cap D)$.

Player 2 in the two-player game, when deciding whether to cooperate or defect, compares the monetary loss of cooperation, $1 - m$, with the increase in payoffs to the other members of the group, in this case m. This trade-off is the same whatever decision the previous player made. Thus, since the decision of player 1 does not affect the decision of player 2, the trade-off is the same at any possible branch of subsequent play, the probabilities being the same at any branch for the type of the other player involved. Consequently, player 1's problem reduces to the same basic trade-off as already described for player 2. The reasoning for the three-player game is basically the same, except that here cooperative action generates a payoff of $2m$ for the group. Therefore, for any given type of player in a three-player game, the propensity to cooperate increases since, although the monetary cost of cooperating is the same, the payoff for the group increases.

4. Experimental Design

The benchmark game used in this study is a two-person sequential prisoners' dilemma of the type in Figure 14.1. The payoffs that appear there, expressed in pesetas, are those used in the experiment.

Subjects in the experiment played this game once. The strategy Method was used. This method allows one, without deception, to obtain complete data on the strategy the player with the second move employs. Brandts and Charness (2000) have shown the use of the strategy method not to affect how a subject responds to a given action by the previous player.

The second game in the experiment was a three-person sequential prisoners' dilemma game. This game is depicted in Figure 14.1. Note that $z = 1500$ and $m = .6$, just as in the two-player game. Although increasing group size to more than three players could be of interest for investigating group size effects, this was not done, since otherwise the game could have been too complex for use of the strategy method. It was adjudged that use of a four-player game or higher would have increased the number of decisions for the last player to take account of excessively. Using a simplified strategy method in which each subject was asked to make decisions for a variety of cases, differing in the number of previous players who had cooperated, would in turn have had the disadvantage of neglecting possible order effects. As a first step, therefore, it seemed more appropriate to start with a strict strategy method.

The results of four sessions run at the Universitat Autonoma de Barcelona in April 2000 are presented. Students with different majors were recruited by posting notices on billboards on the campus, university students with the incentive of obtaining some monetary compensation for participation being asked for. A total of 157 students participated in the experiment. Two sessions of each of the games just described were run. There were 32 two-person groups and 31 three-person groups.

The sessions started by the players being randomly assigned to different seats in a large classroom. In each seat there was the set of instructions presented in the Appendix. The experimenter read the instructions aloud and, after any questions the subjects posed had been answered, assistants gave each subject a decision form. In this decision form each subject received, the randomly assigned role in the game he/she was to have was specified. Subjects made

Table 14.1. Effective results of both the two-person and the three-person games.

	Two-person game		*Three-person game*	
	Obs.	*Rel. Freq.*	*Obs.*	*Rel. Freq.*
Full Cooperation	1	0.031	1	0.032
High Cooperation			4	0.129
Low Cooperation	4	0.125	10[a]	0.322
Full Defection	27	0.843	16	0.516
Total	32		31	

their decisions simultaneously and the assistants collected the forms. The experimenter and the assistants matched the decision forms of different types of players randomly until each of the groups had been formed. Since subjects were asked to make their decisions using the strategy method, the next task was to follow the decisions made in each group. After all the decisions had been made and recorded, each subject was paid privately and the experiment was ended. The sessions were some 30 to 45 minutes in length. Subjects earned approximately $10 on the average.

5. Results

The major descriptive results of the experiment are shown in Table 14.1. Regarding effective outcomes of the games, full defection was, by and large, the most common result in both games. In the two-player game this outcome appeared in 27 of the 32 groups, whereas in the three-player game it appeared in only 16 out of 31 groups. Thus, cooperation was less common in the two-person than in the three-person game. In the three-person game, partial cooperation was usually the result of just one player cooperating. Full cooperation occurred only once in each game.[3]

The reason for adopting the strategy method was that the data just presented does not provide very detailed information on the behavior involved. More adequate insight into how the subjects behaved can be obtained on the basis of individual data, revealing percentages of occurrence of different patterns of behavior. Figure 14.2 indicates the percentage of occurrence of free-riding behavior, which corresponds to a strategy of defection for players 1, 2 and 3 in each of the two types of games. Note that in both games the percentages involved decrease as the order of play increases. In the two-player game, 87.5% of those who make the first move consistently defected as compared with 68.8% of those who made the second move. In the three-player case, as one moves from the first player to the third, the percentages of free-riding are 87%, 61% and 48%, respectively. The percentage of free-riders is smaller generally in the three-player case, 78.1% as compared with 65.5% in the two-player case.

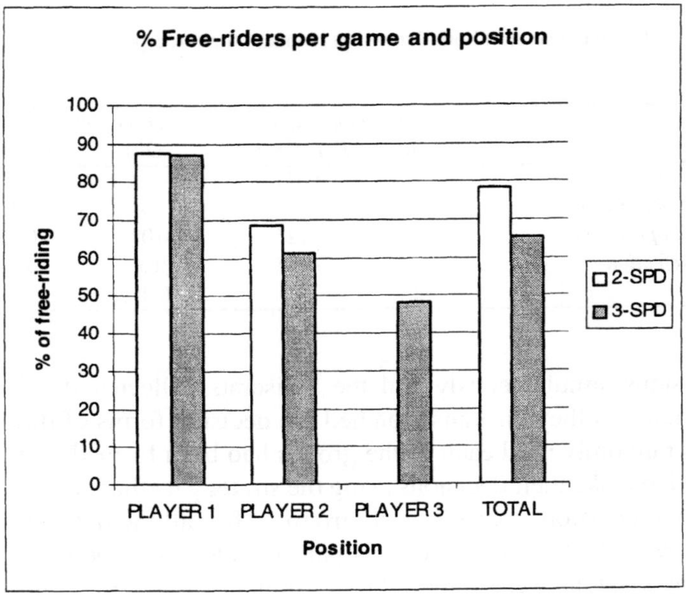

Figure 14.2. Free-riders per game and position.

Table 14.2. Observed frequencies of cooperative behavior per game and position.

	Two-Person Game		*Three-Person game*	
	Obs. (n=32)	*Rel. freq.*	*Obs. (n=31)*	*Rel. freq.*
C	4	.125	4	.129
C/C	9	.281	12	.387
C/D	2	.062	7	.225
$C/C \cap C$			13	.419
$C/C \cap D$			7	.225
$C/D \cap C$			12	.387
$C/D \cap D$			5	.161

Table 14.2 presents the complete results for the experiment. Note that the standard game theoretical prediction would be a table of zeros. It is apparent that this prediction is not supported by the data. All but the proportion of cooperative choices by the second player after defection by the first in the two-player game are significant at the 1% level. The more specific predictions presented in the previous section will now be examined.

Claim 1 (ERC-2) involved predictions for the two-player case based on the ERC model. One can observe that the data obtained are consistent with these predictions. The proportion of cooperative choices by the second player after cooperation by the first is higher than the proportion of cooperative choices after defection (0.281 versus .0.062), a difference significant at the 5% level. (Binomial test, p=0.03). In contrast, the proportion of cooperative choices by the second player after defection by the first, 0.062, does not differ significantly from zero.

Claim 2 (ERC-3) involved hypotheses for the three-person game likewise based on the ERC model. The proportion of cooperation by player 2 after observing cooperation by player 1 is significantly higher than the proportion of cooperation shown by player 1 (0.387 versus 0.129), a difference significant at the 2.5% level (p=0.02). Also, as predicted by the reciprocity model, the proportion of cooperative choices after two prior cooperative choices is higher than the proportion of cooperative choices after two prior defections, 0.419 versus 0.161, a difference significant at the 5% level.

Claim 3 (ERC-2-3) concerned differences in choice that the ERC model predicted connected with differences in group size. The direction of the difference obtained is opposite to that predicted, but the difference is not significant. Although the ERC model is consistent with the data obtained for each of the two games, the comparison between games points out a problem of the inequality concerns hypotheses to explain what we observe.

Claim 4 (Altruism) involves hypothesized relationships that would generate a simple altruism model. None of these relationships is supported by the data. As already indicated, the proportion of cooperative choices was found in part to depend to a significant degree on the prior decisions that were made, in line with the ERC model. The order of play also appears to be an important factor for the proportion of cooperative choices that occurs. The altruism model, finally, generated a prediction of the probability of cooperation being higher in the three-person than in the two-person game. Although this prediction was borne out in some cases, the differences were not significant.

6. Conclusions

Experimental data on sequential prisoners' dilemma games was presented with the aim of studying whether inequality aversion or altruism could best account for behavior here. A model that in various other games has predicted reciprocal behavior to occur, the ERC model of Bolton and Ockenfels (2000) was selected due to its success in explaining a wide variety of experimental findings. A simple model of altruism proposed by Ledyard (1995) was utilized as well. The design involved introducing group size as an experimental factor, since it was expected, on the basis of reciprocity considerations, that the size of the group could affect the behavior of an individual in a way not explainable in terms of either altruism or the inequality aversion model employed.

The major results point in two directions. The one is that the ERC model of Bolton and Ockenfels can account for the results observed in each game, whereas a simple model of altruism is not consistent with the behavior shown, in particular because altruism is unable to explain why persons respond as they do to various actions of players who preceded them. According to an altruism model, a player should be insensitive to what other players have done earlier or to what players may do at a later point.

A second important conclusion that can be drawn is that in a sequential prisoners dilemma game, increasing the number of players does not increase free-riding behavior. In comparing the two-person and the three-person game, the predictions of the ERC model concern the desire to avoid inequity. Players in the two-person game did not appear to be guided by a desire to avoid inequality of a degree that would generate defection after cooperative behavior by the other player. In the three-person game, cooperation was found to occur somewhat more following cooperative actions by the previous players, but the difference is not significant. Although these results are consistent with reciprocity, they are not consistent with inequality aversion. If the tendencies observed here are confirmed in future research, such a conclusion could also be extended to the Fehr and Schmidt (1999) model of inequality aversion, since those authors assume that the number of players does not affect the degree of inequality aversion by the individual. Similarly, Selten and Ockenfels (1998) found experimental evidence against use of a pure inequality aversion model incorporating consideration of the number of players into the utility function.

In conclusion, results obtained are consistent with strategy-sensitive models of behavior and indicate that groups may generate a perceived norm to be followed. It may be appropriate to introduce reciprocity considerations into the models directly in line with what Dufwenberg and Kirchsteiger (1998) have done. It appears that efforts to refine the models employed so as to provide additional predictions could be of interest in future research.

Appendix

Instructions for the two-person sequential game

GENERAL:

Welcome. The object of this session is to study how people make decisions in a given situation. At any time you can raise your hand and a monitor will come to answer your questions. From now on, it's important that you do not communicate with other people in this session. The number that appear in this folder will be used to pay you at the end of the session.

In this session you will make money. This money will be paid to you at the end. Payments are confidential: no other participant in this session will know how much money you make.

Half of the people that came today will play the role of A and the rest will play the role B. In this session you will be paired with another person with a different role from your own role. Nobody will know the identity of the other person in his/her pair.

DECISION TASKS:

In each pair there will be a participant with role A and a participant with role B. The money you'll make depends on your decisions and the decisions of the other participant in your pair, and nobody will know at the time of taking decisions what the decisions of his/her pair are. The participant designated as A will make a decision between two alternatives: A1 or A2. The participant designated as B will make two decisions. B will not know what person A decides, hence B will make a decision for each possible selection of A. B will decide between B1 or B2 for the case in which A would have chosen A1 and B will decide between B3 and B4 for the case in which A would have chosen A2. Each combination of decisions between the two participant in a pair results in different payments in pesetas for each member in the pair. The final result will follow the effective decisions of both participants.

In order to illustrate the situation, the following graphical representation describes the decision process and you will be able to see the consequences of the decisions of both participants in a pair in terms of payments in pesetas.

(We included here a representation of Game 1)

Explanation of the graphical representation:

The letters A and B that appear in the graph indicate where the decision for each member takes places.

The participant with role A decides between A1 and A2.

The person with role B chooses between B1 and B2 for the case in which A would have chosen A1 and chooses between B3 and B4 for the case in which a would have chosen A2.

The pairs of numbers that appear in the inferior part of the graph indicate the consequence of each pair of decisions. The number above corresponds to payment in pesetas for A and the number below to the payment in pesetas for B. Hence, if A chooses A1 and B chooses B1 in that case, participant A gets pta. 1500 and participant B gets pta. 1500, whatever the decision of B for the case in which A would have chosen A2. (*etcetera for each combination in the instructions*).

As you can see, your decisions and the decisions of the other member in your pair determine the payment that each member will receive.

It's very important that you understand perfectly how the process of decisions imply payments in pesetas. If at this point, you are not confident with it, you can raise your hand and a monitor will clarify the situation.

DEVELOPMENT OF THE SESSION:

When everybody has finished to read and received the instructions, decision tasks will start. The monitors will give a decision form to each participant in the session. This registration form contains your identification number and the role that you have been assigned, A or B. In this decision form there will be a graphical representation identical to the one explained before. You will use this decision form to register the decisions that you will choose according to your role. That is, if you have role A you will have to choose between A1 or A2 marking the letter corresponding to the alternative that you prefer in the graphical representation. If you have been assigned role B, you must mark either B1 or B2 for the case in which A would have chosen A1 and you should also mark either B3 or B4 for the case in which A would have chosen A2.

After decisions have been made, you will be able to fill the receipt with your personal data. You cannot fill in the amount of money that we pay you in the receipt because you still don't know it.

The monitors will get all the decision forms from the participants and they will proceed in the following way: they will mix the decision forms from participants with role of A and, separately, those with the role of B. Then they will select one decision form of each type randomly until all pairs will be completed. After this process is completed they will observe for each pair what is the decision of the participant A and what is the decision of participant B that corresponds to the decision of A. So that the complete sequence of effective decisions can be completed. When this process is finished for all pairs, monitors will call apart each participant (identified by the personal identification number in the folder). Each participant will take the folder with all pages inside and she/he will be paid individually.

Notes

1. Rabin (1993) and Fehr and Schmidt (1999) also consider that, as the scale of the payoffs increases, the material payoff will be the main motivation.

2. Equilibrium analysis as well as the proofs for the following claims can be found in Solà (2001).

3. In this table, "low cooperation" means just one player cooperating and high cooperation, just two players cooperating. [a] Five of these cases pertain to a subcase where the last player cooperated after two defections.

References

Anderson, S. P., J. K. Goeree, and C. A. Holt, (1998). "A theoretical analysis of altruism and decision error in public good games," *Journal of Public Economics* 70, 297-323.

Andreoni, J. (1995). "Cooperation in public goods experiments: kindness or confusion?," *American Economic Review* 85, 891-904.

Berg, J., J. Dickhaut, and K. McCabe, (1995). "Trust, Reciprocity and Social History," *Games and Economic Behavior* 10, 122-42, doi:10.1006/game.1027

Bolton, G.E. (1991). "A comparative model of bargaining: theory and evidence," *American Economic Review* 81, 1096-1136.

Bolton, G. E., J. Brandts, and E. Katok, (2000). "How Strategy Sensitive are Contributions?," *Economic Theory* 15(2), 367-387.

Bolton, G. E. and A. Ockenfels, (2000). "ERC: A Theory of Equity, Reciprocity and Competition," *American Economic Review* 90(1), 166-93.

Brandts, J., and G. Charness, (2000). "Hot Vs Cold: Sequential Responses and Preference Stability in Experimental Games," *Experimental Economics* 2(3), 227-238.

Croson, R. T. A. (1998). "Theories of Altruism and Reciprocity. Evidence from Linear Public Goods Games," The Wharton School of the University of Pennsylvania Working Paper.

Dorsey, R. E. (1992). "The voluntary contributions mechanism with real time revisions," *Public Choice* 73, 261-282.

Dufwenberg, M. and G. Kirschsteiger, (1998). "A Theory of Sequential Reciprocity," Center for Economic Research, Tilburg University.

Elster, J. (1989). *The cement of society: a study in social order*. Cambridge University Press.

Fehr, E., S. Gachter, and G. Kirchsteiger, (1997). "Reciprocity as a Contract Enforcement Device," *Econometrica* 65 (4), 833-60.

Fehr, E. and K. Schmidt, (1999). "A Theory of Fairness, Competition and Cooperation," *Quarterly Journal of Economics*. 817-869.

Isaac, R. M. and J. M. Walker, (1988). "Group Size Effects in Public Goods Provision: The Voluntary Contributions Mechanism," *Quarterly Journal of Economics* 103, 179-200.

Isaac, R. M., J. M. Walker, and A. W. Williams, (1994). "Group size and the voluntary provision of public goods: Experimental evidence using large groups," *Journal of Public Economics* 54, 1-36.

Kurzban, R., K. McCabe, and V. Smith, (1999). "The Role of Information in a Real Time Public Goods Game: Reciprocity and Commitment," Economic Science Laboratory, University of Arizona.

Ledyard, J. O. (1995). Public Goods: A Survey of Experimental Research, in *The Handbook of Experimental Economics*, J. O. Kagel and A. E. Roth ,editors,Princeton University Press.111-194.

Olson, M. (1971). *The Logic of Collective Action*. Harvard university Press.

Rabin, M. (1993). "Incorporating Fairness into Game Theory and Economics," *American Economic Review* 83(5): 1281-1302.

Selten, R. and A. Ockenfels, (1998). "An Experimental Solidarity Game," *Journal of Economic Behavior and Organization* 34(4), 517-539.

Solà, C. (2001). "The Sequential prisoners' Dilemma Game: Reciprocity and Group Size Effects," Universitat de les Illes Balears. WP 30.

Chapter 15

COLLUSION IN AUCTIONS WITH STRUCTURED COMMUNICATION: AN EXPERIMENTAL STUDY *

Jana Vyrastekova
Department of Econometrics and Operation Research and CentER
Tilburg University
vyrastek@kub.nl

Maria Montero
Department of Economics
University of Dortmund
maria.montero@wiso.uni-dortmund.de

1. Introduction

This paper is an experimental study of a repeated first price sealed bid auction with private values. Values are drawn independently each round and are private information. In each round of the game, players are allowed to send simultaneously messages about their current value. These messages are cheap talk and have no direct payoff consequences. Moreover, communication is *anonymous* (players do not know the identity of their opponent) and *structured* (the set of possible messages is limited). Players are allowed to stay away from bidding, while retaining the possibility to bid in later rounds; in this way the good can be allocated to the bidder with the highest value at the lowest possible bid. After the object is allocated, the winner can make a sidepayment to the loser; sidepayments can be used to provide incentives for a low value player to stay out from bidding in favor of a high value player.

The repeated game has several equilibria. Some of them are noncooperative and some of them are collusive;[1] some of them are efficient (in the sense of

*We would like to thank Georg Kirchsteiger, Jan Potters, Karim Sadrieh, Eric van Damme, Fredrik Andersson, Håkan Holm and seminar participants at Tilburg University for useful suggestions and discussion.

allocative efficiency: the player with the higher value always gets the good) and some inefficient. The central question is one of equilibrium selection: will players manage to cooperate and if so, will they coordinate on the most profitable collusive equilibrium in which the value messages are informative?

The possibility of sending value messages is (together with the sidepayments) theoretically sufficient for the existence of an efficient collusive equilibrium. However, in the treatment sessions we add one additional cheap talk round: after hearing each other's value message, players can exchange nonbinding bidding proposals. We suggest that the proposals can help the players to coordinate on an efficient equilibrium: first, a player can use the bidding proposals to point out the possibility of collusive bidding to the other player; second, messages can serve for the players to reassure each other that they will bid collusively; third, complying with the bidding proposals can be used to build trust in the truthfulness of value messages.

One may expect that if players can communicate before the game, Pareto efficient equilibria will be played. However, Aumann (1990) points out that communication will not always be helpful: a signal about intended play will not help if the player wants it to be believed regardless of what he really intends to do. A message the sender wants to be believed if and only if it is true is called *self-signaling* (see Farrell and Rabin, 1996). An announcement of collusive bidding is not self-signaling in our experiment.

Aumann's conjecture has been tested in one-shot games by Clark et al. (2001). They investigate the effect of preplay communication in two-player coordination games with two equilibria (one risk-dominant and another Pareto dominant). They compare a game in which messages are self-signaling to a game in which each player always prefers that the other chooses the action corresponding to the Pareto dominant equilibrium. The results support Aumann's conjecture: messages about intended play were more effective when they were self-signaling. On the other hand, communication did not always lead to playing the efficient Nash equilibrium even when messages were self-signaling: quite often players announced their intention to play the risk-dominant strategy. In a related experiment, Charness (2000) studies the effectiveness of cheap talk in a game where messages are not self-signaling and finds that messages are less effective when sent after players have chosen their action, supporting a conjecture of Farrell (1988). Duffy and Feltovich (2000) compare one-shot games in which players can observe the previous period choice of their opponent to one-shot games with cheap talk: when messages are not self-signaling, "actions speak louder than words".

There is relatively little known about communication in more complicated games (e.g., games with incomplete information), or about the interaction of cheap talk signaling of future actions and reputation building in repeated games. A one-shot game with incomplete information is studied by Palfrey and Rosenthal (1991). They implement a three-player public good game in which at least two players have to contribute for the public good to be produced and players have private information about their cost of contribution. Without communication, experiments give support to the play of a symmetric cut-point noncooperative equilibrium: a player contributes when his cost does not exceed the cutoff point. When players are allowed to send binary messages ("I intend to/not to spend") new equilibria with higher expected payoffs appear, though miscoordination can still occur. Players conditioned on messages but message behavior was erratic and efficiency gains low. Forsythe et al. (1999) study a two-person one-shot market where only sellers are informed about the quality of the good. Even though the introduction of cheap talk messages does not change the equilibrium set buyers were highly gullible, though they tended to learn after observing dishonesty in others.

Cooperation is easier to achieve in repeated games: cooperative outcomes that are not equilibria of the one-shot game may be equilibria of the repeated game and players may use current actions to signal future intentions. Palfrey and Rosenthal (1994) find that efficiency increases in the repeated public good game (due to increased cut-points) though players could have done better with rotation schemes. Clark and Sefton (2001) found different first round behavior in coordination games depending on whether they were one-shot or repeated.

What is the role of communication in repeated games? The introduction of messages of intention on future play in repeated games might be viewed as redundant: it does not expand the equilibrium set and players can learn more about senders' intentions from observing the history of play. However, intention messages can be used by the players to build (mis)trust.

Face-to-face communication was successful in the public good experiments by Isaac and Walker (1988) and Cason and Kahn (1999) and in the auction games studied by Isaac and Walker (1985), Artale (1997), and Kwasnica (2000). Since face-to-face communication eliminates anonymity and enlarges the message space, one would expect the communication medium to play an important role. Indeed, different levels of efficiency between face-to-face communication and electronic communication have been observed by Frohlich and Oppenheimer (1998) in a prisoner's dilemma game. Nevertheless, electronic communication has also been successful in experiments like the Hotelling games in Brown-Kruse et al. (1993) and Brown-Kruse and Schenk (2000); Brown-Kruse and Schenk also find that efficiency is easier to achieve in a version of the game with a restricted strategy set. Charness and Garoupa (2000) find that reputation effects often lead to truthful revelation of information. In contrast, in a repeated public good game Wilson and Sell (1997) find that allowing players to announce their intended contributions increases efficiency, but suppressing all information (messages and history of play) leads to even better outcomes. Cheap talk was also unsuccessful in the repeated oligopoly studied by Cason (1995).

In most of the experiments dealing with repeated games communication was face-to-face or electronic but freeform. Communication in our experiment was highly structured but the message space was relatively rich: players send value messages directly and (in the treatment sessions) the bidding proposals include a bid for both players. We observed an overall low proportion of players reporting values truthfully and coordinating on the best collusive equilibrium, despite the possibility of truthtelling being incentive compatible. Average earnings were the same in treatment sessions and in control sessions. There was high variability across sessions, especially across treatment sessions, suggesting that communication can have negative as well as positive effects. From the questionnaire data we infer that the lack of widespread collusion cannot be fully explained by cognitive limitations of our subjects: they often described efficient collusive agreements as a desirable mode of bidding behavior. In practice, however, they behaved regularly in a very myopic way: trying to deceive their partners and not sticking to the bidding proposals they made.

The rest of the paper is organized as follows. In section 2, we present the game. In section 3, we discuss the experiment design and in session 4 we present the data collected in the experiment. Section 5 concludes.

2. The Game

The stage game is a first price sealed bid auction with private values, limited communication between the bidders and sidepayments. This stage game is repeated for a finite number of rounds. The game is played by two bidders, and we will assume in this section that they are rational, risk neutral and care only about their own material payoffs.

In each round, a unit of a good is put for sale. The value of the good for bidder i, v_i, is his private information and can be either high (H) or low (L) with probabilities p_H and $p_L = 1 - p_H$ respectively. Values are independently and identically distributed across players and rounds.

After the players learn their values for the current round, they simultaneously send *value messages* $m_i \in \{H, L\}$; $i = 1, 2$. In the treatment sessions, after receiving each other's value message each player i sends a *bidding proposal* $b_i = (b_i^i, b_i^j)$ where b_i^i represents the bid a player proposes for himself and b_i^j the bid he proposes for the other player for the current auction round; the set of admissible proposals is $A \times A$, where $A = \{H, L, r, N\}$ (see below). Both the value messages and bidding proposals are sent via computer. This structured communication removes the uncontrolled psychological aspects of face-to-face communication.

After learning each other's bidding proposals, the players simultaneously submit bids. We denote the bid of player i by B_i. The set of possible bids is restricted to the following: N (representing no bid or a bid of zero), r (representing the reservation price of the seller, $0 < r < L$), L and H (the latter only allowed for high-value players). Thus, in designing the game we enforce a "no loss" condition, i.e., players are not allowed to bid above their value.

The good is assigned to the bidder with the highest bid, provided that the highest bid is at least r. If both players submit the same bid, each player gets the good with probability $\frac{1}{2}$.

After bidding, the winner is allowed to send a sidepayment s to the other bidder, up to the amount of payoff earned in the current round. The net payoff for the winner is winner's value minus winner's bid minus sidepayments. The payoff to the loser is the sidepayment received from the winner.

We have assumed a discrete type space and a discrete strategy space. Both of these assumptions are made in order to make the game transparent to the subjects. Furthermore, the discrete strategy space plays a role in supporting collusion as an equilibrium of the finitely repeated game.

In our experiment we used the following parameters: $H = 20$, $L = 10$, $r = 2$ and $p_H = p_L = \frac{1}{2}$.

2.1 Nash Equilibria of the Stage Game

An important assumption satisfied by our parameters is

$$L < \frac{1}{2}(H + r). \tag{15.1}$$

Given this assumption, there are two types of Nash equilibria of the stage game. In the first type, $B_i(H) = L$ and $B_i(L) = r$ for $i = 1, 2$; in the second type $B_i(H) = B_i(L) = L$ for $i = 1, 2$. In both types of equilibria sidepayments are zero; value messages and bidding proposals are not restricted.[2] We will denote the first type of equilibrium by e^u (undominated) and the second by e^w (since it involves a weakly dominated strategy for type L) Equilibrium e^u Pareto dominates equilibrium e^w. Both equilibria are Pareto dominated by the bidding strategies $B_i(H) = B_i(L) = r$ ($i = 1, 2$), but assumption (15.1) precludes these strategies being an equilibrium.

2.2 Collusion in the Repeated Game

Strategy combinations resulting in a Nash equilibrium of the one-shot game in each round constitute an equilibrium of the finitely repeated game, and are referred as *noncooperative*.

Our auction game is similar to the prisoner's dilemma in that both players would do better (in expected terms) if they could commit themselves to cooperate with each other (for example, by always bidding the reservation price). However, there is an important difference: the auction stage game has two types of Nash equilibria, e^u and e^w, one of which is better than the other for the players.[3] A "bad" equilibrium can then be used to punish defection and cooperation can be temporarily sustained, even if the game is only finitely repeated. We will briefly discuss two types of collusive strategies: *simple collusion* and *efficient collusion* (the details can be found in the appendix).

Simple collusion. In the cooperative phase of this strategy, players bid the reservation price regardless of their value. If a defection occurs, they revert to the dominated Nash equilibrium of the stage game, i.e., they bid L regardless of their value. This sort of collusion does not require the exchange of any messages.

Efficient collusion. When value messages are possible, players can improve (in expected terms) over the simple collusion strategy in the following way. Each player reveals his value truthfully; if the players have different values, the low value stays out and the high value bids r; if they have the same value, both players bid r. Observable defection from these strategies is punished by reverting to a "bad" equilibrium of the stage game.

Since the actual values of the players are never revealed, these bidding strategies can only be part of an equilibrium if there is a reward for the players who reveal a low value and stay out from bidding. A possible reward is a sidepayment from the winner to the loser (to sustain cooperation, it is sufficient that sidepayments are given after the players have announced different values and the low value player has stayed out, but they could also be given in the case of equal announced values). Notice that bidding proposals are not necessary to sustain efficient collusion, since all the information is already in the value messages.

3. The Experimental Design

Altogether 110 undergraduate students of international business, economics, and leisure studies of Tilburg University participated in 9 experimental sessions conducted in May 2000, February 2001 and May 2001. 46 subjects participated in four control sessions (denoted C1 to C4) without the bidding proposals stage, and 64 subjects participated in five treatment sessions (denoted T1 to T5) with the bidding proposals stage.

In each session, one cohort of 10 to 16 players was matched to play the corresponding repeated game five times, each time to a different anonymous opponent. One game lasted 10 to 15 rounds. After the 10th round, the continuation of the game was determined by a coin flip. We terminated the game as soon as heads occurred, and also if heads did not occur up to the

15th round. Players were informed about the termination rule in advance. At the end of the experiment, two games out of five were drawn at random, and participants were privately paid all their earnings from these two games, plus a 5 NLG participation fee. During the experiment players were shown their earnings in points, and 1 point was worth 25 cents (since the subjects were paid for two games out of five, the expected value of 1 point was 10 cents). Average earnings for the 1.5 hour experiment were around 30 NLG.

In all sessions, the participants were seated in isolated computer cubicles, and any communication besides the computer messages was prohibited. The experiment was fully computerized, with instructions read aloud. After the experiment, subjects answered a questionnaire designed to capture the game understanding, intentions and trust attitudes of the players.[4]

3.1 Hypotheses

We investigate two main hypotheses: on equilibrium selection in the repeated game, and on the role of bidding proposals in the equilibrium selection problem.

We have shown above that the game has several types of equilibria, differing in the role of value messages and sidepayments, and in the conditioning on the history of play. Efficient collusion requires truthful revelation of private information up to a certain maximal round of game repetition (up to round 9 for the lowest sidepayment of $\frac{L-r}{2}$, up to round 6 for the highest sidepayment of $\frac{H-r}{2}$), believing the received private information signals (i.e. trust) and a reward for staying out from bidding in the form of a sidepayment. Players have to condition behavior on the observed history of the game (bidding, private information signals, and sidepayments) and switch to a punishment phase after any observable deviation. Alternatively, simple collusion gives lower payoffs to the players than efficient collusion (though it practically gives the same payoff as the strategy with efficient collusion up to round 6, corresponding to the highest possible value of the sidepayment), but behavior does not have to be conditioned on the (unverifiable) private information signals, and sidepayments need not be used. These equilibria condition only on the history of the observed bidding behavior. And, finally, the game has low-payoff equilibria (noncooperative equilibria), repetition of the stage game equilibria; in their simplest form players do not condition their behavior on either private information signals or on the history of the game.

The strategies supporting the equilibria with higher payoffs are not only more complex but also involve the risk of being exploited by the other player; this risk is greater when trying to play efficient collusion. Thus, if players are constrained by complexity and risk considerations when selecting the equilibrium to play, we hypothesize that they will be more inclined to play noncooperative equilibria rather than simple collusion, and more inclined to play simple collusion rather than efficient collusion. This is our *selection hypothesis*.

The second hypothesis concerns the role of cheap talk bidding proposals in the repeated game. These proposals, while not allowing players to submit a full strategy for the repeated game, allow them to signal immediate intentions for the bidding stage, thus potentially helping them to coordinate on the more efficient equilibria. In particular, we allow two-way (simultaneous) messages in order to give players the necessary tool for mutual assurance of intentions.

Under our *communication hypothesis*, players will be more likely to coordinate on efficient collusion in sessions with bidding proposals. As a consequence, the average payoff in the control sessions would be lower than the average payoff in the treatment sessions.

The game we implement is quite complex, and the bidding proposals might serve as a teaching tool, when one player in the pair is not aware of the collusive bidding opportunities. For this purpose, admittedly, the communication we allow is very scarce. Under the *teaching hypothesis*, players in the cheap talk sessions will submit bids coinciding with the collusive bidding proposal in the initial rounds of the game even if the current bidding proposal was not coordinated, i.e., the players did not agree on how to play the game. The players reap the gains from teaching in the repeated interaction with the same player in one game.

4. Results

In the analysis that follows, we always use for comparability reasons the data from the first 10 rounds of every repeated game. The results include some statistical tests. It should be noticed, nevertheless, that except in the cases where we take each repeated game as an observation and use only game 1 data, the observations are not independent.

4.1 Average Earnings

Before analyzing players' behavior in detail, we first have a look at a rough indicator of players' ability to coordinate on efficient collusive equilibria, the average earnings.

Average earnings in control sessions C1 to C4 (without bidding proposals) and treatment sessions T1 to T5 (with bidding proposals) are presented in table 15.1. We use as a benchmark the expected payoff of the stage game Nash equilibrium in undominated strategies (e^u) played by both players in all 10 rounds. In column "efco" of the table we present the payoff corresponding to the most profitable equilibrium (efficient collusion till round 9 followed by simple collusion at round 10). Column "sc" refers to simple collusion played in all 10 rounds. 1.35 in that column means that by playing simple collusion in

Table 15.1. Average earnings per session and game.

game	*efco*	*sc*	*T1*	*T2*	*T3*	*T4*	*T5*	*C1*	*C2*	*C3*	*C4*
1	1.67	1.35	0.69	0.77	0.74	0.99	0.89	0.59	0.78	0.73	1.00
2	1.51	1.33	0.63	1.08	0.88	1.18	0.91	0.86	1.03	0.93	1.19
3	1.65	1.38	1.02	1.20	0.88	1.35	1.12	0.96	1.01	1.16	1.34
4	1.52	1.30	0.99	1.18	0.85	1.18	1.03	0.96	0.97	0.93	1.30
5	1.65	1.53	0.93	1.09	0.97	1.34	1.23	1.01	0.98	0.99	1.29

all rounds players could earn 1.35 times the benchmark payoff; entries above 1 imply some collusive efforts, and entries below 1 imply the play of dominated strategies. Expected payoffs from a given strategy combination differ across games because of the different frequencies of high and low values, but are the same for all sessions since we generated the values randomly in advance.

Players were (partially) able to collude only in some sessions (T2, T4, T5 and C4). Three of these are sessions with bidding proposals, but the other two treatment sessions are similar to the control sessions C1 to C3. Earnings are highly variable within the same session type, and the differences, if any, between sessions with and without bidding proposals cannot be detected at the aggregate level.

Result 1: Effect of bidding proposals on payoffs. There is no difference between average earnings in control and treatment sessions.

A Mann-Whitney U test comparing individual players' payoffs in control and treatment sessions does not give support for rejecting the null hypothesis that players achieve the same median payoffs in both session types.[5]

Result 2: Variability of earnings. The variability of earnings was higher in the treatment sessions.

An F-test using each pair as an observation rejects the hypothesis of equal variance at the 1% significance level. This seems to indicate the presence of both positive and negative effects of introducing bidding proposals. In sessions where proposals were mostly collusive and complied with, bidding proposals were helpful; in sessions where collusive proposals were often followed by noncooperative bidding, this behavior was seen as deceitful and made players give up any attempts to cooperate.

Do players on average succeed in achieving payoffs significantly greater than 1 if data are pooled from all sessions? Only in the last three games.[6] Average payoffs in the last three games are around 1.11, somewhat above the stage game Nash equilibrium but very far from the maximal equilibrium payoffs.

Result 3: Efficiency. Players' ability to achieve payoffs above the repetition of the stage game Nash equilibrium in undominated strategies is not widespread. After players gain experience with the game, average payoffs are slightly higher than 1, indicating some collusive bidding.

Can the rarity of collusive bidding be due to cognitive limitations of the subjects? In the post-experiment questionnaires, players were asked to advise an agent who will bid in their name in an auction. The round-one scenario, for which we elicited this advice, was such that the agent's own value was 10, he had sent a message of 10 and received a message of 20. In this scenario, around half of the players both in control (52%) and in treatment sessions (48%) advised the agent to submit a bidding proposal according to which he would stay away from bidding. Among them, 91% in control and 73% in treatment sessions indicated that the agent should comply with the bidding proposal.

Observation: Efficient collusion as a desirable mode of behavior. One third of the subjects in treatment sessions and one half of the subjects in control sessions recommended the efficient collusion strategy in the questionnaire.

These numbers provide a lower bound for the fraction of the subjects who eventually understood the payoff dominance of efficient collusion; of course, other players may have realized the payoff dominance of efficient collusion while still preferring to recommend the "safer" noncooperative strategy. In particular, the subjects in treatment sessions, who had actually experienced bidding proposals (and defections from them), were less enthusiastic in the questionnaire about trying to implement efficient collusion.

4.2 Bidding Behavior

Figure 15.1 shows the bid frequency for each player type across games. Treatment and control sessions have very similar frequencies. Bidding 0 by low value players is slightly more frequent in treatment sessions, whereas bidding 2 by high value types is slightly more frequent in control sessions. This suggests that collusive efforts in control sessions were more concentrated in simple collusion.

The bid frequency does not alter dramatically across games. As players gain experience, bidding becomes more cooperative and the proportion of players bidding their own value is reduced (and disappears completely for high value players). For low value players, bidding their own value does not completely disappear, and is consistent with the punishment phase of cooperative strategies.[7]

Observation: Bidding behavior The most frequent bidding behavior corresponds to the undominated Nash equilibrium of the one-shot game.

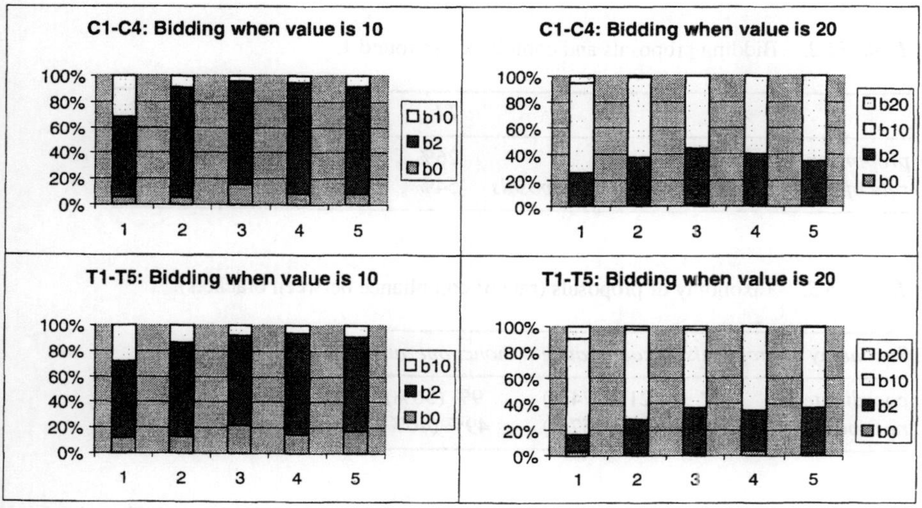

Figure 15.1. Bid frequency in sessions C1-C4 and T1-T5.

The relation of bidding behavior to bidding proposals and value messages is discussed in the next subsections.

4.3 Bidding Proposals

Round 1 data. Looking only at round 1 data across all games with bidding proposals, we are interested in the fraction of bidders who made proposals consistent with the collusive strategies we have described: players who propose $(2,2)$ when both players have announced the same value, and either $(2,2)$ or the low value player staying out and the high value player bidding 2 when the two players have announced different values. 38% of all proposals were collusive in this sense; of them, 44% were coordinated proposals. Compliance with the proposals was relatively low: 66% of all collusive proposals and 61% of coordinated collusive proposals were complied with. This defection rate is rather high for a repeated game, and we expect it to affect the chances of sustaining cooperation in further rounds.

As we saw in section 4.1, collusion took place only in three of the five treatment sessions (T2, T4 and T5). One may wonder whether this was due to a higher frequency of collusive proposals or to a higher rate of compliance with collusive proposals. It turns out that both effects were present (see table 15.2).

Observation: Trying to collude. At round 1, attempts to collude were not widespread, and the defection rate was relatively high. The frequency of

Table 15.2. Bidding proposals and compliance in round 1.

	T1	*T2*	*T3*	*T4*	*T5*
proportion of collusive proposals	26%	40%	32%	49%	38%
rate of compliance with collusive proposals	54%	63%	50%	82%	61%

Table 15.3. Taxonomy of proposals (rate of compliance between brackets).

Taxonomy of proposals	*cooperative*	*noncooperative*
coordinated	21% (74%)	9% (56%)
not coordinated	21% (57%)	49% (40%)

collusive proposals and the rate of compliance with them differed widely across sessions.

It is interesting to compare round 1 bidding behavior in sessions with bidding proposals to round 1 bidding behavior in sessions without bidding proposals. Do players initiate collusion more often in treatment sessions? Players with value 10 who sent a message of 10 and received a message of 20 stayed out more often in treatment sessions (43%) than in control sessions (19%). Differences are smaller in other cases: players with value 20 who sent a message of 20 and received a message of 10 bid 2 41% of the time in treatment sessions and 49% of the time in control sessions; when the message received was 20 the proportions were 42% and 30%.

Observation: Effect of the treatment variable on actual bidding. Games with bidding proposals started with a higher inclination towards efficient collusion on the part of low value players.

Nevertheless, we have seen that average earnings were almost identical in both types of sessions. One can hypothesize that the high proportion of defected proposals creates a negative effect that compensates the positive effect of the bidding proposals. An alternative explanation is that positive sidepayments for bidders staying away from bidding were more common in control sessions (75% of the bidders staying out got a positive sidepayment) than in treatment sessions (62%).

Overall data. Looking at table 15.3, we see that proposals that were cooperative and coordinated were rare, but complied with more often than other proposals.[8]

Table 15.4. Collusive proposals and compliance rates after messages (10,10).

After (10,10)	*propose (2,2)*	*bid 2 after proposing (2,2)*	*bid 2 after both propose (2,2)*
truthtellers	41%	96%	99%
liars	34%	10%	8%

Table 15.5. Proposals of efficient collusion and compliance rates after messages (10,20).

After (10,20)	*propose (0,2)*	*bid 0 after proposing (0,2)*	*bid 0 after both propose (0,2)*
truthtellers	44%	79%	91%
liars	21%	11%	23%

Compliance with own bid proposal was higher when bidders reported their value truthfully: in 68% of cases when value was reported truthfully, the bidder submitted a bid as in his proposal; the rate of compliance was only 28% when value was misrepresented. This is partly due to the fact that truthtelling and value misrepresenting cases are connected to different proposals made, in particular, value misrepresenting players were more likely to make "unreasonable" proposals (like bidding 20, or both players bidding 0); these proposals seem to indicate that players do not want to communicate with the other bidder.

Tables 15.4, 15.5, 15.6, 15.7, 15.8 and 15.9 focus on whether players proposed (and complied with) collusive bidding. Each table refers to a different pair of messages and a different collusive strategy.

In table 15.4 it is interesting to see that only 41% of truthtellers propose $(2,2)$ (which is both the undominated Nash equilibrium and the "nondiscriminatory" collusive outcome); another interesting point is that the liars (that is, the players that really had value 20) almost never complied with their proposals: thus, announcing value 10 and proposing to bid 2 was done to fool the other player.

Players with value 10 who revealed their value truthfully and received a message of 20 were much more likely to propose the efficient collusive strategy (44%, in table 15.5) than the simple collusive strategy (only 11%, in table 15.6); both proposals were serious in the sense that they were very often complied with. On the other hand, truthtellers with value 20 who got a message of 10 were not only unlikely to propose simple collusion (only 8% of the time) but also unlikely to implement their proposals. Other types of proposals were taken more seriously, as tables 15.7 and 15.9 show.

Observation: Bidding proposals and compliance with them. Proposals that were both cooperative and coordinated were rare, but they were imple-

Table 15.6. Proposals of simple collusion and compliance rates after messages (10,20).

After (10,20)	*propose (2,2)*	*bid 2 after proposing (2,2)*	*bid 2 after both propose (2,2)*
truthtellers	11%	91%	100%
liars	16%	17%	33%

Table 15.7. Proposals of efficient collusion and compliance rates after messages (20,10).

After (20,10)	*propose (2,0)*	*bid 2 after proposing (2,0)*	*bid 2 after both propose (2,0)*
truthtellers	55%	74%	92%
liars	21%	85%	83%

Table 15.8. Proposals of simple collusion and compliance rates after messages (20,10).

After (20,10)	*propose (2,2)*	*bid 2 after proposing (2,2)*	*bid 2 after both propose (2,2)*
truthtellers	8%	24%	20%
liars	13%	75%	80%

Table 15.9. Proposals of collusion and compliance rates after messages (20,20).

After (20,20)	*propose (2,2)*	*bid 2 after proposing (2,2)*	*bid 2 after both propose (2,2)*
truthtellers	29%	79%	90%
liars	14%	59%	100%

Table 15.10. Value messages.

Session	*T1*	*T2*	*T3*	*T4*	*T5*	*C1*	*C2*	*C3*	*C4*
v=10 and m=20	37%	29%	25%	15%	27%	23%	15%	12%	13%
v=20 and m=10	52%	52%	64%	41%	39%	40%	50%	65%	51%

mented more often than other proposals. Efficient collusion was more often proposed than simple collusion, and more often implemented.

There is some evidence for teaching (or signaling) effects. Let's consider players with value 10 who tell the truth, receive a value message of 20, propose $(0, 2)$, and receive a different proposal from the other player. Should they bid 0 after all? 52% of the players did it. The reason could be to "teach" the other player or to signal one's willingness to cooperate. If this is the case, the teaching effort should decrease over time. Indeed, the rate of compliance is 62% in the first five rounds versus 39% in the last five rounds. Instead, if we look at *all* uncoordinated proposals the rates of compliance are 49% in the first five rounds versus 43% in the last five rounds.

4.4 Value Messages

Players were consistently more likely to misrepresent their value when it was high, see Table 15.10. Due to this fact, in all sessions the value message 20 is more informative. Reporting a lower value might have been connected with trying to induce the other player to bid 2 and win the auction by bidding 10: indeed, players with value 20 were more likely to bid 10 after reporting a value of 10 (see figure 15.2). We do not find any treatment effect on value messages when looking at the fraction of truthful reports.[9]

Players bid differently depending on whether they are sending truthful messages. After sending truthful messages, players with value 10 stay out more often and players with value 20 bid 2 more often; truthtellers are also less likely to bid their own value (see figure 15.2; this figure pools data from all nine sessions, ignoring possible dynamic effects and treatment effects).

Players also respond to the value message of the other bidder in a different way depending on whether they themselves have told the truth. When we aggregate data from all sessions and games, we observe that truthtelling players with low value are much more likely to bid 0 after receiving a value message of 20 (see figure 15.3). In all other cases (players with high value and players with low value who send a value message of 20) bids are not conditioned on the received message. This is what one would expect: both collusive strategies (efficient collusion and simple collusion) and the undominated Nash

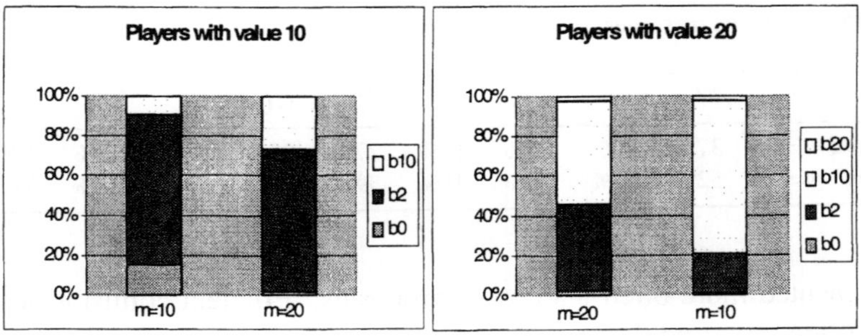

Figure 15.2. Bidding behavior depending on own value message.

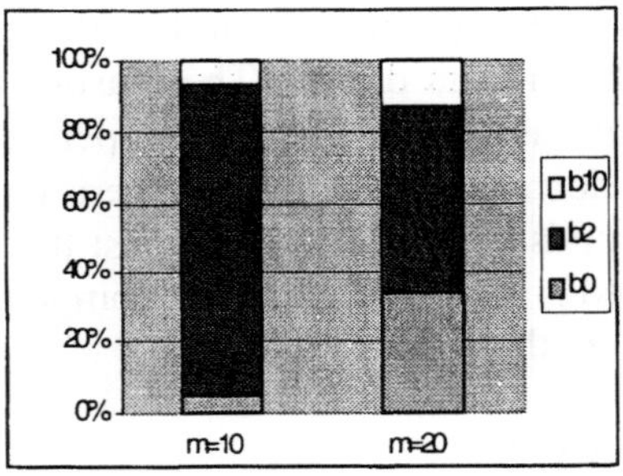

Figure 15.3. Bidding behavior by low-value truthtellers depending on received value message.

equilibrium of the one-shot game prescribe the same bid for high-value players regardless of the message of the other player.

Observation: value messages and bidding. Players bid more cooperatively when they are sending truthful value messages. Only low value players sending truthful messages condition their bidding behavior on the other player's value message.

4.5 Sidepayments

If we look at very aggregate data, control and treatment sessions had very similar average sidepayments (see table 11). We see that players who reported value truthfully gave higher sidepayments, and that sidepayments were higher when the other player bids 0. This is partly due to higher earnings in these cases; to control for this, the table also includes the fraction total sidepayments/total (gross) earnings.

Concentrating on the case of players with value 20 who revealed their value truthfully and won with a bid of 2 we see that higher sidepayments are connected

Table 15.11. Average sidepayments (with sidepayments as a fraction of earnings between brackets).

Average sidepayments	*in control (C1 to C4)*	*in treatment (T1 to T5)*
overall	1.49 (15%)	1.53 (16%)
given that the loser bids 0	5.12 (37%)	4.97 (36%)
by truthtellers	2.11 (22%)	2.54 (24%)

Table 15.12. Average sidepayments by high value truthtellers bidding collusively (average over last three rounds between brackets).

	other bids 0	*other announces 20 and bids 2*	*other announces 10 and bids 2*
treatment	7.30 (7.31)	7.16 (7.00)	4.24 (3.75)
control	8.07 (7.65)	8.21 (7.86)	4.50 (4.00)

with efficient collusion as we would expect. The table also reflects a slight decline of average sidepayments over time, though not as sharp as the theory would predict.

5. Conclusion

In our repeated game experiment, players seemed to coordinate most often on the repetition of the stage game Nash equilibrium in undominated strategies. On the other hand, efficient collusion was more frequent than simple collusion, so that neither complexity nor payoff dominance alone explain the equilibrium selection by the players.

A possible explanation of the low frequency of collusion is that the gains from selecting an efficient but risky equilibrium involving complicated strategies were too small. A possible extension of the present study would be to increase the incentives to cooperate by implementing longer supergames and/or changing the parameters, or alternatively to enlarge the message space. One could also study the effects of simplifying the game even further by making the values public information.

Appendix: Collusion in Equilibrium

Collusive Strategies

Efficient collusion

Suppose the stage game is repeated T times. The efficient collusion strategy has the following three phases:

Phase 1 (cooperative phase)

This phase lasts from period 1 to period $\bar{t} \in (1, T)$. During this phase players send truthful messages about their value ($m_i^t = v_i^t$ for all $t \in [1, \bar{t}]$) and collude efficiently (if $m_1^t = m_2^t$, both players bid r; otherwise the high-value player bids r and the low-value player stays out). Finally, the winner sends a sidepayment s.

Phase 2 (noncooperative phase)

This phase lasts from period $\bar{t} + 1$ till period T. During this phase players send arbitrary messages, bid according to the undominated Nash equilibrium of the stage game ($B_i^t(L) = r$ and $B_i^t(H) = L$) and send no sidepayments.

Phase 3 (punishment phase)

This phase is reached if at least one of the players deviates observably from strategy σ (that is, a player's bidding or sidepayments are not as prescribed). During this phase players send arbitrary messages, bid according to the dominated Nash equilibrium of the stage game ($B_i^t(L) = B_i^t(H) = L$) and send no sidepayments.

Simple collusion

This strategy differs from efficient collusion only in phase 1.

Phase 1 (cooperative phase)

Players bid r regardless of value.

We now turn to the question of under which conditions collusion is an equilibrium. Since players play equilibria of the stage game in phases 2 and 3, we only have to check whether the cooperative phase can be sustained.

Efficient Collusion as an Equilibrium Strategy

The cooperative phase of this strategy consists of three elements: messages, bidding and sidepayments. We consider the incentives to deviate at each of the three moments in turn. It suffices to check that a deviation is not profitable at time $\bar{t}$, since this is the time at which punishment is smallest.

Incentives to tell the truth. Since the actual values of the players are never revealed, players may send untruthful messages without triggering any punishment. Thus, the value of s has to be set in such a way that players find it profitable to tell the truth.

If a player has value L and reports value L, he expects a payoff of $\frac{L-r}{2}$ if the other players says L and s if the other player says H. If on the other hand he reports H, he expects $L - r - s$ (if the other player reports L) or $\frac{1}{2}(L - r)$ (if the other player reports H). Thus, he will tell the truth if $p_L \frac{L-r}{2} + p_H s \geq (L - r - s)p_L + p_H \frac{L-r}{2}$ or $s \geq \frac{L-r}{2}$. Analogously, in order for a high value to be reported truthfully, $s \leq \frac{H-r}{2}$.

Thus, players have an incentive to tell the truth if

$$\frac{L-r}{2} \leq s \leq \frac{H-r}{2}. \tag{15.A.1}$$

Incentives to bid low.

Players with a high value. Consider the possibility of a deviation of the high type to bid L rather than r (this makes sense only when the opponent has announced a high value). If he does so, he wins the auction for sure and gets $H - L$. However, this deviation triggers the punishment phase and his expected payoff is only $p_H \frac{H-L}{2}$ in each subsequent period. If instead he bids r, he expects $\frac{H-r}{2}$ in this period and $(p_H p_L(H-L) + p_H^2 \frac{1}{2}(H-L) + p_L^2 \frac{1}{2}(L-r))$ in each of the remaining periods. Thus, in order for bidding r to be an equilibrium for a high-value player we need

$$H - L - \frac{H-r}{2} \leq (T - \bar{t})\, p_L \left[p_L \frac{1}{2}(L-r) + p_H \frac{1}{2}(H-L) \right]. \tag{15.A.2}$$

Players with a low value. Given that sidepayments are at least $\frac{L-r}{2}$, the low value player has an incentive to stay out when prescribed. If he instead bids r, his expected payoff is no larger than the sidepayment and moreover he triggers the punishment phase.

Incentives to give sidepayments. Does the winner have an incentive to give sidepayment s? If instead he gives zero, his gain is s and his loss is as in the previous section. Thus, in order for the winner to have an incentive to give a sidepayment, we need

$$s \leq (T - \bar{t})\, p_L \left[p_L \frac{1}{2}(L-r) + p_H \frac{1}{2}(H-L) \right]. \tag{15.A.3}$$

Clearly, this inequality is more likely to be satisfied the lower the value of s. Notice also that incentives to give sidepayments do not depend on the value of the player.

There are also equilibria in which players achieve efficient collusion without sidepayments in the first rounds of the game: a low value player will have an incentive to stay out if by doing so he is more likely to win in future rounds (the increase in the probability of winning in future rounds is an implicit sidepayment, cf Athey and Bagwell, 1999). This type of collusion involves more complex and less profitable strategies than collusion with sidepayments; moreover, the risk of being exploited is higher: since the reward for staying out does not take place in the current round cheating is not immediately discovered. We did not observe this type of collusion in our experiment.

Simple Collusion as an Equilibrium Strategy

For the low value player, bidding r is automatically an equilibrium since it is a weakly dominant strategy. For a high value player, inequality (15.A.2) should be satisfied.

Collusion as an Equilibrium Strategy in our Experiment

For the parameters we used, equation (15.A.3) implies equation (15.A.2). If we take into account that in our experiment the stage game is repeated $T = 10$ times for sure and after this it is repeated with probability $\delta = \frac{1}{2}$ up to a total number of 15 rounds, we obtain the following inequality

$$s \leq p_L \left[p_L \frac{1}{2}(L-r) + p_H \frac{1}{2}(H-L) \right] \left[T - \bar{t} + \frac{\delta(1-\delta^5)}{1-\delta} \right].$$

Efficient collusion can then be sustained up to round 9 for the lowest possible value of the sidepayment ($\frac{L-r}{2} = 4$) and up to round 6 for the highest possible value of the sidepayment ($\frac{H-r}{2} = 9$). Thus, the most efficient equilibrium corresponds to the lowest value of the sidepayment.

As for simple collusion, we only have to check for incentives to bid low and thus we only need

$$H - L - \frac{H-r}{2} \leq p_L \left[p_L \frac{1}{2}(L-r) + p_H \frac{1}{2}(H-L) \right] \left[T - \bar{t} + \frac{\delta(1-\delta^5)}{1-\delta} \right].$$

For the parameters we use, this inequality is satisfied up to round 10 (after round 10, it can be checked that cooperation can be sustained up to round 14).

A combination of efficient collusion (played until round 9) and simple collusion (played until round 14) is clearly also an equilibrium.

We have assumed risk-neutral players. The presence of risk aversion does not change the equilibria of the one-shot game or the bounds on the sidepayments which ensure truthtelling, but it affects the incentives to bid low for high value types and the incentives to actually pay the sidepayment. Since the short run gain is sure and the punishment is only probabilistic, sustaining cooperation is more difficult with risk aversion.

Notes

1. Collusion in auction models usually requires an infinitely repeated game (see McAffee and McMillan, 1992). However, we consider an auction in which collusion can be sustained for the initial rounds if the game is finitely repeated: players may punish defection by switching between different stage game Nash equilibria differing in desirability.

2. In particular, truthful revelation of values is an equilibrium since players would have no incentive to change their bid if they knew the other player's value.

3. Here the discrete bidding space plays a role. If players could make any bid, the only equilibrium would be type L bidding L and type H playing a mixed strategy (cf. Athey and Bagwell, 1999).

4. Instructions and questionnaire can be found at Vyrastekova's homepage (currently http://cwis.kub.nl/~few5/center/phd_stud/vyrastek/).

5. Using data from the first game and taking each repeated game as an observation, the two-tailed p value is 0.762. Using data from all five games, $p = 0.809$.

6. At a 5% significance level using a t-test. The t-values in the games 1 to 5 are, in sequence, $-4.289, -0.173, 3.164, 1.848, 2.493$. Notice that in the first game payoffs are significantly *lower* than 1.

7. Bidding their own value was correlated with higher bids and lower sidepayments by the other player in the previous round. Nevertheless, some of the bids occurred in the first round of the game (even in latter games), so they cannot be associated with punishment strategies.

8. Noncooperative but coordinated proposals that were not complied with were often (coordinated) "babbling": one third of them were clearly "not serious" (involving a bid of 20 by one of the players, or a bid of zero by both, or a bid of 0 for one player and 10 for the other) and one half involved one of the players staying out when he didn't announce a lower value than the opponent. In most of these cases *both* players played the undominated stage Nash equilibrium, supporting the idea that proposals were just babbling.

9. Remember that we used in all sessions the same randomly pre-generated sequence of valuations, so that the data are directly comparable. Using a two-tailed Mann-Whitney U test for all games, the p-value is 0.327; if considering only game 1, $p = 0.966$.

References

Artale, A. (1997). *Rings in Auctions: An Experimental Approach.* Berlin: Springer Verlag.

Athey, S., and K. Bagwell. (1999). "Optimal Collusion under Private Information," forthcoming in *RAND Journal of Economics.*

Aumann, R. J. (1990). "Nash Equilibria Are Not Self-Enforcing," in *Economic Decision Making: Games, Econometrics and Optimisation* (ed. by J. J. Gabszewicz, J. F. Richard, and L. A. Wosley), 201-206. Amsterdam: Elsevier.

Brown Kruse, J., M. B. Cronshaw, and D. J. Schenk. (1993). "Theory and Experiments on Spatial Competition," *Economic Inquiry* 31, 139-165.

Brown Kruse, J., and D. J. Schenk. (2000). "Location, Cooperation and Communication: An Experimental Examination," *International Journal of Industrial Organization* 18, 59-80.

Cason, T. N. (1995). "Cheap Talk Price Signalling in Laboratory Markets," *Information Economics and Policy* 7, 183-204.

Cason, T. N., and F. U. Khan. (1999). "A Laboratory Study of Voluntary Public Goods Provision with Imperfect Monitoring and Communication," *Journal of Development Economics* 58, 533-552.

Charness, G. (2000). "Self-Serving Cheap Talk: A Test of Aumann's Conjecture," *Games and Economic Behavior* 33, 177-194.

Charness, G., and N. Garoupa. (2000). "Reputation, Honesty, and Efficiency with Insider Information: An Experiment," *Journal of Economics and Management Strategy* 9, 425-451.

Clark, K., and M. Sefton. (2001). "Repetition and Signalling: Experimental Evidence From Games with Efficient Equilibria," *Economics Letters* 70, 357-362.

Clark, K., S. Kay, and M. Sefton. (2001). "When are Nash Equilibria Self-Enforcing? An Experimental Analysis," *International Journal of Game Theory* 29, 495-515.

Duffy, J., and N. Feltovich. (2000). "Do Actions Speak Louder Than Words? An Experimental Comparison of Observation and Cheap Talk," forthcoming in *Games and Economic Behavior*.

Farrell, J. (1988). "Communication, Coordination and Nash Equilibrium," *Economics Letters* 27, 209-214.

Farrel, J., and M. Rabin. (1996). "Cheap Talk," *Journal of Economic Perspectives* 10, 103-118.

Forsythe, R., R. Lundholm, and T. Rietz. (1999). "Cheap Talk, Fraud, and Adverse Selection in Financial Markets: Some Experimental Evidence," *Review of Financial Studies* 12, 481-518.

Frohlich, N., and J. Oppenheimer. (1998). "Some Consequences of e-Mail vs. Face-to-Face Communication in Experiment," *Journal of Economic Behavior and Organization* 35, 389-403.

Isaac, R. M., and J. M. Walker. (1985). "Information and Conspiracy in Sealed Bid Auctions," *Journal of Economic Behavior and Organization* 6, 139-159.

Isaac, R. M., and J. M. Walker. (1988). "Communication and Free-Riding Behavior: the Voluntary Contributions Mechanism," *Economic Inquiry* 26, 99-126.

Kwasnica, T. (2000). "Collusion in Multiple Object Simultaneous Auctions: Theory and Experiments," *Journal of Economic Behavior and Organization* 42, 323-346.

McAfee, R. P., and J. McMillan. (1992). "Bidding Rings," *American Economic Review* 82, 579-599.

Palfrey, T. R., and H. Rosenthal. (1991). "Testing for Effects of Cheap Talk in Public Goods Game with Private Information," *Games and Economic Behavior* 3, 183-220.

Palfrey, T. R., and H. Rosenthal. (1994). "Repeated Play, Cooperation and Coordination: An Experimental Study," *Review of Economic Studies* 61, 545-565.

Wilson, R. K., and J. Sell. (1997). " 'Liar, Liar...', Cheap Talk and Reputation in Repeated Public Good Settings," *Journal of Conflict Resolution* 41, 695-717.

MIX
Papier aus verantwortungsvollen Quellen
Paper from responsible sources
FSC® C105338

If you have any concerns about our products,
you can contact us on
ProductSafety@springernature.com

In case Publisher is established outside the EU,
the EU authorized representative is:
Springer Nature Customer Service Center GmbH
Europaplatz 3, 69115 Heidelberg, Germany

Printed by Libri Plureos GmbH
in Hamburg, Germany